GEOMORPHOLOGY TEXTS

General Editor: K. M. CLAYTON, University of East Anglia

4

GEOGRAPHICAL VARIATION IN COASTAL DEVELOPMENT

This book examines ways in which the morphological development of coasts varies from one part of the world to another, and tries to isolate the factors involved. These factors include global and smaller scale geological structures, lithology, subaerial climates, waves and tide regimes, and the effects of a wide range of plant and animal organisms. Throughout, an attempt is made to look at things from a world viewpoint and to suggest the existence of broad patterns on a global scale.

Although the special importance of biological effects in the tropics has long been recognized, coastal processes generally have been thought of as being largely independent of climate, in contrast to geomorphological processes on land. This book concludes that, while the fundamental influence of geological structure and lithology and the legacies derived from past conditions must be recognized, it *is* possible to distinguish broad climatically determined zones within which shore development varies significantly.

J. L. Davies is Professor of Geography in the School of Earth Sciences at Macquarie University, Sydney, Australia. He has worked for over twenty years on coasts in Europe and Australia, and has travelled widely, gaining first-hand experience of a variety of environments in other continents as well. The book reflects these experiences, and also his extensive study of the vast amount of available literature and of maps and air photographs from different parts of the world.

Professor Davies has reorganized and updated the second edition in order to provide a more balanced account without losing the global viewpoint characteristic of the first edition.

J. L. DAVIES

Professor of Geography
School of Earth Sciences
Macquarie University
Sydney, Australia

GEOGRAPHICAL VARIATION IN COASTAL DEVELOPMENT

2nd edition

Edited by K. M. Clayton

LONGMAN
London and
New York

LONGMAN GROUP LTD
London
Associated companies, branches and representatives
throughout the world

Published in the United States of America
by Longman Inc., New York

ISBN 0 582 49000 5

First published 1972 by Oliver and Boyd Ltd.
Second impression and first paperback edition,
with revisions and corrections, published by
Longman Group Ltd., 1977
2nd edition, 1980

British Library Cataloguing in Publication Data

Davies, John Lloyd
  Geographical variation in coastal development. -
  2nd ed. - (Geomorphology texts; 4).
  1. Coasts
  I. Title   II. Series
  551.4'5   GB451.2   79-41082

ISBN 0-582-49006-5

Printed in Great Britain by
Lowe & Brydone Printers Limited, Thetford, Norfolk

PREFACE

In this book I have tried to assess the present state of knowledge on how and why the morphology of coasts varies from place to place, and in writing it, I am aware of metaphorically swimming against the present geomorphological tide in at least two respects. In the first place it is a book full of attempted synthesis and generalization in which words such as 'probably' and 'likely' occur with more than commendable frequency and in which very few statements are made in adequately quantified fashion. I have conceived it as an effort at stocktaking, in which the generalizations represent hypotheses erected with varying degrees of confidence on the basis of available fact and needing critical examination. I hope that I have managed to convey something of the degree of confidence which seems applicable in individual instances. It will be a long time before a definitive work on this theme is written: in the meantime a first attempt at assessing present knowledge and thought and pointing to 'probabilities' and 'likelihoods' seemed a worthwhile project. The 'probabilities' and 'likelihoods' will disappear only when we have far more data and can quantify the inputs and outputs of the world's coastal systems.

The book also deals with a topic which has become rather unfashionable in subaerial geomorphology, where the trend in recent years has been to be increasingly sceptical of many ideas on the climatic zonation of landforms. Until quite recently, coastal processes and forms were thought of as being essentially azonal and attempts, particularly by French geomorphologists, to introduce the idea of climatically controlled distributions have come comparatively late. It is to be hoped that this will enable climatic coastal geomorphology to profit from the mistakes of climatic subaerial geomorphology and in the discussion which follows I have tried to give due weight to all factors of locational variation.

Because it is part of my thesis that the development of thought on coastal processes and forms has been strongly influenced by the location of authoritative workers, it is desirable that I declare my own experience. Although I have seen at least something of the coast of every continent except Antarctica, and have visited extensive stretches of the North American coast, I am most familiar with the shores of Europe and Australia and this familiarity has possibly coloured some subjective judgements which are made in what follows. The Australian coast in particular, incorporating as it does a very wide range of environments, is a very profitable field for the study of coastal variation. Within the tropics I can claim only to have worked for short periods in Ceylon and Barbados and to have made more fleeting visits to other low-latitude shores in Australia, the West Indies, Malaya, Hawaii, Samoa and Fiji. I have not seen coasts in the Arctic or Antarctic and my only experience of ice action has been during a winter and spring spent on the shores of Lake Huron.

Much of the discussion in this book is based on map and air photo work and on a reading of the now very extensive literature in coastal studies, but for practical reasons

v

only a small fraction of this literature has been cited.   Often the choice of a reference or references has been an invidious one, but as far as possible I have tried to pick those which will lead on to further reading.   I have assumed familiarity with at least one of the basic English language texts in coastal geomorphology such as Guilcher (1958), King (1959), Zenkovich (1967) or Bird (1968), and have attempted in the main to proceed from where they stop.   In places, however, it has been necessary to review briefly some old ground.

The maps and diagrams have almost all been drawn or redrawn by Guus van de Geer, to whom I am grateful for his interest in the work.   Our wide use of Mercator's projection was determined by the desirability, where climatic factors are involved, of a cylindrical projection showing parallel straight lines of latitude and the additional desirability in many cases of being able to show true directions.   In the result of course, high latitude coasts receive disproportionate prominence, but this disadvantage did not seem to outweigh the advantages.   The frequently used base map (Fig. 1, for instance), emphasizing the continuity of oceans rather than land areas seemed to us to give a better perspective view of coastal distributions than do more conventional layouts and it has the fortuitous but, to an Australian worker, gratifying result of placing Australia near the centre of things.   Because the aim has been to examine variations along oceanic shores, no attempt has been made to plot distributions in enclosed seas such as the Caspian, the Black Sea and the Great Lakes, in spite of the important work which has been carried out there.

Appropriate acknowledgement has been made where photographic illustrations have been provided from other sources and I am glad to be able to thank Eric Bird, David Hopley, Joe Jennings, Brian McCann and John Small for their help in this respect.

I am appreciative of the assistance of Joe Jennings and Keith Clayton, who read the manuscript and suggested improvements: they are in no way to blame for the imperfections which remain. I would especially like to acknowledge the encouragement given to me in the early stages of this work by the late David Linton and, in particular, the lengthy discussions I had with him on terminology, which helped greatly to clarify my ideas.

PREFACE TO SECOND EDITION

The first edition of this book was not written with the object of providing a text in the traditional sense. My aim had been to present coastal geomorphology from a particular viewpoint and as a result the treatment was in places deliberately unbalanced. In the event it appears that the book has been used widely as a text and so I have tried in the second edition to give a more balanced account, without making the book significantly bigger and without losing the global viewpoint characteristic of the first edition.

In practice this has mainly involved re-organizing the material dealing with beach processes and forms and bringing it up to date in the light of the substantial advances that have been made since the first edition was prepared. The treatment of erosional forms has been amplified and that of tidal flat shores reorganized and to some extent rewritten.

                                                                    J. L. D.

CONTENTS

ACKNOWLEDGEMENTS

We are indebted to the following for permission to reproduce copyright material:

Academic Press Inc. and the author, Dr. A. L. Bloom for data from pp. 185–205 to compile a Fig. from an article 'Quaternary sea level fluctuations on a tectonic coast: new ^{230}Th/^{234}U dates from the Huon Peninsula, New Guinea' from *Quaternary Research* No. 4, 1974; American Society of Civil Engineers and the author, A. D. Short for Fig. 2 'Three dimensional beach model' and Fig. 10 'Beach-stage curves for global wave environments' from a paper *Wave Power and Beach Stages: A Global Model* 1979 in press with the Proceedings of the 16th Conference on Coastal Engineering.

I | INTRODUCTION

Early work in coastal geomorphology, as in geomorphology generally, was overwhelmingly concentrated in the temperate latitudes of the northern hemisphere and it was inevitable that the concepts which developed were derived from this background. In Europe the more northern countries—Britain, France, Holland, Denmark, Germany —rather than those bordering the Mediterranean contributed most to early ideas.   In North America it was New England and the Maritime Provinces of Canada which provided most of the inspiration for D. W. Johnson's two influential books of 1919 and 1925.   Russian work too was inevitably concentrated in northern middle latitudes with much of the early work being carried out in the Caspian or on the north coast of the Black Sea.

The environment in which these early studies were made cannot be thought of as particularly representative of most of the world's coasts.   It was one of low temperatures and stormy seas, where glacial and periglacial processes were active during the Pleistocene.   Mostly too it was one of semidiurnal tides and relatively large tidal ranges.   In some cases arguments were developed from studies in large lakes, such as the Great Lakes, and from enclosed seas, such as the North Sea and the Baltic.   Many early American ideas stem directly from Gilbert's studies (1885, 1890) of the fossil shorelines of glacial Lake Bonneville.   It followed naturally that the early text books dealt essentially with coastal processes and forms prevalent in these regions.   Johnson's great systematisation of 1919, *Shoreline processes and shoreline development,* dealt essentially with the North Atlantic only, yet was reissued in 1939 and had virtually no competition as a standard text right down into the 1950s.   Beginning in the 1940s, but increasingly in the last two decades, the picture has changed radically with reports of detailed work from areas as diverse as California, the Gulf of Mexico, Surinam, West Africa, Madagascar, Australia, New Zealand and the Pacific islands.   In 1958 McGill published a world map showing the distribution of major coastal features.   More recent texts, such as those of Guilcher (1954, 1958) and Bird (1968), have been written by authors experienced in a variety of environments and this is reflected in their coverage.   Zenkovich (1967), while taking the bulk of his examples from northern shores, pointed to the need to study the wide problem of coastal processes in relation to latitude.   In a number of writings Tricart (1956, 1957, 1959, 1962) has been a leader in climatic coastal geomorphology and, in a series of geomorphological texts organized on a climatic basis, has devoted sections to the coast (notably Tricart and Cailleux, 1965).

FACTORS OF GEOGRAPHICAL VARIATION

Three broad groups of factors may be recognized as important in influencing geographical variation in coastal development.   They are physical factors operating from landward, physical factors in the sea, and, thirdly, biological factors operating along the shoreline itself.

PHYSICAL FACTORS OF THE LAND

The first group includes factors such as lithology, structure, tectonic stability and subaerial denudation and accretion, and it is these that have been most widely identified in the past. One of the earliest distinctions—between 'Atlantic' and 'Pacific' type coasts made by Suess (1892)—was made on a structural basis and virtually all classifications proposed since have leaned heavily on variations in structure and subaerial erosion as methods of differentiation. Through the first half of the twentieth century, a supposed distinction between 'shorelines of submergence' and 'shorelines of emergence' was widely adopted. Suggested by Davis (1898) and developed first by Gulliver (1899) and more extensively by Johnson (1919), it was abandoned following the realization that the massive marine transgression of postglacial times had affected all coasts and that perhaps only the coasts of Hudson Bay and the Gulf of Bothnia and those of some tectonically active area such as New Guinea are rising at a rate sufficient to justify the appellation 'of emergence'. We now recognize that Johnson's 'shoreline of emergence' is really a special type of 'shoreline of submergence', formed where the post-glacial sea rose against a gently sloping, relatively undissected land mass. This, then, was really another distinction made on the basis of structure and subaerial erosional history.

Many classifiers, including Valentin (1952) and Shepard (1963) whose systems are probably most widely known, have differentiated coasts on the basis of other terrestrial factors.   Control by volcanic and fault structures and the nature and extent of fluvial and glacial erosion and deposition have especially been used to divide coastal types.

That subaerial climates—and particularly Pleistocene climates—have differentiated coasts has also been appreciated to some extent for a long time, although usually in implicit fashion.   Johnson (1919) for instance divided his 'shorelines of submergence' into 'ria shorelines' and 'fiord shorelines', so acknowledging the effect of a difference in Pleistocene climate.   The contrast between coasts influenced by fluvial processes and those influenced by glacial processes has been noted by almost every classifier since.

One of the few attempts to be more explicit in outlining the role of subaerial climate was that of Aufrère (1934) who distinguished the following regions:

(*i*) Permanent ice cover—development virtually halted because of apparent absence of marine agents of modification.

(*ii*) Seasonal ice cover—coastal activity intermittent, glacial sediments important in supplying beaches.

(*iii*) Temperate humid—the coastal type considered 'normal' and inhabited by most geographers.

(*iv*) Hot, wet—characterized by the presence of corals, constructional features tend to grow in the wet season.

(*v*) Deserts—estuaries and deltas are absent, littoral sediments exclusively marine in origin.

(*vi*) Semi-arid—seasonal continental influence, littoral lagoons take on the character of sebkhas.

The tentative and brief attempt by Aufrère has never been developed and seems to have been consistently overlooked in textbook discussions of classification systems.

PHYSICAL FACTORS OF THE SEA

Physical factors in the sea include wave regime, tidal type and range, and seawater characteristics. In strong contrast to the first group, they have been almost completely ignored by coastal classifiers. There seems to have been no explicit recognition of the part played by variations in wave energy in giving rise to differences in coastal type until the writings of Price (1954a, for instance), although it has often been invoked since and is now generally recognized as a fundamental factor in causing shorelines to evolve in different ways (for example Tanner, 1960). Differences brought about by tidal variations have received perhaps even less attention and there has been little attempt to discuss systematically the effect of different tidal types and ranges. My own tentative discussion (Davies, 1964) is amplified and developed in later pages.

Seawater characteristics of significance include salinity, especially in estuarine, lagoonal or deltaic environments, carbonate content and temperature. As a corollary of temperature, the nature and distribution of sea ice is of obvious importance.

The apparent neglect of marine factors and the absence of much systematic discussion of their effect may be due in part to the way in which they influence the shoreline itself rather than the coastal zone as a whole. In consequence they often make a less obvious impact on the landscape than do subaerial factors. The question of scale in coastal categorization has been examined by Inman and Nordstrom (1971), who suggested that at least three major orders can be distinguished. They envisaged first-order features with dimensions of something like 1000 km long, 100 km wide and 10 km high and owing their form to factors of global tectonics. Second-order features might have a scale of about 100 by 10 by 1 km and be associated with large-scale processes of deposition and erosion as in the case of deltaic or fjord coasts. Third-order features include such forms as beach berms and shore platforms, and higher orders could be introduced to incorporate microforms. First- and second-order features characterize the coast, third- and higher-order features the shore. In terms of our present discussion terrestrial factors are most important in relation to the coast, marine and biological factors in relation to the shore.

Another important reason for the relative neglect of marine factors is undoubtedly our general ignorance of their nature and significance until a surprisingly late date. It is true that there have existed for some time abundant data on variations of tidal range and type and that a great deal is known about associated current systems in constricted waters where they are most in evidence and constitute a navigation hazard: but our knowledge of waves and wave-induced currents has remained largely at the qualitative stage in spite of the big advances made in the last two or three decades. In the latter part of the nineteenth century and in the earliest part of this, constructional shore forms were widely interpreted in terms not of waves but of conveniently invoked currents and, as discussed by Jennings (1955), for instance, this way of thinking survived in some quarters until relatively recently.

Some workers have attempted to assess wave parameters from deduced relationships with other measurable features: Price (1955), for instance, suggested that wave energy could be broadly categorized by its relationship with the steepness of the offshore ramp. He used gradients of 1·5 and 2·5 feet per mile to separate low, moderate and high energy conditions. Since the 1950s a start has been made in collecting wave statistics derived from both ship-borne and shore-based instrumental wave recorders, and during the 1970s transmitting waverider buoys have been used increasingly. Towards the end of 1976 for instance there were eleven such recorders tethered along the east coast of Australia between Cairns and Port Kembla, and by applying corrections for refraction and shoaling effects it is becoming increasingly possible to use the deep water wave data so recorded to calculate the nature of wave impact on the shore.

On a world scale however, the amount of this information is so small that we are still dependent on visual observations of very varying quality in order to attempt an assessment of spatial and temporal variations in wave incidence. A large number of observations made on board ship has been collected in marine atlases, such as the *Monthly Meteorological Charts of the Oceans* issued by the British Meteorological Office and the US Navy *Marine Climatic Atlas of the World* (Washington, 1955-1959). Such data have been used as the basis of such regional accounts as that for the North Atlantic by Schubart and Mockel (1949) and that for South American coasts by Russell (1969). Judiciously modified by wave hindcasting techniques, they were used by Meisburger (1962) to assess world wave height distribution and were the basis of the attempt by Bruns (1953) to review wave regimes generally. From the point of view of the coastal worker, shipboard observations have many limitations, some of which have been discussed by Burkhart and Cline (1961) and by Russell (1969).

Organized attempts to record visual information from the shore have so far been few, but where they have been made, as along coasts in the USA (Helle, 1958), they are potentially more useful than ship records because of the way in which they portray conditions on the shore itself. They have been used, for example by Tanner (1961), to assess energy variation.

My own attempt (Davies, 1964) to present a world picture of wave environments was based on a deductive approach, using the data of marine meteorology in conjunction with what is known of the factors of wave generation and propagation and comparing the conclusions thus reached with the observational records in existence. This sort of approach, used again in Chapter III, is also clearly limited by the data available, but it may be by following this line of attack that a really satisfactory inventory of world wave regimes will eventually be built up. Meanwhile, it must be freely admitted that here lies one of the fundamental weaknesses of any exercise in relating the distribution of shore forms with those of wave parameters.

Although they rate barely three paragraphs in Johnson's text of 1919 and do scarcely better in the much more modern work of Zenkovich (1967), coral reefs have long been appreciated as a feature giving rise to geographical variation. In fact, if one takes a world view, one of the most fundamental divisions is that between coralline and non-coralline coasts. This is virtually the same as the division made by Valentin (1952) between biogenous and non-biogenous coasts, and the fact that his coastal classification brings out this distinction clearly is one of its many virtues.

Salt marsh plants and mangroves have received considerable attention in relation to shore accretion and so have the plants of beaches and dunes. The part played by algae of a great number of families in building up or helping to destroy rocky coasts is well appreciated, even if not properly understood, and the same may be said for a great variety of animals which are active in rock destruction. Less is known of the significance of micro-organisms such as bacteria in modifying depositional and erosional processes.

However, whereas mangroves and reef-building corals are generally recognized as being distinctly zonal in distribution and effect, there has been very little discussion of the extent to which the influence of other organisms may be thought of as reflecting locational variables.

BASES OF DISCUSSION

In the four chapters which follow, an attempt is made to examine in greater detail the extent to which it is possible to adduce geographical variation in the effect of all these factors. Then, in the next six chapters, comes a discussion of ways in which variation in the effect of the factors appears to be related to variation in process and form. Basically, three approaches have been used.

The safest and most acceptable method of approach is to compare reports of actual studies made on different sections of coast. This must clearly remain the basic method in any assessment of regional variation and the fundamental way in which hypotheses, suggested by other lines of evidence, must be tested. Unfortunately, there are at present severe limitations to this method of approach, mainly due to the very unbalanced distribution of regional coastal studies and the way in which they often examine only a part of the shore system and are therefore not very useful for comparison. There are many more studies from Europe and North America than from elsewhere and, on coasts where studies have been more numerous, more of them have also been carried out in greater detail and on a higher plane of sophistication. Conversely, the less well-known coasts have been the sites of studies which have commonly been of a reconnaissance nature. Not only has this led to a frequent lack of comparability, but it has also presented the same traps into which some proponents of subaerial climatic geomorphology may have fallen. Initial generalizations made during reconnaissance studies have not always appeared so valid in the light of subsequent more detailed work (Stoddart, 1969b).

These limitations of the strictly inductive approach have convinced some workers that it is unwise to attempt further generalization until many more regional studies have been carried out.   But it is common practice in science to use deductive procedures in which *a priori* models and working hypotheses are progressively tested and rejected until apparently correct explanations are attained.   In the present context a major advantage of erecting hypotheses and attempting generalizations at this stage would seem to be that it enables further detailed studies to be directed to locations where such hypotheses may be tested and resources are thus used most economically.   The study by Bird and Hopley (1969) on a hot, wet section of the Australian coast is an example of an attempt to test hypotheses of geographical variation by selecting what appears to be a critical stretch of coast.

EXTRAPOLATION FROM SMALLER
TO LARGER SCALES

The second approach involves extrapolation from the small scale to the large scale. One method involves using the results of model experiments.   It can be demonstrated in a wind tunnel for instance that, if atmospheric humidity and sand moisture are increased, then threshold velocities for sand movement by wind are raised and from this it can be deduced that, in humid climates, winds of higher velocity are needed to move sand of given characteristics.   In similar fashion, but perhaps with less confidence, many of the variables introduced into wave tank experiments may provide data capable of being matched in nature at the larger scale.   This is an approach which has by no means been fully exploited and a good deal of work remains to be done.

A second way is by extrapolating from small scale to large scale in nature.   Islands are often profitable places to study the effects of different environmental conditions in close proximity and many of the ideas put forward in the present book owe at least something to experience of the contrasting coasts of islands—in particular the different sides of Britain, Ireland, Sri Lanka, Barbados and Tasmania.   That strongly developed single berms are characteristic of the east coast of Tasmania with a tidal range of about a metre, while double berms are found along the north coast with ranges of three to four metres is used as one argument for suggesting that this association may tend to occur on a world scale.   One small basalt islet off the northwest corner of Tasmania has a sloping intertidal shore platform on its seaward exposed side and this changes to a sub-horizontal high tide platform on the sheltered landward side: this is used to support the idea that the development of sloping platforms generally is encouraged by high wave energy.   These examples could be multiplied considerably.

Because of the greater difficulty of isolating particular variables, extrapolation within nature is clearly more dangerous than extrapolation from model to nature, but both methods provide valuable food for thought and appear worth pursuing, provided that their inherent limitations are constantly borne in mind.

DISTRIBUTION OF KNOWN FACTORS

The third approach consists of using knowledge of the distribution of known factors affecting known processes. An example of this sort of thought sequence might be— wave abrasion increases with wave energy and tool supply, wave energy and tool supply are less in the tropics, so wave abrasion must be less. Or one could argue— water layer weathering is promoted by the frequent drying out of rock surfaces between tides, this in turn is favoured by high rates of evaporation, so water layer weathering is likely to be a more important process on coasts where humidity is low.

This sort of approach is obviously the most dangerous of the three, is susceptible to circular argument and needs continual checking by actual experience; yet it may throw up hypotheses which can be tested in the field and eventually yield more soundly based results.

PROCESS VERSUS FORM

Convergence of form, whereby different processes may produce landforms of apparently similar appearance, is now widely recognized in geomorphology. It has led to the realization that it is often necessary to look for more than one mode of origin for a particular landform, and that such landforms are more safely defined descriptively than genetically. In coastal geomorphology for example, the many hypotheses which have been erected to explain the extensive barrier systems which occur on such coasts as those of eastern USA are not necessarily mutually exclusive (Schwartz, 1971). There have almost certainly been more ways than one in which barriers have been formed in different parts of the world, and we should not expect to find a simple correlation between barrier construction and a single environmental factor. However, there are identifiable processes which are conducive in different combinations to barrier formation and it is possible to attempt spatial analysis of these. In reviewing the history of climatic geomorphology, Stoddart (1968, 1969b) concluded that form is an ambiguous guide to origin and pointed to the desirability of identifying climatic parameters associated with particular processes rather than forms.

Features which owe their origin to a number of processes acting in combination may display a bewildering variety and be difficult to categorize for general discussion. In coastal geomorphology a good example is the shore platform, a common but very variable feature for which no universally acceptable classification exists. A great range of combinations of lithology, structure and process gives rise to an equally great range of possible forms. In spite of some brave attempts which have been made to classify by form, it seems much more meaningful and satisfying to try to isolate the genetic factors involved and to attempt to categorize these. At the same time the descriptive term 'shore platform' is preferable to terms like 'abrasion platform' and even 'wave-cut platform', which have definite genetic connotations.

In what follows, then, the emphasis is placed on geographical variation in factors and processes rather than in form, although it often appears possible to suggest that certain forms are clearly associated with certain environments.

PHYSICAL FACTORS OF THE LAND

The old distinction made by Suess (1892) between Pacific type coasts, where the structural grain is parallel to the coast, and Atlantic type coasts, where it is discordant, has taken on a new significance since the development and wide acceptance of the concepts of plate tectonics (for example, Le Pichon, 1968; Isacks, Oliver and Sykes, 1968). These concepts envisage lateral movement of enormous crustal plates away from zones of spreading towards zones of convergence, a process which has fundamentally affected

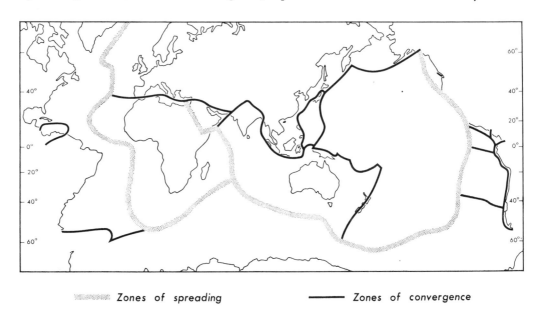

               Zones of spreading   *Zones of convergence*

FIG. 1. Disposition of present-day world crustal plates. Movement is from the zones of spreading towards the zones of convergence or collision.

the evolution of world coasts on a grand scale (Fig. 1). Crustal material is being added along zones of spreading, mainly associated with mid-oceanic ridges, but also occurring in the Red Sea and Gulf of California. It is disappearing along zones of convergence, normally associated with mountain chains and oceanic trenches. Some coasts lie along the edges of plates at zones of convergence and correspond closely to the Pacific coasts of Suess: others, which correspond to his Atlantic coasts, are imbedded in the plate and located away from zones of active crustal addition or subtraction.

Inman and Nordstrom (1971) have discussed first-order coastal evolution in relation to the ideas of plate tectonics and have proposed a broad resulting classification which is given below. Fig. 2 is based on their distribution map for these categories, but with some amendment.

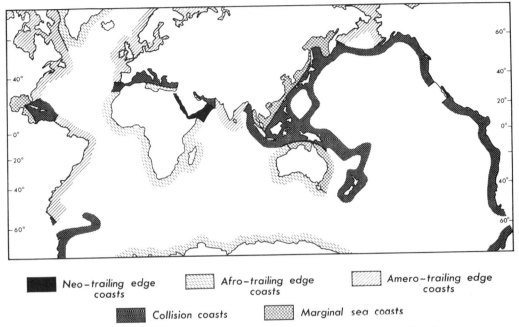

Neo-trailing edge coasts

Afro-trailing edge coasts

Amero-trailing edge coasts

Collision coasts

Marginal sea coasts

FIG. 2. A geophysical classification of coasts in terms of plate tectonics, mainly after Inman and Nordstrom (1971), but with some amendments and additions as discussed in the text. The outer coast of Baja California does not fit into any of the listed categories.

(*i*) *Collision coasts:* formed where two plates converge.
    (*a*) *Continental collision coasts:* where a continental margin is located along the zone of convergence.
    (*b*) *Island arc collision coasts:* where no continental margin is located along the zone of convergence.
(*ii*) *Trailing edge coasts:* where a plate-imbedded coast faces a spreading zone.
    (*a*) *Neo-trailing edge coasts:* where a new zone of spreading is separating a land mass.
    (*b*) *Afro-trailing edge coasts:* where the opposite continental coast is also trailing.
    (*c*) *Amero-trailing edge coasts:* where the opposite continental coast is a collision coast.
(*iii*) *Marginal sea coasts:* where a plate-imbedded coast faces an island arc.

COLLISION COASTS

On island arc collision coasts, a relatively thin but dense oceanic plate is plunging beneath a relatively thin but less dense continental plate some distance from the edge of the continent. A deep linear oceanic trench is produced with which island-forming volcanoes are associated. On continental collision coasts, an oceanic plate is moving under a thicker but less dense plate at the continental edge, so that the crust bordering the continent is folded and raised (Fig. 3). Because the Pacific Ocean is underlain by the only oceanic plates, collision coasts with trench and mountain formation are very largely found along its periphery. Collision coasts elsewhere include those of the East and West Indies, which have associated trenches, and those of the Mediterranean and Baluchistan coasts, which do not, presumably because they lie at the convergence of continental plates where only mountain building by crustal buckling takes place.

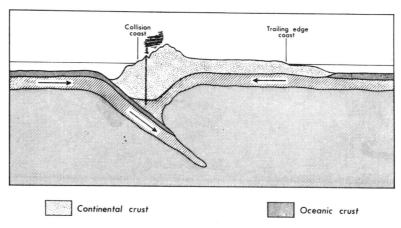

FIG. 3. Diagrammatic representation of a section through collision and trailing edge coasts, adapted from Inman and Nordstrom (1971). Arrows indicate the direction of movement of crustal plates.

Collision coasts are characterized by structural lineations parallel to the shore. They are relatively straight with high, tectonically mobile hinterlands and are fronted by narrow continental shelves. They are by far the most important loci of world volcanic and earthquake activity. The steep mobile hinterland is a potentially strong source of coastal sediment, and earthquake activity along associated trenches is a major cause of the catastrophic waves known as tsunamis (see Chapter IV).

It is along collision coasts that neotectonic effects are most evident and the direct interplay of endogenic and exogenic factors may be observed (Fig. 4). Stanley (1968) described changes along the Alaskan coast as a result of the 1964 earthquake and illustrated the effects of local emergence and submergence. There are numerous references to the way in which post-Pleistocene earth movements have changed Japanese coastal landscapes within historical time, some of them given by Yoshikawa and others (1968). Cotton (collected, 1955) has studied effects of similar deformation on New Zealand coasts. Neotectonic warping may affect the evolution of estuaries, as described by Pimienta (1953) from the Algerian coast, and uplift of the adjoining shelf may possibly bring sea floor sands within the range of onshore wave drifting, so leading to unusual accretion (Snead, 1967).

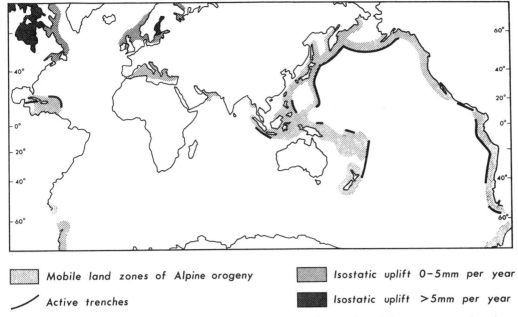

Mobile land zones of Alpine orogeny   Isostatic uplift 0–5mm per year

Active trenches   Isostatic uplift >5mm per year

FIG. 4. Major types of coastal instability. Active trenches and mobile zones are related to zones of plate convergence, major areas of isostatic uplift to the removal of Pleistocene ice masses.

TRAILING EDGE COASTS

Trailing edge coasts are plate-imbedded and contrast strongly with collision coasts in degree of tectonic activity. There is some volcanic and earthquake activity along neo-trailing edge coasts but the remaining categories show very low levels of movement. Neo-trailing edge coasts may have more or less precipitous hinterlands with virtually non-existent shelves, but in general the other categories are backed by plateau-like, hilly or low-lying areas and fronted by wide shelves. Major alignments along Afro- and Amero-trailing edge coasts reflect the alignment of zones of spreading and the occurrence of what have been termed transform faults (Wilson, 1965). Important changes in direction along the Atlantic coasts of Africa and South America, for instance, appear to be related to transform faults along the South Atlantic zone of spreading. As pointed out in earlier years by proponents of the continental drift hypothesis, structures dating from Precambrian and Palaeozoic orogenies are truncated, so that the grain of the country is markedly discordant with the coast.

The distinction between Afro- and Amero-trailing edge coasts is fundamental, because of its effect on global patterns of fluvial sedimentation (Mitchell and Reading, 1969). Where the coast on the other side of a continent is a collision coast, the high, tectonically active, rim yields a large sediment load to rivers flowing towards the trailing edge coast: where the opposite coast is itself a trailing edge coast this factor does not operate. Clear examples are the coasts of Africa, where rivers like the Zaïre and Niger carry relatively small loads, and the eastern coasts of North and South America, where the Amazon, Orinoco and Mississippi have much higher load to discharge ratios (see Fig. 12 p. 20).   As a result Amero-trailing edge coasts are lower lying, with more extensive sedimentary plains and wider continental shelves.

Along trailing edge coasts local coastal flexure may take place because of the imposition of differential sediment loads, as in the well-documented case of the Mississipi and Niger deltas.   Such effects are likely to be more important along Amero-trailing coasts, where very large sediment bodies are being built.   However some trailing edge coasts are thought to be very stable and, in particular, the shield coasts of Africa, Australia and parts of eastern South America have been widely conceived as the most stable of all.   Along the western coast of Australia for instance, unflexed Pleistocene shore features have been traced for something like 2000 km (Russell, 1963b).

MARGINAL SEA COASTS

Inman and Nordstrom recognized that their marginal sea coasts are the most diverse in character of all categories.   They are frequently modified by fluvial plains and deltas, their hinterland may vary considerably in relief and their adjoining shelves vary much in width.   Their characteristics are so much more like those of Afro- and Amero-trailing edge coasts than those of neo-trailing edge coasts that it seems doubtful whether they are worth raising to a separate third major category: the only important reason seems to be that, while some of them are near trailing edges of plates, others are near leading edges and cannot therefore be grouped in trailing edge coasts.   Some other difficulties of applying the Inman-Nordstrom scheme in detail can be illustrated by a consideration of Australian coasts, which receive no discussion in their paper.   The map (their Fig. 4) accompanying the scheme shows the southern part of the east coast as a collision coast, although it is hard to think of one reason why it should be so categorized.   It does not lie along a zone of convergence and has none of the vital characteristics of collision coasts.   In the map reproduced here (Fig. 2) it has been reclassified as a marginal sea coast lying behind the Tonga-Kermadec-New Zealand convergent line. This makes the whole coast from near Cape Bougainville in the northwest to Tasmania in the south-east a marginal sea coast, but because Inman and Nordstrom have no category for trailing edge coasts where the opposite continental coast is a marginal sea coast, a problem arises with respect to the remainder of Australia.   Left with a choice of available categories, it appears preferable to classify the trailing edge coast of a continent without young tectonically active mountains as being of Afro- rather than Amero-trailing edge type, and it has been so reclassified in Fig. 2.

It seems clear that the important distinction is between collision coasts lying along a zone of convergence and all the others which do not.   The first big group comprises plate edge coasts: the second comprises plate-imbedded coasts.   In turn, these groups approximate to the Pacific and Atlantic coasts of Suess.

ZONES OF SPREADING

The direct importance to coastal geomorphology of the existence of oceanic zones of spreading lies in the way in which islands are formed by the volcanic activity associated with magmatic upwelling (Fig. 5). Along slowly spreading zones, such as those typical of the Atlantic, where combined plate velocities are less than 6 cm per year, volcanic material tends to accumulate relatively close to the locus of spreading so that there is a marked mid-oceanic ridge, with relatively massive mountainous islands like the Azores. However, where the rate of spreading is rapid, as it is in the Pacific, growing volcanic

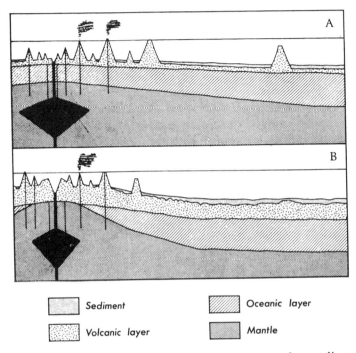

FIG. 5. Diagrammatic sections through zones of spreading: *A* – more rapid spreading typical of the Pacific; *B* – less rapid spreading typical of the Atlantic. (After Menard, 1969).

structures are moved considerable distances from the zone of origin, eventually sinking and becoming dormant. As a result the floor of the Pacific is covered by very large numbers of submarine sea mounts, some of them truncated by wave attack before they sank and so producing the flat topped sea mounts called guyots. Some of these sea mounts and guyots have provided platforms on which coral atolls have evolved: the absence of oceanic atolls in the Atlantic is due in part therefore to the slower rate of crustal spreading in that ocean.

COASTAL LITHOLOGY

The nature of coastal lithology changes so rapidly and often so subtly along most coasts that it is difficult to attempt any discussion on a world scale. Where bedrock meets the sea along erosional coasts, physical and chemical characters of the rock fundamentally affect shoreline evolution. Such characters include degree of consolidation and cohesiveness, distinctness and closeness of jointing, bedding and pseudo-bedding, (all of which affect the efficiency of wave quarrying), and permeability, grain size and chemical reactivity which influence the extent to which marine weathering processes may proceed. The effect of such factors is discussed in Chapter VI.

Russell (1967) has forecast that lithology may prove eventually to be the soundest basis for coastal classification, and in particular has pointed to the uniform appearance of crystalline rock coasts in all latitudes. Curvilinear jointing in granites, for instance, gives a characteristic appearance to sea cliffs in Scandinavia, Brazil and south-western Australia which is quite independent of climate. As in subaerial landscapes, limestones of varying nature produce especially distinctive forms along the coast. In part these are due to the special action of shoreline processes on carbonate-rich rocks: in part they are due to the drowning of subaerial karst landscapes. Drowned karst coasts include such features as some of the calanques of the French Mediterranean (Nicod, 1951), the submerged solution forms of Bermuda (Bretz, 1960) and many characteristics of coral atolls (MacNeil, 1954).

Particularly striking on a world scale is the way in which bedrock characteristics appear to carry more direct significance in high latitudes than they do in the tropics. This is because, as Tricart and Cailleux (1965) have pointed out, along extraordinarily long stretches of tropical coast the country rock is separated from the shore by a depositional fringe of varying width and of fluvial, marine or fluvial-marine origin. Possible reasons for this are suggested later (Chapter IX): meanwhile, it can be exemplified by contrasts between the coasts of Precambrian shield areas in high and low latitudes. Along the coasts of Brazil, tropical Africa, India and western Australia the old shield rocks are separated from the sea for a large proportion of their length by coastal plains of varying width, but this is certainly not so in the case of shield areas of North America and northern Europe. Even along plate-edge coasts in the tropics a narrow coastal plain or apron of sediment is commonly present.

Within the tropics two very characteristic groups of youthful rocks are commonly juxtaposed with the sea, especially on islands. On the one hand are found volcanic rocks, young lavas and pyroclasts, and on the other limestones and lime cemented sandstones and conglomerates produced by the organic secretion of carbonate and by the lithification of dune and beach sands. A large part of the literature on hard rock coasts in the tropics deals with erosional processes on these two rock groups.

PRESENT SUBAERIAL CLIMATE

The present atmospheric climate affects coastal evolution in three main ways—through its direct effect on shore processes, such as platform weathering and dune building, in the littoral zone; through its effect on subaerial geomorphic processes in the coastal zone behind the shore, and through its influence on the nature and rate of supply of sediments from the coastal hinterland—sometimes at great distances from the coast itself.

THE LITTORAL ZONE

The evolution of shore platforms, coastal dunes, tidal plains and to a small extent even beach structures is influenced by subaerial climate. Some of these effects will be discussed later, but there are two major difficulties to discussion which have been widely recognized as difficulties facing climatic geomorphology generally. The first is that we often know too little of the exact operative processes to be able to pinpoint with any certainty the really appropriate climatic parameters. The second is that, even where we can pinpoint them, the properly applicable climatic data are very rarely available: the nature of the macroclimate changes rapidly near the coast and there are not enough strictly coastal recording sites for a truly reliable picture to emerge. In the final analysis it is microclimatic effects which are usually relevant and these we must estimate crudely from what is known of the macroclimatic differences.

Maps of climatic elements reproduced here (Figs 6 to 11) share these defects and limitations. They give only a general impression of how the apparently more important elements—precipitation, insolation, evaporation, frost occurrence and wind incidence—vary around the coasts of the world.

THE COASTAL ZONE

In the zone behind the shore climate influences the processes of weathering, mass movement and erosion as well as biological processes. This is the familiar ground of subaerial climatic geomorphology to which much attention has been paid. Generally, it is obvious that coasts undergoing contemporary glaciation, periglacial solifluction and extreme desiccation are likely to develop special characteristics; however, the consideration of less extreme environments leads us on to more debatable ground. The most important effects everywhere are along bedrock coasts, where the extent and nature of cliff evolution is much affected, and in coastal inlets where variations in stream discharge and plant cover have significant repercussions.

THE COASTAL HINTERLAND

The critical effect of climate here in the coastal hinterland is to influence the nature and rate of supply of sediment to the shore. On a world scale, there are enormous variations in the extent to which shore sediments are derived from the land by river transport and these reflect not only differences in discharge but also in the denudation systems over the catchment as a whole. Fig. 12 superimposes two attempts to map regions with maximum rates of erosion, and indicates comparative rates of supply of solid material to the coast by major rivers. Working in USA, Schumm (1963) concluded that sediment yield is at a maximum with rainfall totals of 250–350 mm per year, in what are usually termed semi-arid areas, but the work of Fournier (1960) and Douglas (1969) strongly suggests that another major maximum may occur with high precipitation aggregates and intensities in the hot, wet zone—probably where aggregates exceed 1500 mm (Stoddart, 1969a). Such river load data as exist certainly imply that fluvial sediment supply to the coast is greatest where catchments lie in tropical wet or semi-arid

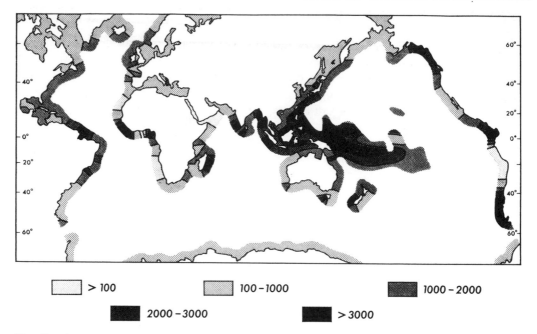

> 100   100 – 1000   1000 – 2000

2000 – 3000   > 3000

FIG. 6.   Average annual precipitation in the coastal zone in millimetres.

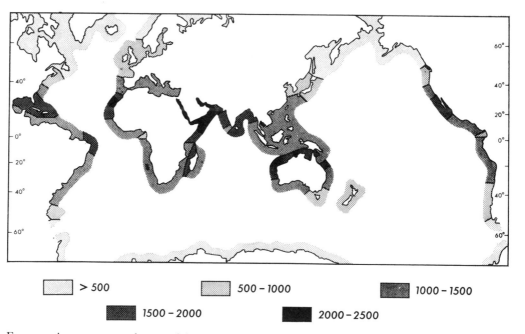

> 500   500 – 1000   1000 – 1500

1500 – 2000   2000 – 2500

FIG. 7.   Average annual potential evaporation in the coastal zone in millimetres. (Data from *Physical Geographic Atlas of the World*, Moscow, 1964.)

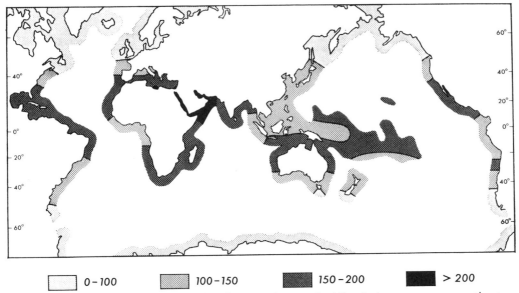

0-100   100-150   150-200   > 200

FIG. 8. Average annual solar radiation in coastal zones in kilocalories per square centimetre. (Data from *Physical Geographic Atlas of the World*, Moscow, 1964.)

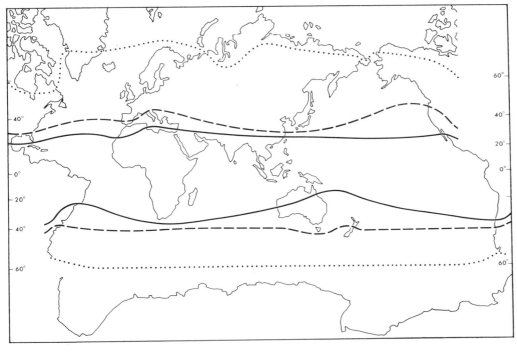

······ 60 frost-free days per year   — — Limit of coasts where frosts
——— Limit of frost-free coasts   do not occur every year

FIG. 9. Air frost frequencies in the coastal zone. (Data from *Physical Geographic Atlas of the World*, Moscow, 1964.)

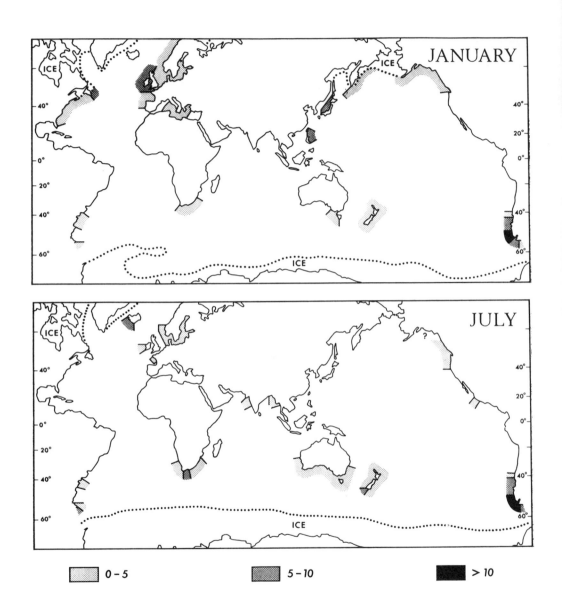

Fig. 10. Average percentage frequency of occurrence of onshore winds of Beaufort Force 8 and over for January and July. (Data from *Monthly Meteorological Charts of the Oceans*, British Meteorological Office.)

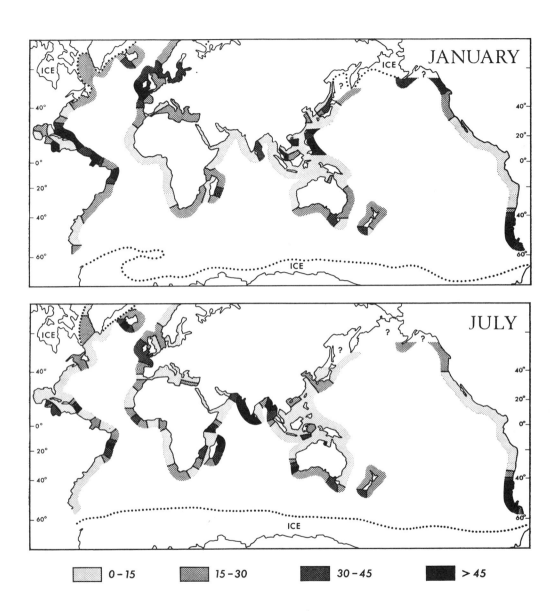

FIG. 11. Average frequency of occurrence of onshore winds of Beaufort Force 4 and over for January and July. (Data from *Monthly Meteorological Charts of the Oceans*, British Meteorological Office.)

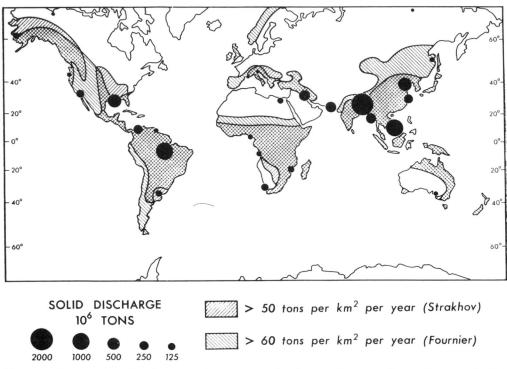

SOLID DISCHARGE
10⁶ TONS

2000   1000   500   250   125

▨ > 50 tons per km² per year (Strakhov)

▨ > 60 tons per km² per year (Fournier)

FIG. 12.   Distribution of major areas of greatest mechanical erosion according to Fournier (1960) and Strakhov (1967). The circles are proportionate to the amount of solid discharge per annum by the world's larger rivers. (Data from several authors.)

zones of high, geologically youthful mountain relief, and the coasts of northern South America and Monsoon Asia are outstanding on a world scale.   Putting it in another way, while the Amero-trailing edge and marginal sea coasts of Inman and Nordstrom (1971) are typified by great bodies of fluvial sediment, these bodies are notably greater on low latitude sections than on high latitude sections.

Although other variables, notably lithology, are of great importance locally, the climate of the hinterland also has an overall effect on the particle size of sediments being supplied to the coast (Fig. 13).   In particular, the greater rate of clay production in warmer, wetter climates (Rateev and others, 1969) helps towards a higher mud fraction, sometimes with a high humus content, while the sediment yield from semi-arid or seasonally dry catchments seems to comprise a larger proportion of sand.   Proportionately the most effective sand supply to the coast may occur in semi-arid, tectonically active areas such as the Makran coast of Baluchistan, a plate-edge or collision coast where Snead (1967) reported the rivers to be carrying enormous amounts of coarse alluvium at flood stages and supporting the construction of large beach ridge complexes. As discussed later, in Chapter VIII, zonal tendencies in the nature of fluvially supplied sediments are reflected in the distribution of offshore bottom materials and in the evolution of the coast.

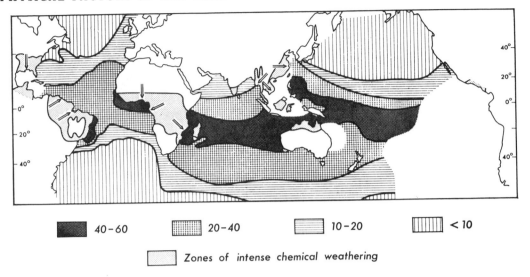

40-60   20-40   10-20   < 10

Zones of intense chemical weathering

FIG. 13.   Latitudinal variation in chemical weathering as indicated by percentage of kaolinite in ocean floor clays, kaolinite being a product of intensive chemical rock breakdown. (After Rateev and others, 1969.) The continental zones of intensive chemical weathering are from Strakhov (1967) and the arrows indicate major river discharge points within these zones.

PLEISTOCENE INHERITANCE

It is widely recognized that many coastal landforms owe something, and sometimes very much, to conditions which have operated in the past.   In particular, climatic factors generally functioned differently during the Pleistocene and along some coasts the difference was very marked indeed.   The factors discussed in the last section not only had a different distribution but, because of the concomitant Pleistocene sea level changes, they also acted at different heights in relation to the present shore.   In this way cliffs and shore platforms have usually to be thought of as being multicyclic in origin, beaches may contain relict sediments, old dune systems may extend behind their modern counterparts, and coastal inlets owe much of their form to downcutting in glacial or even preglacial times.

In spite of postglacial modification, the broad outlines of most coasts owe much to the nature of the subaerial landscape against which the postglacial sea encroached and in this there are strong zonal implications.   Former glacial conditions have clearly left their mark on fjord coasts and those of morainic origin but the effects of other climatic swings are not so easily identified.   Indeed, until there is agreement on the nature of contemporary climatic effects, positive identification will be impossible (Fig. 14).

A very important Pleistocene legacy along many coasts is represented by varying proportions of the sediment body.   Some coasts, of which the southern part of the east coast of Australia is almost certainly a good example, are receiving little material from rivers today but are carrying apparently substantial amounts derived from Pleistocene

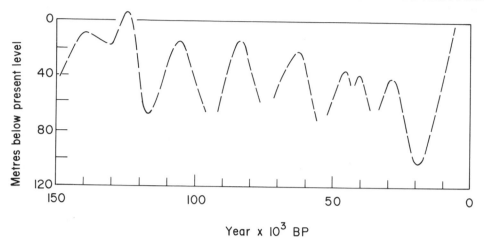

Fig. 14. Late Quaternary sea level fluctuations inferred from coral reef terraces on tectonic coasts. (After Bloom and others, 1974.)

rivers.   Fluvial sediments were deposited on what is now the continental shelf and concentrated on the present shore by the rising postglacial sea.   Phleger and Ewing (1962) thought that a large part of the sand on the coast of Baja California was brought by rivers in former pluvial periods and, in a discussion on West Africa, Grove (1968) has suggested that much transport of sand to the coast in the drier tropics may have occurred during a pluvial phase approximately 10 000 to 5000 years ago, which was thus contemporary with the last great rise of the sea to its present general level.   On other coasts, such as in much of western Europe, big quantities of pebble and boulder material were derived from Pleistocene glacial and periglacial deposits, either similarly concentrated on the shore by the postglacial transgression or produced by recent marine erosion of sea floors or cliffs.   Examples are numerous and the question is reopened in Chapter VIII.

SEA LEVEL CHANGE

The sea level changes of the Pleistocene were primarily eustatic and to this extent were worldwide in effect.   In the study of present-day coastal morphology the changes of the last 150 000 years are most important and a more detailed picture of these is beginning to be constructed (Fig. 14) as a result of studies on tectonically active coral coasts, principally in New Guinea and Barbados (Bloom and others, 1974).   This suggests that the last time that world sea level was higher than the present was about 120 000 years ago.   During the intervening glacial episode sea level has fluctuated below its present level and reached a lowest point about 18 000 BP.   The last great submergence brought the sea to its present level but there has been considerable controversy over the details of fluctuation on the most recent part of the curve.   Around Australian coasts there now seems abundant evidence to show that present sea level was reached about 6000 BP and there has not been much change since that time.   This conclusion contrasts markedly with those reached from North Atlantic coasts for instance, where submergence seems to have gone on at a reduced rate for much longer. On other coasts, especially those adjacent to the Pacific Ocean, small higher postglacial sea levels have been postulated.

It is in looking at these low amplitude fluctuations that geographical variation becomes apparent and local, non-eustatic factors significant. Differential sea level changes which are due to vertical movements along plate-edge or collision coasts, isostatic rebound following the removal of large Pleistocene ice bodies and local sedimentation near river mouths have long been accepted. More recently the idea of hydro-isostasy or differential weighting of continental shelves by sea water has been developed, especially by Bloom (1967). Isostatic readjustment of the littoral zone has been envisaged as a response to loading and unloading of the shelf by the big eustatic sea level fluctuations. The amount of this readjustment should vary from section to section according to the width and depth of the shelf, which would in turn control differences in the weight of water at glacial and interglacial times. By constructing 'isomesobaths' of the continental shelf of eastern USA, Bloom was able to explain discrepancies in records of postglacial coastal submergence between different places in terms of the expectable differential downwarping of the adjacent shelf. His hypothesis is that 'the water load of the postglacial rise of sea level has isostatically deformed the Atlantic coast of the United States in proportion to the average weight of water at the present shoreline'. On a world scale, differences in the structure of the continental shelf may be involved.

If this hypothesis survives further testing it introduces intriguing possibilities. It may help to resolve conflicts of opinion on the nature of postglacial sea level changes and in particular the longstanding argument relating to the existence or otherwise of a higher mid-Recent sea level. On a broader scale, it suggests further speculations. Have shallow shelves everywhere submerged less and is this an added reason why they tend to promote the formation of barrier systems, while, conversely, steep coastal ramps have submerged more and encouraged deep ria development?

The world ocean current system causes the hypothetical still water surface of the seas to be uneven within a range of about 1·5 metres (Fig. 15). In general terms the effect is to raise sea level in the western parts of the oceans in lower latitudes. Since this uneven surface is related to the strength and trajectory of the various currents, it seems a logical deduction that any change in global climate, giving rise to a change in oceanic circulation, would change the relief pattern of the sea surface. Fairbridge and Krebs (1962), for instance, suggested that it would be worthwhile considering whether part of the anomalously rapid contemporary sea level rise along the east coast of North America may be due to a long-term deceleration of the Gulf Stream. The same authors have reviewed possible effects of long-term cyclic changes in the pattern of atmospheric pressure on local sea level changes as revealed by tide gauge records. These small spatial and temporal variations in the height of the sea surface are probably negligible in terms of major eustatic shifts, but they may well be pertinent to the study of minor postglacial movements of a metre or two, which have been postulated for some coasts and particularly those adjacent to the Pacific Ocean.

Other possible causes of small differential sea level changes include variations in the earth's rate of rotation, which affect the amount of the equatorial bulge so that a slowing of the rate would increase water level at the poles relative to the equator, and variations in the position of the axis of rotation, which would relocate the bulge in relation to the present equator.

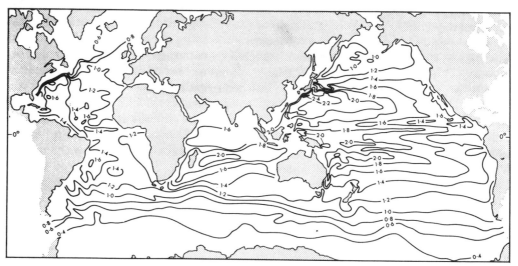

FIG. 15.   Levels of the sea surface in metres above an arbitrary level surface. (From a map by Stommel, 1966.)

III PHYSICAL FACTORS OF THE SEA: WAVES

Since waves are by far the most important agents of coastal modification, any attempt to examine world variations in coastal processes must pay particular attention to wave climates. We ought to know something of variations in their direction of approach, their length, height, energy and steepness and the degree to which these characteristics change seasonally. In fact, of course, we have very few statistics and in this respect coastal geomorphology differs from subaerial geomorphology where there is at least a modicum of data pertaining to the hydrologic cycle, wind velocities and directions, and the dynamics of glaciers. Only since World War Two have instrumental wave recorders been developed and operated, and even now the amount of information which has been derived from them is very small. It is true that there is a great deal of non-instrumental observational data available, much of it summarized in marine atlases, but this has to be treated with a certain amount of caution. For example, observations at sea tend to ignore long low swell which may peak up and become of vital significance on the shore and this is a grave limitation for present purposes of publications like Hogben and Lumb (1967), primarily designed to aid in ship routing. On the other hand, observations on the shore tell little of what is happening outside the surf zone. What we now know of wave generation and propagation suggests that the actual state of affairs is almost always much more complex than it appears to the eye.

On the credit side, there has been a vast advance in wave theory over the last quarter of a century, and there now exist reasonable methods for wave forecasting, the most generally used being those given by Pierson, Neumann and James (1960). At the moment of writing the best summary of progress in wave theory is probably that provided by Kinsman (1965). The ability to make local forecasts of wave weather at specific points on the coast, by using particular synoptic situations, implies at least some ability to reconstruct wave climates for longer lengths of coast by using the data of atmospheric climatology, and this is the approach which will be attempted in this chapter. World wave climates will be deduced from wave theory and wind data and these deductions will be compared with the actual observations—both instrumental and non-instrumental—which are available. Such an approach has its limitations and it will be necessary to keep these in mind all the time, but the broad picture which results is not likely to be seriously wrong even though we are unable to fill in all the details.

WAVE GENERATION

The potential energy of wind-generated gravity waves on the surface of the ocean is a function of the wind velocity, the duration of time through which it blows in one direction and the fetch or distance over which it has operated.   Changes in fetch are important up to about 1500 km, and for higher wind speeds it may take up to about two days before the effect of the duration factor ceases to be significant and the sea surface is fully aroused.   However, the length of time taken for a fully aroused sea to be produced depends in part on its initial condition, in that it will take less time where a sea surface is already disturbed than where the sea is smooth.   The wind generates a spectrum of waves of different heights and periods, giving rise to a confused jumble of short-crested waves within the storm area, but as the waves move out from here the individual components tend to segregate as the faster longer frequency waves draw further ahead. These more-travelled waves become longer crested and more regular in appearance, and begin to approach the form of the 'model waves' which need to be assumed as a mathematical basis for wave theory.   Although the wave spectrum may have a large range of wave periods, the great bulk of the energy is carried within a particular band where wave height is greatest and it is the waves of this optimum energy band which are of prime geomorphic significance.

The wave crests generated by a particular wind can probably be thought of as arcuate in plan, because appreciable amounts of energy are transmitted at an angle to the wind direction itself.   Arthur (1949) concluded that wave height is likely to vary as the cosine of the angle of divergence of the main wind direction, and on this basis waves travelling at 40 degrees to the wind direction would still be about three-quarters the height of those travelling in the wind direction.   The waves travel in a direction perpendicular to a line tangential to the wave crest.   Because wave travel involves very little mass transport and effectively it is only the wave form which moves, there is insignificant deflection as a result of the Coriolis effect and wave groups may be thought of as following great circle tracks over the surface of the oceans.

Waves actively being impinged on by the wind are termed *sea waves* and are contrasted with *swell waves* which have travelled out of the zone of generation.   This use of the term 'sea' is perhaps a bit unfortunate—in the colloquial sense all ocean waves are sea waves—but it is now firmly fixed in this more restricted and technical sense and no better alternative seems to exist.   Sea waves include not only the storm waves of obvious geomorphic significance but also the small choppy wavelets produced by the slighter breezes.

As swell travels, energy, which may be taken to vary as wave length times the square of wave height, decreases with distance, mainly because of attenuation, dispersion and angular spreading.   Estimates of rates of swell decay may be obtained from relationships developed by Bretschneider (1952), which suggest that something of the order of 80 to 90 per cent of energy is lost in about the first 2000 km but that, after this, the rate of loss is much reduced (Fig. 16).   Some additional loss of energy may occur where waves move through regions of opposing winds, which may cause breaking into white caps, but this seems to be most important in the earlier stages of travel when the wave forms are steeper.   Very low and smooth old swell is not likely to lose energy in this way and may carry for thousands of kilometres until it is arrested by a coastline.

It is not too difficult to get some idea of the broad spatial variation in wave energy input over the world's oceans because of the way in which this is related to wind

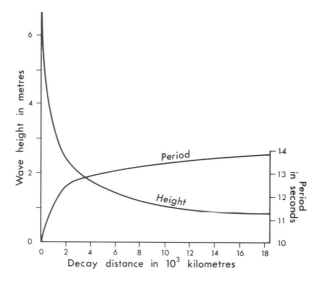

FIG. 16. The effect of swell decay on wave period and height in the case of a 10-second wave, 6·1 m high, generated over a fetch distance of 735 km. (Based on the values of Bretschneider, 1952.)

velocity. We have seen that duration and fetch are also factors, but much the most important variable is likely to be the proportion of time that winds of given speeds are recorded at particular localities and there is a great deal of information on this in various forms. In Fig. 17 percentage frequencies of occurrence of gale force winds (Beaufort Force 8 and over) are mapped for the oceans in two representative months. Such winds have mean velocities in excess of about 17 m/sec^{-1} and, according to all proposed forecasting formulae, there is a tremendous increase in energy input in this range. The relationships suggested by Pierson, Neumann and James (1960), for instance, are illustrated in Fig. 18. The regions with a relatively high frequency of occurrence of gales are therefore the principal regions of high wave generation and high energy input. Fig. 17 shows that these are overwhelmingly the regions of frontal activity in the higher mid-latitudes of both hemispheres. In the high polar regions and the tropical zone, gales are infrequent, although important major exceptions are those associated with ephemeral tropical cyclones in which wind velocities are very much higher even than in the normal gale.

In 1958, Holcombe presented an analysis of somewhere around twenty-five and a half million observations of winds at sea, from which he obtained figures for location and abundance of gale force winds, and some of his conclusions are summarized in Fig. 19. He found that in the southern hemisphere the mean latitude of the zone of maximum number of gale force winds is remarkably stable and varies only between 54°S in winter and 56°S in summer. The corresponding figures for the northern hemisphere are 62°N in summer and 46°N in winter. Greater seasonal variation in the north is also reflected

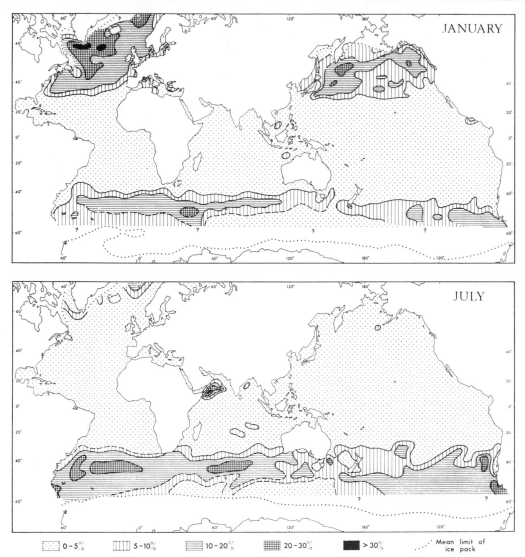

FIG. 17.   Percentage frequency of occurrence of gale force winds (Beaufort Force 8 and over) in oceanic areas for January and July. (Data from *US Navy Marine Climatic Atlas of the World*.)

in the mean monthly extremes of latitude of the zone of maximum abundance, which are 47° and 60° in the south but 16° and 76° in the north.   The southern hemisphere zone is more stable in time as well as in space since the proportional abundance of gales in the zone of maximum frequency of occurrence varies only between 24 per cent in winter and 17 per cent in summer.   The corresponding figures for the northern hemisphere zone are 24 per cent and 5 per cent.

These differences between the north and the south also appear in Fig. 17, and are

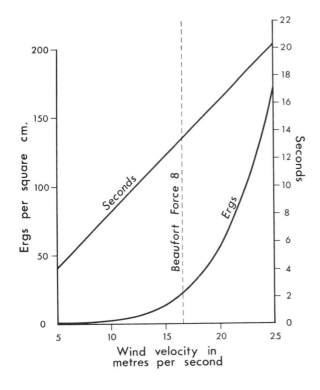

FIG. 18. Average potential wave energy, in ergs per square centimetre, of a fully arisen sea at different wind velocities, and period in seconds of the optimum spectral energy band related to generating wind velocity. (data from Pierson, Neumann and James, 1960.) Note rapid rise in energy above Beaufort Force 8.

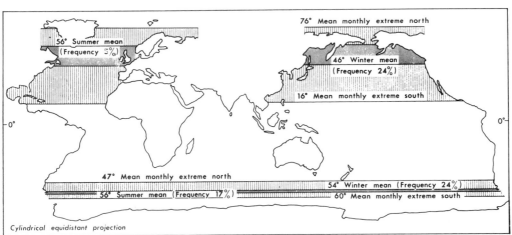

FIG. 19. Latitudes of mean maximum occurrence of gale force winds for summer and winter and of mean monthly extremes north and south. (Data from Holcombe, 1958.) Mean frequencies of occurrence are also indicated.

clearly due to the influence of the great northern land masses in widening the zone of development of the polar front and producing a massive seasonal change in the climatic picture between the summer and winter seasons. Except where it intersects the extremity of South America the southern zone lies virtually entirely over the sea, and the south coasts of South Africa, Australia and New Zealand are only marginal to it.

The consistent occurrence of a large number of gale force winds (around one-fifth of all winds recorded), their relative persistence in location and the long sea distances over

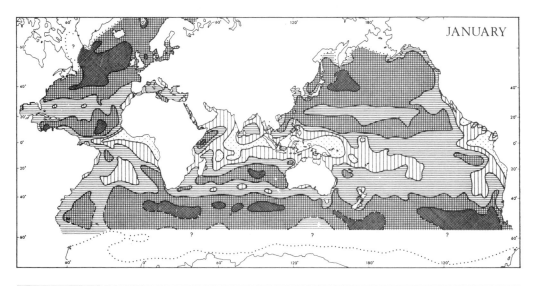

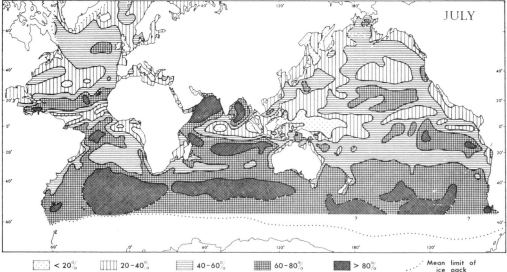

FIG. 20.   Percentage frequency of occurrence of winds at Beaufort Force 4 and over in oceanic areas for January and July. (Data from *US Navy Marine Climatic Atlas of the World*.)

which they blow make the southern storm belt much the most important and clearly definable wave generating area in the world. Although very few of these southern gales impinge on the coast or produce storm waves impinging on the coast, they produce a very high proportion indeed of world ocean swell; as we shall see, there is direct evidence that the effect of this swell is felt even along coasts in the northern hemisphere.

If we turn our attention now to winds of lower velocity, it seems most meaningful to take Beaufort Force 4 (moderate breeze with minimum speed 5 m/sec^{-1}.) as a cut-off point below which waves of normal geomorphic significance are unlikely to be generated. By convention, Force 4 winds are those which give rise to small waves with fairly frequent white caps: winds which produce only large wavelets with perhaps scattered white caps are designated Force 3. In Fig. 20, the percentage frequency of occurrence of winds of Force 4 and over is given; of course, the northern and southern storm belts are again prominent, but it is now possible to identify other regions of likely wave production and, in particular, zones in both hemispheres around about 10 to 20° from the equator. These are the zones of the tropical easterlies, often called the trade wind belts. Between them is the doldrum belt, a discontinuous zone where even winds of 5 m/sec^{-1} are infrequent, and lighter breezes and calms may be observed for over 80 per cent of the time.

The nature of the tropical easterlies was examined in a series of papers by Crowe (1949, 1950, 1951), whose diagrams show that velocities lie almost exclusively in the range of 3 to 10 m/sec^{-1}. Wind speeds greater than this are rare, except in the Indian Ocean, where they may more usually rise to 13–14 m/sec^{-1} during the time of the southwest Asiatic monsoon. The monsoons may be considered as extensions of the system of the tropical easterlies, and it is relevant to note that their velocities are generally comparable. Only the Arabian Sea monsoon winds commonly reach speeds of 13–14 m/sec^{-1}. Because by far the greater number of observed velocities in the tropical easterlies and their associated monsoons are less than 11 m/sec^{-1}, the waves they produce are considerably lower, and shorter, than those produced in the temperate storm belts, and they carry much less energy.

The remaining important wave-producing winds to be mentioned are those generated by tropical cyclones during summer and autumn in either hemisphere. They differ from other wind regimes in their extreme irregularity of occurrence, direction and velocity. Each individual cyclone may have a life of a week or more and follows a more or less well defined path (Fig. 21). In assessing the significance of data for the average number of occurrences per year, it is important to bear in mind that the same paths are not followed every year and, on a given coast, the interval between successive cyclones may be several or many years.

WAVE PROPAGATION

Having outlined in broad fashion the major pattern of wave generation over the oceans, it is necessary to turn next to consider the effect of this in terms of the propagation of waves reaching the coast. In order to simplify the discussion, the behaviour of sea waves is considered separately from that of swell.

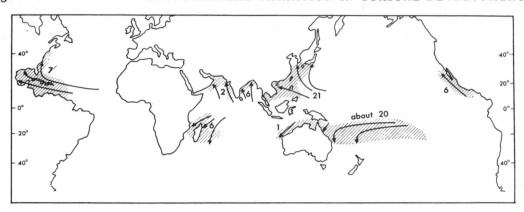

FIG. 21.   Coasts subject to tropical cyclones (hatched), major cyclone tracks and average annual frequency of occurrence within each region. (Data from a number of sources.)

STORM WAVE ENVIRONMENTS

We have seen that, with the exception of tropical cyclones, the highest sea waves are produced in the temperate storm belts, where much the greatest number of high waves is generated.   We have not yet taken into consideration the fact that the dominant direction of winds in these temperate storm belts is westerly, so that big sea waves reaching the west coasts of continents in temperate latitudes are certain to be more numerous than those reaching the eastern shores.   They may also be higher, because the more disturbed state of the ocean surface off west-facing coasts should lead to the more rapid development of a fully aroused sea.   Kinsman (1965), for instance, has suggested that such a difference may exist between the western and eastern sections of the North Atlantic.   In some opposition to this is the tendency of winds to produce bigger waves where sea surface temperatures are significantly higher than those of the air above.   According to Brown (1953), waves produced by winds of Beaufort Force 6 for instance, are 25 per cent higher for water $5\frac{1}{2}$°C warmer than the overlying air than for cases where water and air temperatures are the same (see also Burling, 1955).   Regions favourable to such temperature differences occur at the western sides of temperate oceans and particularly in association with the Gulf Stream and Kiro Siwo currents.   The most we can conclude with any degree of certainty is that west-facing coasts in Europe and temperate North America are likely to be affected by relatively frequent storm waves in winter and infrequent ones in summer, whereas the east-facing coasts of temperate North America and Asia are liable to suffer less frequent storm wave attack in winter and very little at all in summer.   The west coast of Patagonia is probably the most consistently attacked by storm waves all year round and contrasts with the east coast, where storm wave attack is of considerably lower intensity.   Something of this picture is brought out in Figs 10, 25 and 26.

In spite of the differences which have been outlined, all these coasts can be grouped into what may be termed storm wave environments because big, steep storm waves are common only along these coasts.

SWELL-WAVE ENVIRONMENTS

Outside the storm wave environments, open coasts are likely to be influenced by swell waves travelling away from the gales generated in these regions and by other locally produced wind waves, which, if common, are relatively small and, if large, are relatively rare.

The swell emanating from the temperate storm belts travels great distances. The direction which these waves take up is controlled by the direction of the generating wind, their tendency to fan out on either side of this direction and the fact that they travel along more or less straight lines on the globe. This last property is of particular importance because it means that the swell waves follow great circle courses, and this permits some prediction of subsequent history. Fig. 22 shows that waves generated in the southern storm belt by winds blowing from any direction between north-west and south all tend to take a general course from south-westward as they move away from their area of origin. A north-westerly gale off the Cape of Good Hope will eventually produce south-westerly swell on the coast of Tasmania. Similarly, gales from between north-east and south will give swell from a generally south-easterly direction. For the median paths of swell to reach Antarctica the generating winds must blow from the sector between north-west and north-east. The Antarctic coasts therefore remain relatively sheltered from heavy swell and the great bulk of energy transmitted by southern hemisphere gales is directed northward towards the equator. In a similar way, swell generated in the northern storm belt will tend to move along tracks suggesting a north-westerly or north-easterly origin and relatively little of the winter swell in the northern Pacific and Atlantic Oceans will travel towards the Arctic. Fig. 22 illustrates some examples of this phenomenon.

Because the westerly component in temperate latitude gales is much more important than the easterly, it is in fact south-westerly swell which is of particular importance in the south and north-westerly swell in the north (Fig. 23). This westerly swell has been extensively recorded instrumentally and by general observation along considerable stretches of the world's coasts. It is particularly in evidence along coasts such as those of Peru and West Africa, where strong winds are few or offshore in direction so that there are not many locally produced waves of geomorphic consequence. South-westerly swell from southern ocean storms is known to occur along the west coast of the Americas, from California to Chile (Munk and Snodgrass, 1957; Schweigger, 1959; Gierloff-Emden, 1959; James, 1961), along the west coast of Africa from Ghana to the Cape of Good Hope (Jessen, 1951; Guilcher, 1954c, 1959; Darbyshire, 1957b; Sitarz, 1960), and in southern Australia (Silvester, 1956; Davies, 1958, 1960; Noye, 1967). The propagation of southern swell across the Pacific was studied by Snodgrass and others (1966), who set up a chain of six wave recording stations from New Zealand to Alaska and were able to track different energy spectra over a period of two and a half months. They found that most energy was lost shortly after the waves left the generating area in the southern ocean; there was little loss from interaction with, for example, trade wind seas. In view of its extensive penetration in the Pacific and Atlantic, it seems certain that southern swell reaches the south coasts of Asia.

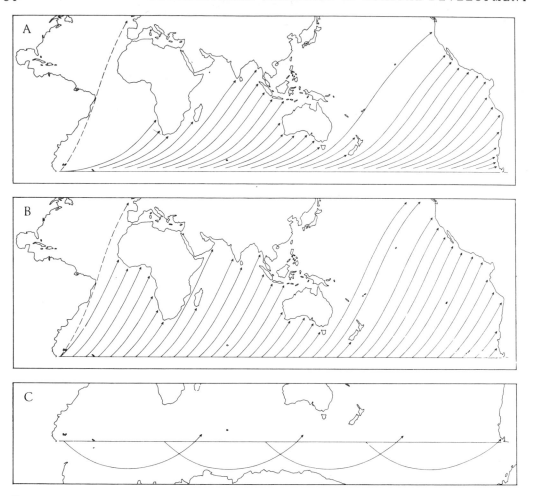

FIG. 22. Typical great circle paths followed by swell generated at latitude 55°S by (A) westerly, (B) southwesterly and (C) northwesterly gales. The broken line indicates the great circle path from the Falkland Islands to Cornwall travelled by swell recorded by Barber and Ursell (1948).

Along the west coasts of Africa and the Americas, south-westerly swell waves decrease in height from south to north and also from southern winter to southern summer. In southern California, at a latitude of about 30°N, they are reaching the margin of their geomorphic influence, but heights of up to a metre have been recorded regularly for waves which have been shown to have travelled from the neighbourhood of 55°S (Munk and Snodgrass, 1957). On the south-west coast of England waves with a maximum height of about 30 cm were shown to have originated in the region of the Falkland Islands (Barber and Ursell, 1948 and Fig. 22). Sitarz (1960), summarizing records to that date for the Bight of Benin in West Africa, gave the height as rising to 2 m or even 3 m in July and exceptionally 4 m, but dropping to 40 to 60 cm in January.

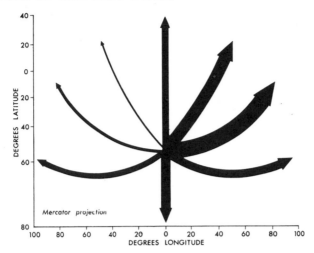

FIG. 23. Great circle paths travelled by swell generated at latitude 55°S by gales from main compass points. Line thicknesses are proportional to frequency of occurrence in the South Pacific.

A report by Nedeco (1961) on the Nigerian coast gave period and height of the typical swell as 12 seconds and 1·5 m. This swell was calculated to have energy levels sixteen times that of the typical locally generated wave trains. These figures are representative of marginal areas and are of course exceeded further south.

Coasts influenced by westerly swell from the north are much more restricted in extent and may be taken to comprise the east coast of the Atlantic from the Bay of Biscay south to Senegal, and the east coast of the Pacific in Oregon and California. The Atlantic coast of Morocco has long been known to be subject to consistent attack by north-westerly swell (Jessen, 1951; Guilcher, 1954c). Darbyshire (1957a) has published wave records taken at Casablanca for short periods in September 1953 and February 1954 when there was no local wind and the waves could be shown to have originated in storms 650 to 3000 km away. The heights recorded were up to about five metres. Jessen's observations suggested that wave heights varied between about 1·5 and 5 m for between 12 and 19 days of the month in the northern winter but rarely exceeded 3 m during the rest of the year. His data suggested that the year can be rather sharply divided into a winter period, when big swell is common, and a summer period when it is rare, and this agrees well with the known behaviour of the northern storm belt, described earlier as tending to disappear in summer.

The north-westerly swell of the Oregon and Californian coasts has been described by a number of authors, from Munk and Traylor (1947) onwards. It is highest and most continuous during the northern winter, when it reaches heights of 1 to 2 m as far south as southern California. Further north it is much heavier, and the spectacular north-westerly swell of the Oregon Coast has been described expressively by Bascom

(1964).   Wave characteristics are very similar to those for north-westerly swell on the African coast, with a notable drop of energy in the northern summer.

Wave regimes on the east coasts of the continents are distinctly more complex than those on the west.   Evidence suggests that swell from extra-tropical storms penetrates equatorward much as it does along west coasts, but its frequency of occurrence and height is markedly less.   On the east coast of Australia, McKenzie (1958) noted that big swell of southern origin is sporadic in appearance; this is certainly true of the east coast of Tasmania, where only occasionally is the height of the continuous west coast swell attained and there are long periods when breakers are under 1 m in height. However, this small swell tends to persist throughout the year.   Swell from the northern North Atlantic has been recorded instrumentally at Barbados in the West Indies (Donn and McGuiness, 1959).   A northerly swell is a well-known phenomenon on the island and is an important factor in the wave regime, especially on the west coast where it is not masked by trade wind generated waves.   As might be expected, its occurrence is limited more or less to the northern winter.   Munk and Snodgrass (1957) thought that southerly swell recorded by Donn (1949) at Bermuda was likely to have had an origin in the southern storm belt, since its constituent wave periods of up to 18 seconds are difficult to explain in terms of any other source.

Superimposed on this background of swell are waves from more local sources, notably the tropical easterlies and the ephemeral tropical cyclones.   Maps compiled by Crowe (1951) and on which Fig. 24 is based show that the truly consistent trades affect only comparatively small sections of tropical east coasts.   From these maps it is easy to see why workers in the West Indies such as Donn and McGuiness (1959) and in the central Pacific islands such as Inman, Gayman and Cox (1963), place special stress on the importance of trade wind generated waves.   Anyone who has seen these waves coming in on the north-eastern coasts of Oahu and Barbados, for example, cannot fail to be impressed by their obviously supreme importance in the local wave regime.   However, comparison of Fig. 24, which shows the consistency of trade wind direction, with Fig. 20, showing the abundance of winds of Force 4 and over, suggests that the only extensive stretches of continental coast strongly influenced by waves generated by tropical easterlies lie in tropical Brazil and East Africa.

Munk and Sargent (1948) invoked trade wind waves with a period of about 7 to 9 seconds and a height of 2 or 3 m to explain the orientation of coral features in mid-Pacific. Such figures are comparable with those of 7 to 10 seconds in period and 1 to 3 m high quoted by Gurtner (1960) for monsoon generated waves along the Indian coast. The figures agree well with those of an 8 seconds maximum energy period and 3 m highest one-tenth of waves which are obtained for a 10 m/sec^{-1} wind using the Pierson–Neumann–James method of forecasting. They may be taken as typical of the geomorphically most effective tropical easterlies and their monsoonal derivatives.

Monsoon generated waves are of major importance along the coasts of India and South-east Asia where there is sufficient fetch.   The north-east monsoon generates important wave trains along the east coast of the Malayan peninsula (Nossin, 1961), but it is the south-west Indian monsoon which is of major wave generating significance.

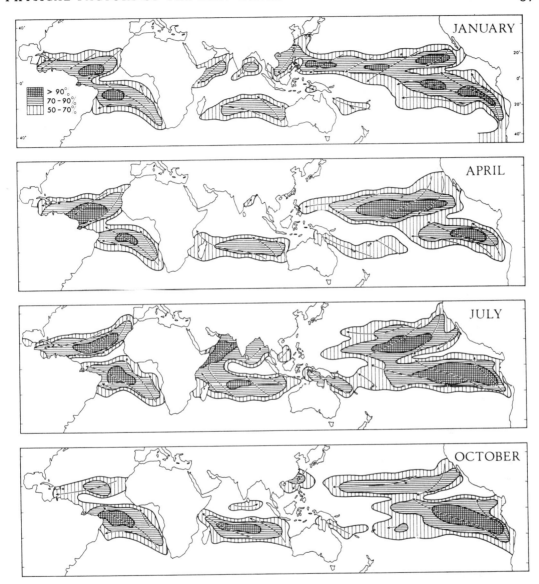

FIG. 24. Percentage frequency of persistence of oceanic trade winds. The arrows indicate major tracks of the true persistent trades and their monsoonal derivatives. (After Crowe.)

Indian workers, such as Manohar (1958, 1961) and Joglekar, Gole and Apte (1958), have described the seasonal reversal of wave direction on the coast of India attributable to the monsoon regime, but we should bear in mind that a good deal of southern ocean swell may be mixed up in the monsoon generated spectra. Pilot's Handbooks published by the British and German Admiralties refer to a perennial southerly swell on the oceanic coasts of India, Sri Lanka and Sumatra which is quite independent of local weather conditions.   This swell increases in height and persistency at the same time as southern swell in the Pacific and Atlantic, an increase which coincides both with the more intensive storm activity further south in the southern winter and with the incidence of the south-west monsoon.

Relative energy levels in the tropics of swell from temperate latitudes and waves generated by trade winds can be approximated by using the forecasting relationships of Pierson, Neumann and James (1960) and the decay relationships of Bretschneider (1952).   Average potential wave energy in the complete spectrum in a fully arisen sea generated by a 18 m/sec^{-1} wind is likely to be about 20 times that generated by a 10 m/sec^{-1} wind, while the energy carried by the biggest waves in the spectrum will be something of the order of 50 times as great for a 18 m/sec^{-1} wind as for a 10 m/sec^{-1} wind. Even though the waves from polar front gales may lose about 90 to 95 per cent of energy by the time they reach the equatorial zone, they will still be potentially more energetic. However if, as is usual, they are following approximately the same tracks as trade wind and monsoon generated waves, they may not be particularly evident to crude observation.

Swell waves are of most geomorphic consequence where the coast is fronted by a moderately shallow shelf, which allows the wave form to peak up and generate maximum forward translation of energy towards the shore.   On steep coastal ramps, especially where reef barriers occur, much of the energy of long flat waves is reflected and they play little part in shore modification.   This seems to be why southern swell is of overwhelming importance along the west coast of southern Africa and in southern and western Australia but, as exemplified by the work of McIntire and Walker (1964), is of minor importance on the island of Mauritius, which lies in the same latitudinal relationship to the zone of origin, around 55°S.   In the Pacific, the dominant nature of southern swell along the west coast of South America and its ready identification north as far as California contrasts with the way in which it is rarely mentioned by writers on oceanic island morphology, except for more southerly groups like some of the Tuamotos (Newell, 1956; Wiens, 1959).

Fig. 21 shows the location of coasts affected by very high energy waves from tropical cyclones and, with the exception of western Mexico and north-western Australia, it will be seen that like the trade wind coasts these are also on the eastern sides of continents. Individual stretches of coast will suffer the effect of waves from this source for very short periods at irregular intervals so that, even in the east Asiatic typhoon area where tropical cyclones are most abundant, a particular locality will not necessarily be subjected every year to waves being actively driven by hurricane force winds.   The summary of hurricane wave statistics for the Gulf of Mexico compiled by Wilson (1957) may be taken as exemplifying the general situation.

However, the effect of swell waves originating in tropical cyclones is far wider, and most sections of the coasts distinguished in Fig. 21 can expect to receive swell from most of the storms which occur in any part of the whole region.   Coasts outside the tropical cyclone regions are reached by swell from this source: for instance swell from a west Atlantic hurricane has been recorded off Cornwall (Barber and Ursell, 1948).

DISTRIBUTION OF WAVE PARAMETERS

Wave parameters of geomorphic significance are energy, height, length, steepness and direction.   Both energy and steepness are functions of height and length, but energy is mainly correlated with height, and steepness mainly with length.

WAVE ENERGY

As noted previously, few direct measurements of wave energy are available and the picture which has been presented here relies on knowledge of the distribution of energy input by wind and the behaviour of the resulting waves.   This suggests that high energy waves are to be found mainly in the storm wave environments; that, on west coasts in the swell environments, high to medium wave energy is generally experienced; that, on east coasts in swell environments, energy varies from low to medium high; and that, in major enclosed seas and along Arctic and Antarctic coasts, mean energy levels are low. This highly qualitative and subjective picture has limitations which have already been outlined and it obviously cannot take into account local variations in exposure to wave attack.

Because mean energy levels tell only part of the story, it is necessary also to take into consideration variations about the mean.   Extreme cases might be exemplified on the one hand by west coast swell environments such as Guinea, where Sitarz (1960) remarked on 'cette houle d'une régularité presque déconcertante', and on the other by low energy environments with occasional tropical cyclones, such as the Gulf of Mexico, where studies like those of Morgan, Nichols and Wright (1958) in Louisiana, and Stoddart (1965) off Honduras, provide illustrations.   In the first case there is little energy variation around the mean and wave induced processes tend to be continuous in operation and effect: in the second there is enormous departure from the mean and wave processes operate on distinctly different energy levels at different times.   Between these extremes lies a host of other regimes in which seasonality and range of wave energy vary.

A study reported by Ball, Shinn and Stockman (1967), on the effects of a hurricane in south Florida, suggested that a bias exists for the preservation in the geological record, and also presumably in the landscape, of the effects of high energy events.   Such a conclusion is of particular pertinence in environments with wide energy deviation.

WAVE HEIGHT

The energy of a particular wave is taken to vary as the length times the square of the height, so we see that height and energy must be closely related.   The relationship is even closer if a train of waves is taken because it is then necessary to divide energy by the period in order to attain comparability.   The geographical pattern of wave height is therefore much the same as that for energy, but with an even greater contrast between storm wave and swell environments.   It is only in storm wave environments and on coasts subject to tropical cyclones that waves exceeding about five metres are of expectable normal occurrence.

A study of the frequency of occurrence of waves of given height around the coasts of the world was made by Meisburger (1962). Figs 25 and 26 are based on his conclusions, which in turn were derived from observational data for individual Marsden squares and supplemented by some hindcasting from known meteorological conditions. They support the general picture of relatively common high waves in temperate latitudes of polar front activity.

WAVE LENGTH

Analysis of records of southern swell made on numerous coasts over the last twenty years shows a marked consistency of optimum periods in and near the 14 to 16 second band, probably representing optimum energy periods of about 10 to 12 seconds in the generating area. Swell records in the North Pacific and North Atlantic suggest that optimum periods there may be somewhat shorter, as might be expected from the generally less favourable conditions for sea and swell production. The contrast is with the storm wave environments, where waves are generated over the continental shelf towards the shore and a complex situation results (see for example the discussions by Todd and Wiegel, 1952, and by Bretschneider, 1956). Both height and period are limited by the much more restricted fetch, but, in comparison with swell waves, it is the shorter period and therefore shorter wave length which is significant, optimum periods being generally in the range of 6 to 12 seconds.

This contrast in dominant wave periods between two major groups of environments has important direct geomorphic effects. The shorter significant waves of storm environments have a shallower depth of action or 'wave base', so that they are less prone to lose energy, modify the bottom or refract as they approach the shore. They also produce high values for wave steepness.

WAVE STEEPNESS

Although steepness, expressed as height divided by length, varies with both these values, in practice it is mainly a function of length. Again, the fundamental contrast is between the steep waves of the storm environments and the flat waves of the swell dominated coasts. Laboratory and field work in the 1950s suggested that steepness was an important wave parameter, particularly in relation to beach processes, and model work suggested that an important change takes place at steepness values of about 0·020 to 0·025 (Johnson, 1956 for example). More recent explanations of surf dynamics rely far less on the steepness factor, which now appears important mainly for its effects in the swash zone.

Kemp (1961) and Kemp and Plinston (1968) have used the phase difference or ratio between time of uprush and wave period to explain important differences in beach profile. Swell environments are characterized by low phase difference values, so that the backwash is able to return before the next wave reaches the shore. In storm wave environments high phase differences are more prevalent as bigger shorter waves move

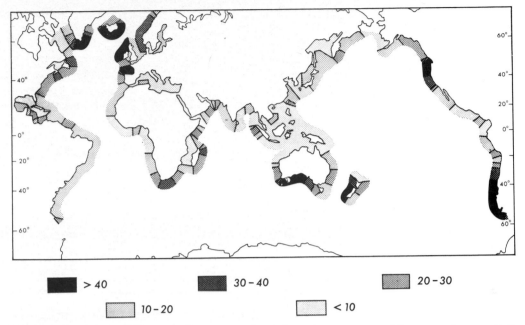

> 40   30 – 40   20 – 30

10 – 20   < 10

FIG. 25.   Percentage frequency of occurrence in at least two quarters of the year of waves 8 ft high or higher. (Data compiled by Meisburger, 1962.)

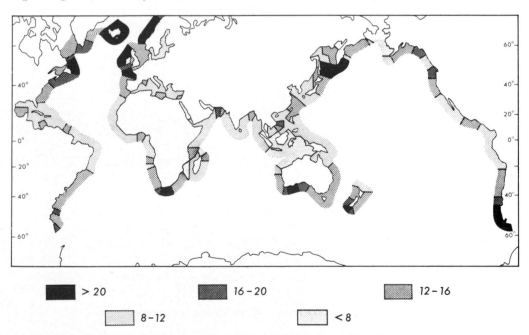

> 20   16 – 20   12 – 16

8 – 12   < 8

FIG. 26.   Greatest height in feet reached by waves occurring with a frequency of 3% or greater in at least two quarters of the year. (From data compiled by Meisburger, 1962.)

water into the shore zone with greater rapidity.   In the laboratory a phase difference of about 0·7 appears critical.

The direction of approach of waves depends on the location and direction of generating winds and the configuration of the coast.   For a number of reasons wave direction is more consistent on swell dominated coasts.   As Silvester (1956) has pointed out, waves originating in storms thousands of kilometres away will not change direction markedly even though the storm centre moves a few hundred kilometres.   The property of great circle travel of swell also tends to promote consistency of direction of waves generated at a distance because, as discussed previously, it results in eventual movement to the north in the southern hemisphere and to the south in the northern hemisphere.   Southern swell is probably particularly consistent in direction because of the great stability, both spatial and temporal, of the southern storm belt (Fig. 19).   In contrast, coasts subject to frequent storm waves generated locally experience a great range of potential directions because of the rapidity of relative change in position of the storm locus.   In these circumstances, local coastal configuration, as it influences immediate fetch, is liable to be the controlling factor.

The final direction from which waves approach the shore is strongly influenced by refraction and here again there is a contrast between swell and storm dominated environments.   The longer swell waves refract more and this tends to eliminate smaller variations in deep water direction.   The short storm waves, refracting less, are more likely to retain their greater variety of potential approach directions.

WAVE ENVIRONMENTS

The main conclusions of this chapter are summarized in Fig. 27, which attempts to define genetically certain broad wave environments.   It is a revised and somewhat refined version of a map published in Davies (1964) and must be considered as trying to present a model on the same level as the simple models of atmospheric wind and pressure systems used in elementary meteorological textbooks.   Like all simple models, it may appear misleading in detail, but essentially it is a conceptual starting point capable of further refinement as more information becomes available.   The dominant quadrants of wave approach which are indicated have been checked against the British Monthly Meteorological Charts of the Oceans, the Sea and Swell Charts produced by the US Navy Hydrographic Office, and such assemblages as those of Becker (1936), Schubart and Mockel (1949), Bruns (1953) and Helle (1958).   In practice, the alignment of the coasts themselves normally filters out all but a few possible directions of wave approach and this often simplifies compilation.

The major environments which Fig. 27 appears to delineate may be briefly characterized as follows.

A significant proportion of waves is generated in local waters by gale force winds, these being short, high energy waves of varying direction.   Swell waves form a background,

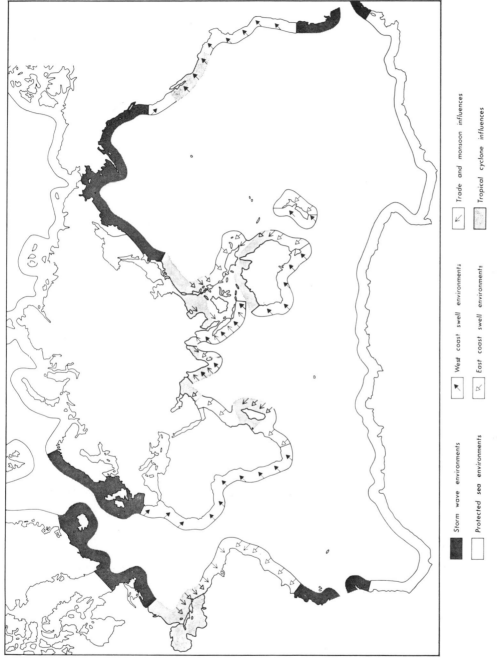

Fig. 27. Major world wave environments. For explanation see text.

Storm wave environments

Protected sea environments

West coast swell environments

East coast swell environments

Trade and monsoon influences

Tropical cyclone influences

persistent in the southern hemisphere, but tending to disappear from the northern hemisphere during summer months.   Energy levels are high virtually throughout, but there may be considerable variation about the mean, especially in the northern hemisphere.

WEST COAST SWELL ENVIRONMENTS

Gale force winds are rare and, within the tropics, local winds tend to blow offshore.   In tropical South America and Africa these are the doldrum coasts.   Big waves are provided by swell, emanating from temperate storm belts, and therefore diminishing in energy away from these sources.   These waves are long and low and relatively consistent in frequency of occurrence and direction, particularly where they come from the southern hemisphere.   Mean wave energy varies from high levels in the higher latitudes to moderate levels in the tropics and low levels around the Gulf of Panama and between Dakar and Freetown in West Africa.   However, there is relatively little variation around the mean throughout.   In spite of differences in mean energy values, these coasts may be the most homogeneous as regards wave environment, but part of the Mexican coast must be distinguished as being subject to tropical cyclones and, on Indian coasts, the swell is reinforced seasonally by monsoon generated waves.

EAST COAST SWELL ENVIRONMENTS

Gale force winds are rare but swell from the temperate storm belts is weaker and less regular in occurrence.   However, it remains relatively consistent in direction.   Winds are generally onshore within the tropics and on certain sections of coast, such as in the West Indies and north-eastern South America, waves produced by the onshore trades outweigh far-travelled swell in importance: in essence they are generated over the same approaches.   Many tropical segments are subject to waves generated by tropical cyclones, giving extremely high energy input for short durations at infrequent and irregular intervals.   With these exceptions, mean energy levels are low to moderate throughout and, apart from cyclone-prone coasts, there is comparatively little deviation from the mean.

PROTECTED SEA ENVIRONMENTS

'Protected' implies that these are coasts of seas where little oceanic swell penetrates and which are either outside the temperate storm belts or are protected by ice cover. Generally they are protected by the seas being more or less enclosed, but the major exception is the coast of Antarctica which is sheltered from much swell by the way in which waves tend to be deflected equatorward along great circle courses, and by the damping effects of sea ice.   Generally these are low energy environments, but some, such as the east coast of Malaya, are subject to seasonal monsoon generated waves of higher energy and others, such as the Gulf of Mexico, are liable to occasional very high energy waves from tropical cyclones.   As already suggested, these last represent the most extreme deviation of wave energy from the mean.

OTHER PHYSICAL FACTORS OF THE SEA

This chapter reviews physical marine factors other than the short and medium period waves discussed in the preceding pages. The factors which appear particularly significant in coastal geomorphology and vary distinctly in a locational sense are tsunamis, tides, storm surges, currents and seawater characteristics.

TSUNAMIS

Cox (1963) defined tsunamis as 'a train of progressive long waves generated in the ocean or a small connected body of water by an impulsive disturbance'. The impulsive disturbance is some displacement of the sea floor, which may perhaps be a volcanic eruption or submarine sliding or slumping, but is in the great majority of cases attributable to shallow focus earthquake activity. In terms of plate tectonics, Isacks, Oliver and Sykes (1968) noted that really effective tsunami generation seems to be related to large dip-slip motion along zones of convergence and more particularly along the zones of rapid convergence which create deep oceanic trenches (Fig. 28). In the terminology of Chapter II they are produced almost entirely along plate-edge or collision coasts and this explains their overwhelmingly Pacific distribution (Compare Fig. 28 with Fig. 4, p. 11).

Even within the Pacific there is very great variation in the extent to which particular

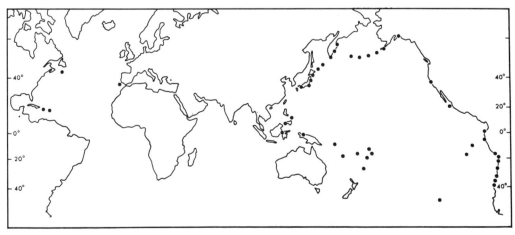

FIG. 28. Distribution of known tsunami-producing earthquakes. (After Isacks and others, 1968.)

coasts are subject to tsunami attack, and the behaviour and effect of the long waves on the shore differs from place to place. Those coasts which are particularly important generators of tsunamis also tend to be important receivers. Because they have comparatively simple outlines and are fronted by deep water, the long waves arrive with little loss of energy by refraction and diffraction. Japan, the Kuriles, Kamchatka, the Aleutians and Chile are vulnerable and so are larger islands, such as those of Hawaii, which lie between the Asian and South American sources. Smaller islands, and especially those with a small diameter in relation to the wave length of the tsunami are very little affected, as are those surrounded by coral reefs. On other continental coasts of the Pacific, tsunami incidence is much less catastrophic. On the USA coast and in New Zealand, sea level may be raised temporarily but rarely more than about 2 metres, while the east Australian coast appears well protected by offlying oceanic rises and island groups. The very long wave length of tsunamis—of the order of 150 km—means that they are refracted in relatively deep water and their energy is redistributed in complicated and still not completely understood fashion over the continental shelf. They may just raise the sea surface so that normal waves can operate for a time at a higher level or they may form very high breaking waves which can send swash to 20 m or more above normal, in the manner graphically described by Shepard (1963). In these ways their effects on coastal morphology may be very similar to those of tropical cyclones.

Other impulsively generated waves caused by rapid subaerial mass movement into the sea are not true tsunamis and produce catastrophic waves of very local incidence. They have been reviewed by Miller (1960) and are again characteristic of plate-edge coasts because of their normal association with earthquakes. Miller records one such wave in Lituya Bay, Alaska in the mid-nineteeth century as having reached a height on the shore of about 525 m, or eight times the height reached by the highest known tsunami. Rather unusual small-scale catastrophic waves were recorded by Nielsen (1969) from a Greenland beach, where sudden disintegration of an offshore iceberg caused a short series of waves, which, although small, completely changed the profile of the foreshore.

STORM SURGES

Storm surges or storm tides are occasioned by the piling up of water against the coast by very strong onshore winds and waves. In this way the sea level may be raised by as much as seven metres, but most commonly rather less, so that wave attack is lifted to an unusually high level. They most often occur in relation to tropical cyclones but may also be generated in temperate storm regions if wind velocity, direction and duration are propitious. Coastal configuration is also important, because, although open coasts such as the east coast of USA may be affected (Fig. 29) and small surges may occur in enclosed seas like the Baltic and Black Sea, the incidence of storm surges is particularly severe in gulfs or gulf-like seas which are enclosed on all sides except that from which the big winds come. The southern part of the North Sea has a long and well documented history of storm surges of varying intensity, that of 1953 having been described in detail

FIG. 29. Foredunes washed back over *Spartina* marsh by hurricane-generated waves accompanying storm surge, Sapelo Island, Georgia. Note the marsh deposits outcropping on the lower beach face.

FIG. 30. Chenier type barrier at Holly Beach, Louisiana, flattened by waves resulting from hurricane Audrey. (Photo by J. N. Jennings.)

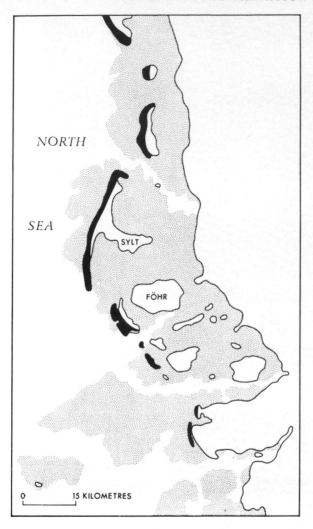

NORTH

SEA

SYLT

FÖHR

0   15 KILOMETRES

FIG. 31. Land lost on the North Sea coast of Schleswig-Holstein in the storm surge of 1362. Land lost is shown stippled with the modern barrier system in black. (After a map by Ingenieurbüro Strunk-Husum.)

by a number of authors (Robinson, 1953; Rossiter, 1954 for example). Other coasts on which large surges are known to occur at intervals include those of the Gulf of Mexico, the Bay of Bengal and the Gulf of Tonkin.

Surges help to produce catastrophic modification of the coast by raising the level at which the large associated storm waves attack (Fig. 30) and the effect is magnified in strongly tidal environments if they happen to occur in conjunction with spring tides. Along low-lying coasts the effect may be carried for great distances inland from the shore (Fig. 31), as in the well-documented case of the 1957 hurricane in Louisiana, which affected country as much as 50 km inland (Morgan, Nichols and Wright, 1958). On steep coasts the effect is much more limited. Sauer (1962) and McIntire and Walker (1964) reported on the effects of two tropical cyclones in Mauritius which occurred in 1960 after a quiescence of 15 years and remarked that topographic changes were of a much lower order of magnitude than those observed in the Gulf of Mexico with comparable meteorological conditions. The shoreline was not displaced and shore vegetation recovered rapidly.

TIDAL TYPE

Fig. 32 gives the general world distribution of tidal type on the basis of a threefold division into diurnal, semi-diurnal and mixed. Mixed regimes are predominantly either diurnal or semi-diurnal, but this subdivision has not been shown because it does not seem to be geomorphically significant and its inclusion tends to obscure the basic

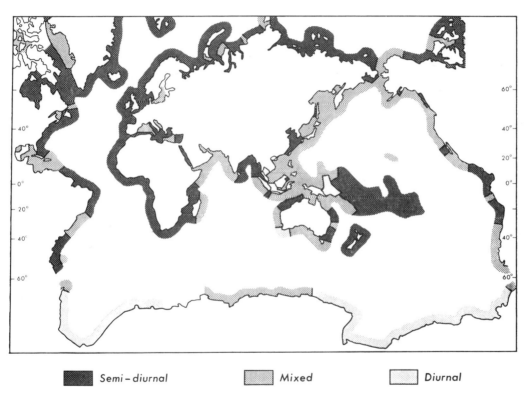

Semi-diurnal   Mixed   Diurnal

FIG. 32. Distribution of tidal types.

patterns. It may however be obtained from maps provided by Dietrich (1963), for instance.

In the diurnal regime there is one high and one low tide in approximately twenty-four hours: in the semi-diurnal regime there are two highs and two lows in the same period. In the mixed regime the situation is more complex because, although there are two highs and two lows per day, the highs and lows are not of the same magnitude. Most commonly, as on the west coast of USA, the sequence is low low, low high, high low and high high; but on some shores a sequence of high low, low high, low low and high high may be found.

Semi-diurnal tides are particularly characteristic of the Atlantic Ocean, where almost all oceanic coasts are subject to this regime. Diurnal and mixed tides are found mainly along Pacific and Indian Ocean coasts. Another major contrast on a world scale is between the semidiurnal tides of the Arctic and the diurnal and mixed tides of Antarctic shores.

Tidal type is of great significance in determining variations in the length of the drying period between tides—an important variable in relation to intertidal weathering and biological zonation, for instance. The major contrast is between semi-diurnal tides, where this period is always less than twelve hours, and diurnal and mixed tides, where in the higher parts of the intertidal zone it is normally longer. It is also of significance in its effect on the intensity of tidal currents: for any given tidal range and cross-sectional condition current velocities must always be less in diurnal and mixed regimes than in semi-diurnal regimes, because of the greater time available for movement of the water mass. This factor particularly affects coastal inlets of various kinds, where different transfer times for tidal prisms vitally influence the speed of currents.

TIDAL RANGE

The other important characteristic of the tide is its height range between high and low water. Although some generalization has been necessary because of the small scale of the map, the world pattern emerges from Fig. 33, which shows tidal range at springs. On open oceanic coasts ranges of two metres or less are common, but range increases where the semi-diurnal component becomes important and also in funnel-shaped embayments where it reaches extreme values. In large, estuary-type embayments tidal range is amplified to varying extents by the development of local seiches. Where the seiche period coincides approximately with that of the tide very large ranges are generated (Marmer, 1926), as in the well-known case of the Bay of Fundy, and these are often associated with the occurrence of tidal bores. At the opposite extreme some large, almost totally enclosed seas, most notably the Mediterranean, the Red Sea, the Baltic and the Gulf of Mexico, are virtually tideless, and temporary movements of sea level due to local meteorological conditions are more significant.

The significance of tidal range as a geographical variable in coastal development has been widely recognized. It directly affects the evolution of shore platforms, beaches and coastal inlets in particular, and a number of less well-defined effects are suggested in succeeding chapters. It is also a main factor in determining the strength of tidal currents.

TIDAL ENVIRONMENTS

Superimposition of Figs 32 and 33 gives a crude picture of world tidal environments which is instructive despite the very complex pattern which results. An attempt to reduce this pattern to its essential components was made earlier (Davies, 1964) and was based on the conclusion that two extreme environments are identifiable and between

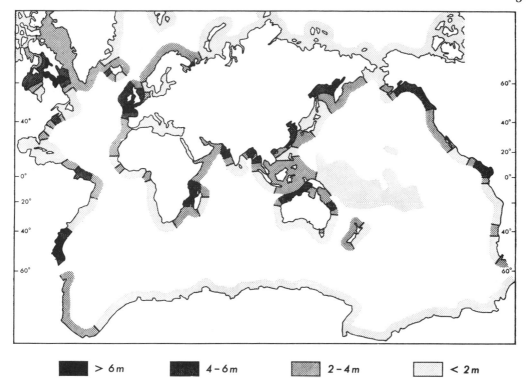

> 6m   4-6m   2-4m   < 2m

FIG. 33.   Distribution of tidal range, given in metres at springs.

them lie a number of environments with variable but intermediate characters.   The two extremes were labelled 'macrotidal' and 'microtidal', while the intermediates were lumped in a category called 'mesotidal'.   The macrotidal environment was defined as having semi-diurnal tides with ranges of over 4 m at springs, the microtidal environment being that with diurnal or mixed tides with ranges less than 2 m.   These values were chosen subjectively as appearing to be critical in relation to coastal landforms. Much of the evidence appears later in discussions of particular geomorphic processes and forms, but broadly speaking macrotidal coasts are subject to strong tidal currents and very wide vertical dispersion of wave attack, while microtidal coasts have the attributes of virtually tideless shores.

In practice the strong distributional relationship which exists between semi-diurnal regimes and high tidal ranges and between diurnal or mixed regimes and low ranges makes the combination of characters particularly meaningful in terms of location. Because of this and because tidal range is a more important overall factor than tidal type, there is much to be said for defining tidal environments purely in terms of tidal range, as was done by Bird (1968).   The biggest anomalies occur around the Gulf of Cambay in north-western India, in the Gulf of Tonkin and on some shores of the Sea of Okhotsk, where diurnal or mixed diurnal tides have ranges of over 4 metres, and on some western oceanic coasts of Africa and South America, where semi-diurnal tides have ranges of less than 2 metres.

TIDAL CURRENTS

Tide-induced currents vary as already discussed with tidal type and range, tending to be most powerful with semi-diurnal tides of large range and least with diurnal tides of small range. The local disturbing factor is that of coastal and shelf configuration. In macrotidal environments tide-induced currents may have a marked geomorphic effect even on the floor of the open shelf, where large-scale rectilinear current ridges may form as described and mapped by Off (1963). Such ridges have now been shown to occur extensively on the west European continental shelf and to be related to large-scale tidal current systems (Kenyon, 1970). The movement of ridges close to the shore may even influence the morphology of the coast itself (Hardy, 1966).

On coasts where the tidal effect is less, the influence of currents becomes progressively more restricted to constrictions between islands, around promontories and in inlets where colks or scour holes may form and sigmoidal banks arise between ebb and flood channels, until in microtidal environments their effect becomes minimal. On the microtidal shores of southern Tasmania, with mixed tides ranging little more than a metre at springs, it is difficult to identify morphologic effects of tidal currents even in the most apparently favourable locations and, in a review of coastal regimes in USA, Saville and Watts (1969) regarded tidal currents as negligible factors in sediment transport.

Although tidal currents are reversing, inequalities between flood and ebb streams may often be significant in terms of net transport and, on coasts with mixed tides, the normal sequence of highs and lows may be of especial importance in producing such inequalities. Thus, if the sequence is low low water, low high water, high low water, high high water, the two flood currents are essentially equal in magnitude and duration but the two ebb currents are unequal so that velocities in the great ebb between high high water and low low water may be much greater than at either of the flood stages. Conversely a sequence high high, high low, low high, low low, high high gives one exceptionally strong flood current between low low and high high water.

In coastal inlets the size, and particularly the length, of the inlet may affect the phase relationship between tidal stage and current velocities. Normally the highest velocities occur at mid-tide, but in long estuaries there may be considerable divergence so that, near the mouth, low tide may be associated with the fastest ebb and high tide with the fastest flood. This may have a morphologic effect by influencing the height at which strongest currents operate.

SEAWATER CHARACTERISTICS

The chemistry of seawater is important principally in relation to weathering and solution processes on rocky shores, and also to beach cementation. The significant parameters are overall salinity (Fig. 34), which may vary sufficiently to be significant

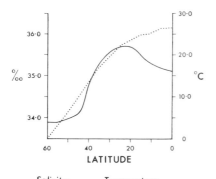

Fig. 34. Mean latitudinal distribution of sea surface temperature and salinity. (Data from Dietrich, 1963.)

Salinity ——— Temperature ·········

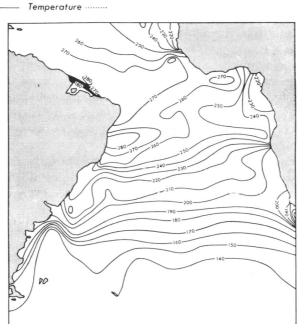

Fig. 35. Percentage saturation of surface seawater with calcium carbonate in the southern Atlantic Ocean, based on a constant carbon dioxide pressure of 3×10^{-4} atmospheres. (Data from Wattenburg, reproduced in Dietrich, 1963.)

geographically in such processes as salt crystallization on platforms and cliffs, and degree of calcium carbonate saturation (Fig. 35), which may be pertinent to the distribution of solutional, constructional and cementational phenomena. Although salinity varies by a factor of two between the Red Sea and the Baltic, the general range along open coasts lies only between about 30 and 37 parts per thousand. As an average over the globe as a whole, maxima of 3·57 per cent occur between latitudes 20 and 25°. Average figures decrease to 3·51 per cent at the equator and to 3·39 per cent at 55° (Dietrich,

1963).   Deviations from latitudinal norms occur mainly because of current systems and discharge from very large rivers.   It seems doubtful, however, whether such small relative differences are of great significance in coastal geomorphology, except perhaps in lagoonal, estuarine or deltaic conditions.

Calcium carbonate distribution is of more general importance.   Seawater is normally supersaturated in respect to calcium carbonate and this supersaturation

FIG. 36.   Talus fringed cliffs and ice cored, debris mantled mounds on beach at Cape Ricketts, Devon Island, Canadian Arctic Archipelago.   The photograph was taken in July after the disappearance of sea ice.   (Photo by S. B. McCann.)

increases with increasing water temperatures, so that it is about twice as great in the tropics as in high latitudes (Fig. 35).   It is also higher off the east coasts of continents than off west coasts.   The pattern is of fundamental biologic and geomorphic significance because it leads primarily to the greater abundance of lime secreting organisms in the tropics, and is pertinent to considerations of carbon dioxide cycles and solution processes (Chapter VI), and cementation processes (Chapter VIII).

Although it has many indirect effects, notably through controlling biological distributions, the temperature of seawater is of interest principally because of its effect on water density and on rates of chemical reaction, and because of its control of the occurrence of sea ice.   Relative variation geographically is very great indeed (Fig. 34) and superimposed on this average latitudinal picture is the well-known contrast between east and west coasts in the ocean basins resulting from water circulation.

Working under controlled laboratory conditions, Fairchild (1959) obtained some interesting data on the effect, presumably because of viscosity differences, of water temperatures on sediment movement by waves. He found that, regardless of sediment type, model beaches reacted more quickly to wave processes in cold water than in warm. With colder water, more material was moved offshore, beach berms were maintained at a lower level and bars and troughs were not so well marked. A similar effect has been computed for river flow, where lower water temperatures are correlated with greater sediment discharges because the associated increase in water viscosity causes a decrease in the fall velocity of sand particles (Colby, 1964).

It would be surprising if sea temperatures had no effect on the rapidity of chemical weathering, even though this will also depend on air and groundwater temperatures. Other processes such as the cementation of beach material are likely to be influenced in rate, or even triggered off, by higher sea temperatures.

Drift ice has a damping effect on ocean waves (Hunkins, 1962) and effectively protects the shore from attack during the season of occurrence (Fig. 37). Along almost all of the Antarctic coast and the northern coasts of Greenland and the Canadian Arctic archipelago, the coast may be so protected for all the year. On remaining Antarctic and Arctic coasts there are distinct seasons of alternating attack and protection, although, as noted in Chapter III, these tend to be low energy coasts in any event. Rex (1964) has described the effect of alternating seasons on Arctic beaches near Point Barrow in Alaska, where ice pushing and rafting dominates for part of the year and wave action for the remainder. He noted that northward in the Canadian archipelago where the period of open water is less, wave processes become more limited and ice processes more dominant. Owens and McCann (1970) have also stressed the variation in extent of marine action on Arctic beaches, depending on the length of the ice-free period and the degree of wave exposure (Fig. 36).

A prominent feature of high latitude coasts is the phenomenon known as icefoot, which mantles the seaward edges of beaches and rocky shores during the season of freeze-up (Fig. 38). It is produced by successive adfreezing of water on rock and ice surfaces in a number of ways. Seven main forms have been described—five by Priestley (1922) and a further two by Joyce (1950). These are listed below with the three most important varieties first.

Tidal platform icefoot—formed by tidal rise and fall between tide marks;
Storm icefoot—built above high water mark by spray;
Drift icefoot—made from snow consolidated by freezing seawater;
Pressure icefoot—over-riding slabs of sea ice pushed onshore;
Stranded floe icefoot—incorporating beached pieces of bergs;
False icefoot—formed from freezing precipitation above high water;
Wash-and-strain icefoot—formed by waves washing over and straining through pebbly beaches.

As will emerge in Chapter VI, icefoot has generally been thought of as a feature of

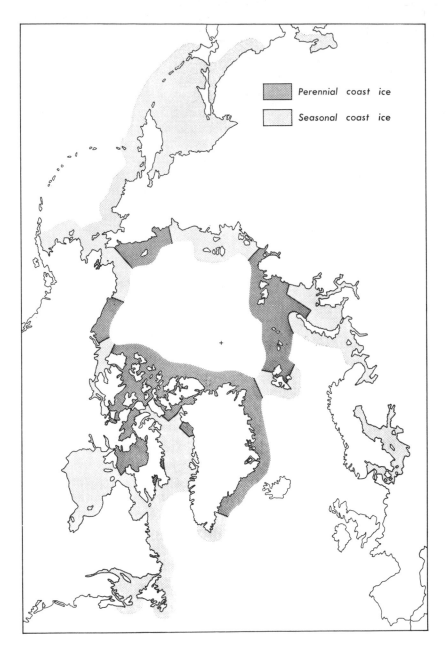

Perennial coast ice

Seasonal coast ice

Fig. 37. Average distribution of perennial and seasonal coast ice in arctic seas. (Data from *Ice Atlas of the Northern Hemisphere*.)

FIG. 38. Coast ice and ice foot near Mawson, Anatarctica. (ANARE photo by P. G. Law.)

rather than a factor in shore development. However, it may prove necessary to distinguish between that formed wholly from seawater and that (drift icefoot and false icefoot) in which there is an important freshwater constituent. Unfortunately there is very little distributional information but the freshwater types might be expected *a priori* to be more characteristic of coasts with higher precipitation aggregates.

The significance of sea and land ice in the evolution of features peculiar to Arctic and Antarctic shores has been examined by John and Sugden (1975) who have provided a general review of coastal geomorphology in high latitudes.

V | BIOTIC FACTORS

Although the general influence of plant cover in landscape evolution is well recognized, biological processes play a more direct and active part in coastal geomorphology than they do in subaerial geomorphology. The constructive effects of marsh and dune plants, of coral and calcareous algae, and the destructive effects of rock-destroying organisms are measurable over relatively short periods of time. Since all these organisms are distributed in different ways around world coasts, geographical variation in the extent and degree of their operation is often, as in the case of coral, relatively simple to demonstrate. In other cases, for example many of the rock destroyers, existing information makes it hard to appreciate how biological distributions affect landforms.

SALT MARSHES

Salt marsh plants grow between tide marks in quiet depositional environments, usually in coastal inlets, but sometimes on the open shore as on the 'zero energy' coast of

FIG. 39. Salt marsh on the open coast of the Gulf of Mexico in the 'zero-energy' environment of northwest Florida.

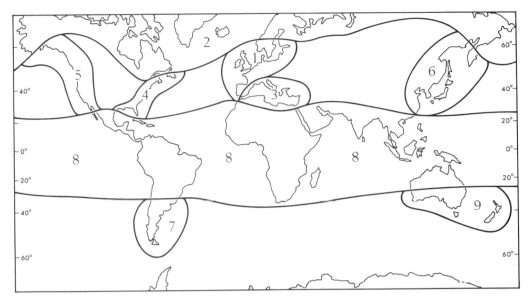

FIG. 40. Major salt marsh groups of the world according to Chapman (1960). 1. North European; 2. Arctic; 3. Mediterranean; 4. Atlantic North America; 5. Pacific North America; 6. West coasts of Pacific; 7. Temperate South America; 8. Tropical; 9. Australia and New Zealand.

north-west Florida (Tanner, 1960) (Fig. 39). As in the case of mangroves, their geomorphic importance as agents of construction has undoubtedly been exaggerated in some of the literature: to a large extent they must be thought of as taking advantage of locations where sedimentation is occurring in any event because of physical conditions. At the same time there is no doubt that they do promote deposition, both organic and inorganic, and inhibit erosion, and they have important effects on minor relief forms such as channel systems.

A major review of salt marshes in different parts of the world was provided by Chapman (1960), who distinguished nine main groups, which are mapped in Fig. 40. Some differences between the groups are due to factors of historical plant geography. The important genus *Spartina*, for instance, has its largest concentration in the Atlantic, from western Europe to north-west Africa and from eastern Canada to Brazil. Outside this region it is of limited occurrence except where introduced by man. Other differences result from environmental factors such as substratum, tidal range and climate. Generally the richest floras are found on the muddy marshes of macrotidal, humid temperate coasts. Although they are salt tolerant, few salt marsh plants appear actually to thrive better under saline conditions than under more normal ones and in warm temperate and tropical marshes, where the ratio of evaporation to precipitation increases, the flora becomes much impoverished. *Salicornia*, perhaps the most ubiquitous of tidal marsh genera and one of those apparently incapable of growing except in halophytic conditions, becomes overwhelmingly dominant on the large majority of lower latitude marshes. *Salicornia* is favoured by other factors giving rise to excessive salinity.   Its importance on west coast marshes in the United States for instance may be attributable to relatively high salinities resulting from the long periods of exposure to drying out which are associated with diurnal or mixed tides.

Many of Chapman's world groups show obvious affinities: the *Salicornia-Arthrocne-mum* marshes of southern Australia and the Mediterranean, for example, show marked similarities and indeed they exist in very similar environments.   Trying to look at distributions zonally and ignoring as far as possible more local effects, it appears that temperate marshes are most varied floristically.   As one goes poleward from here, grasses tend to become dominant in a habitat where temperature is a limiting factor. According to Chapman, Arctic marshes are dominated by *Puccinellia* grasses and Nielsen (1969) has described an apparently typical *Puccinellia* marsh in Greenland.   In the other direction, towards the equator, with extreme salinity as the limiting factor, shrubby marshes with such plants as *Salicornia* and *Arthrocnemum* become more important.

In hot wet regions, where mangroves reach their fullest development, salt marsh is totally excluded and mangrove trees extend completely over the area that it would normally occupy.   Chapman, in discussion on Fosberg (1966), has explained this in terms of reduction of light beneath the woodland canopy.

Ecological studies of salt marsh vegetation have stressed the zonation of species which is commonly discernible and have often interpreted this in terms of succession on a prograding shore.   As noted by Russell (1959), zonation is more clearly marked on coasts with a high tidal range and where the range is low the picture may be more complex.   The successional interpretation needs consideration in terms of the geomorphic history because the existence of a zonation may imply merely a more or less static adjustment to zonal factors of distribution such as tidal exposure and salinity of the substratum.   Sauer (1961) has pointed out in relation to other coastal vegetation types the dangers of implying progradation and succession just from surface zonation of species.

Generally associated with salt marsh zonation, but growing below and around low tide mark and rarely emerged is a group of marine angiosperms, colloquially known as 'sea-grasses'.   All but one of the eleven genera usually recognized are tropical or warm temperate in distribution and only *Zostera* extends into cooler climates.   No total assessment of the geomorphic significance of these plants has yet been made, but their role in the development of accreting shallows on warm-water coasts has been described by a number of authors (Ginsburg and Lowenstam, 1958; Taylor, 1968; Logan and others, 1970, for example).

That floristic differences affect marsh morphology is not in doubt, although a great amount of proof remains to be established.   Different species vary in their efficiency as sediment traps and in the ability of their root systems to withstand erosion (Pestrong, 1965).   Experiments in the introduction of species into areas from which they are naturally absent have produced spectacular results, as in the Tamar estuary of northern Tasmania, where the establishment of *Spartina* in what was originally a virtual ecological vacuum has led to striking geomorphic changes.   Some other effects of floristic variation are alluded to in Chapter XI.

MANGROVES

The appearance of mangrove trees in the quiet depositional environments of the tropics has been one of the facts of climatic coastal geomorphology most generally recognized and yet, paradoxically, this 'recognition' has tended to obscure some essential homologies between tidal landforms in higher and lower latitudes. The terms 'salt marsh' and 'mangrove swamp' are mainly botanical in connotation and there is a need for agreement on strictly morphological terms which will enable proper comparison to be made. Stoddart (1968) has suggested that some of our subjective impressions of zonal landscape differences may result from vegetation contrasts rather than from true variation in the landforms themselves and this suggestion may well apply to tidal plains.

Mangrove trees can be divided physiognomically into three broad groups, depending on the way in which the root systems are adapted to life in anaerobic environments. In one group, typified by such genera as *Rhizophora*, *Bruguiera*, *Ceriops* and *Lumnitzera*,

FIG. 41.   A stilt-root mangrove, *Rhizophora mangle*; Fiji.

arching stilt roots grow out from the lower part of the trunk (Fig. 41) or surface roots develop conspicuous projections usually termed 'knees'. In a second group, exemplified by *Avicennia* and *Sonneratia*, horizontal roots just below the ground surface send up vertically projecting, periscope-like pneumatophores (Fig. 42). In a third group, of which *Conocarpus* is an example, there are no subaerial roots, although, as in *Xylocarpus*, the horizontal roots may appear at the surface. The division between the second and third groups is not a hard and fast one, because genera such as *Avicennia* may not produce pneumatophores at higher levels where the ground dries out periodically, and *Laguncularia* for instance is extremely variable. In general the forms which do not develop 'breathing' roots grow furthest inland so that it is the stilt-root and periscope-root species which are of most significance and interest in geomorphology.

The general distribution of mangrove species is controlled by temperature, or more specifically by the occurrence of frost. They are killed at temperatures below about —3°C so that their poleward limit lies where such temperatures occur at shorter intervals than the reproductive cycle. However, well-developed mangrove is more restricted

FIG. 42.   A periscope-root mangrove, *Avicennia marina*; New South Wales.

than this and, according to West (1956), is found only where average temperatures for the coldest month exceed 20°C and the seasonal range does not exceed 5°C. Stilt-root mangroves are less tolerant of low temperatures than periscope-root species and are more tied to equatorial regions. It is possible to distinguish coasts dominated by 'high' mangroves, where well-developed relatively tall forest occurs, from those dominated by 'low' mangrove. The general disposition of these two coastal types is given in Fig. 43, based on West (1956).

Within the general distribution area of mangroves, two major floristic regions are distinguishable—a relatively rich oriental region stretching from East Africa to the western Pacific, and a relatively impoverished occidental region comprising tropical America and the west coast of Africa. Some more important genera, notably *Rhizophora* and *Avicennia*, are distributed through both these regions and it is doubtful whether the division is significant geomorphically, but the greater availability of species in the oriental region is worth bearing in mind when making spatial comparisons. It has its counterpart among many other groups of tropical organisms, in particular, from our point of view, those which build coral reefs.

The detailed distribution pattern of mangroves depends upon other factors, of which

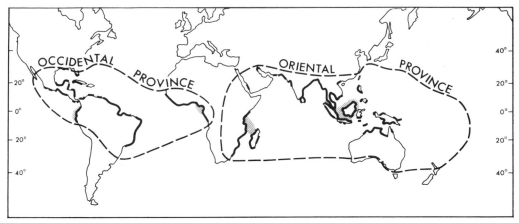

FIG. 43. Distribution of mangroves, mainly after West (1956), but with additions. Broken lines enclose the total range; thick lines denote major stretches of coast dominated by tidal woodlands; hatched areas denote 'high mangrove'.

the most important are substratum and wave climate. Although mangrove species will grow in a variety of sediments, including coral sand, they attain full development on fine-grained, soft organic muds deposited in estuarine or deltaic locations. Because they are vulnerable to wave action at all stages of their life history, they are absent from exposed stretches of shore and can occur on the open coast only in very low energy environments. The viviparous habit of many mangroves enables them to drop ready-grown seedlings, but these can only root given a limited range of water movement. In marginal parts of their range, distribution of mangrove species may be affected by the direction of inshore currents which transport floating seedlings, and this may help to explain their absence from updrift coasts. They are best developed on rainy coasts; high mangrove is restricted to regions of heavy, all-season precipitation, but there is doubt as to how this factor operates. Mangroves are known to be able to extract water requirements from the sea and are thus independent of freshwater (Walter and Steiner, 1936), so that West (1956) suggested that the apparent precipitation factor might operate through affecting the supply of mud. As we noted in Chapter II, it is in the perennially wet tropics that mud supply by rivers is at a maximum. Apart from its function as a favourable substratum for growth, mud may also act as a wave damping agent, since considerable reduction in energy occurs where waves have to travel over extensive shallow seas with muddy bottoms (Gade, 1958). Along desert coasts, where mangroves are stunted or absent, it does seem probable that coarse sediments and exceptionally high salinity of the substratum are important controls, but the extensive development of mangrove away from the shore in hot, wet regions must owe something to increased water availability.

Zonation of species away from the shore has been suggested by many ecological studies, but such zonation is commonly difficult to demonstrate and where it does exist, the species do not always occur in the same order. As in the case of salt marsh, floristic zonation may imply zonation of environment rather than true ecological succession and, where discernible plant zonation is absent, this may be due to the complexity of interaction of environmental factors.

There has been division of opinion on how far mangroves can be thought of as agents of geomorphic change. Davis (1940) followed Vaughan (1909) in ascribing considerable land-building importance to mangrove plants, but his thesis was vigorously denied by van Steenis (1941), who quoted a formidable list of authorities, in particular Watson (1928), for the opposing view. The present consensus would probably be that mangroves are significant factors of shoreline evolution, but that their significance has sometimes been overstressed. In particular, we need more studies like that of Thom (1967), examining the two-way inter-relationship between plants and landforms.

BEACH AND DUNE PLANTS

Plants which establish themselves towards the rear of beaches and on coastal dunes live in a less stable environment than do those of salt marshes and mangrove swamps. Although some, typified by such genera as *Cakile*, are salt tolerant annuals, the important forms from a geomorphic point of view are vigorous perennials with extensive, commonly rhizomatous root systems. Most of these perennials are grasses but in the tropics creeping vines, notably species of *Ipomoea* and *Canavalia* take their place.

The halophytic annuals are widely distributed and so, within the tropics, are the vines. Species of *Cakile*, for instance, extend from the North Atlantic through the Mediterranean to western Asia, and from Australia to the west coast of North America. The *Ipomoea-Canavalia* community is virtually pantropical. In contrast, the natural distribution of dune grasses is more restricted. Species of *Ammophila*, perhaps the most effective of all sandbinding plants in temperate latitudes, did not occur naturally outside the North Atlantic. The coastal *Spinifex* of Australasia is native only to that part of the world, while on the west coast of the United States there are no indigenous dune grasses of equivalent effectiveness. The reason for the contrast may lie in different capabilities for transoceanic dispersal. The first group of plants produces buoyant and impermeable seeds or seed cases which may float for months if not years and remain viable (Guppy, 1906; Muir, 1937). The tiny seeds of grasses do not seem to float for significant lengths of time (Sauer, 1967) and may travel by other means. The broad picture of distribution suggests however that they do not disperse so successfully, although some like *Sporobolus virginicus* have a wide range through the tropics. One result of this is that, whereas there is a basic floristic similarity of tropical beach plants from the West Indies to West Africa and right through the great Indo-Pacific region, there was until recently much greater diversity on temperate coasts. This diversity has been obscured during the last one hundred years or so by man's intervention and most particularly by the introduction of marram, *Ammophila arenaria*, from its native home in western Europe to temperate shores of all continents, where it has almost always proved a more efficient sand binder than native species. This sequence of introductions had the avowed intention of influencing the development of dune morphology and its effects have been widespread.

Among the plants which are important in influencing the accretion and stabilization of dune sand, two broad growth forms can be distinguished which seem to be of geomorphic significance (Fig. 44).   The first is that most generally recognized by those who live in temperate regions and is exemplified by *Ammophila*.   In this genus, long underground rhizomes spread laterally, but above ground the plant develops a characteristic tussocky shape as explained by Greig-Smith and others (1947), and is able to maintain upward growth to keep pace with an accreting sand surface.   The second growth form

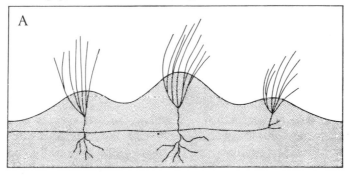

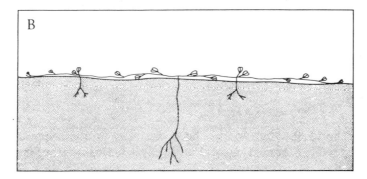

FIG. 44.   Typical growth habits of *A* rhizomatous, tussock forming *Ammophila* and *B* stoloniferous *Ipomoea*.

occurs in the trailing vines such as *Ipomoea*, but also in some grasses like the Australian *Spinifex*.   In this case lateral growth is by means of long stolons which creep over the ground surface, sending down adventitious roots, so that the dominant surface form is that of a sheet.   Since the surface form of dune plants affects the pattern of sand deposition by altering the microclimatic wind field, it seems likely that these two identifiable growth forms may have differing effects.   The suggestion is taken up again in Chapter X: meanwhile, it may be observed that, whereas the rhizomatous form is dominantly temperate in distribution, the stoloniferous form is clearly associated with the tropics.   In part this association may reflect the lower rates of sand movement by wind in low latitudes, so that accumulation is not so important, but it is mainly a reflection of the way in which tropical plants are able to expose more vulnerable vegetative parts, and particularly growth renewal buds, in a frost-free environment. The general phenomenon is illustrated by the following table of dune plant species in the various Raunkaier life form categories counted on equivalent dune areas at Skallingen in Denmark and on the island of St Croix in the West Indies (Raunkaier, 1934).

	Skallingen	St Croix
Number of species	105	80
Percentages		
Phanerophytes (aerial plants)	1	74
Chamaephytes (surface plants)	7	16
Hemicryptophytes (half-earth plants)	47	4
Geophytes (earth plants)	19	1
Therophytes (annuals)	26	5

One of the most striking features of sandy shores in the humid tropics is the way in which tall trees may grow right down to the back of the beach and present the appearance of an abrupt wall of vegetation. The best known species is undoubtedly the coconut palm which has spread naturally and with man's help throughout the tropics. Other broad leaved evergreen trees are of importance regionally, notably species of *Barringtonia* in the Indo-Pacific and *Hippomane* in the tropical west Atlantic. Although this phenomenon must be partly due to the generally greater vigour of woody vegetation in warm climates and the larger pool of floristic genes, the main factor is undoubtedly reduced exposure to wind and waves at the rear of tropical beaches when compared with temperate ones. In turn the presence of tall trees at the rear of the beach must affect the velocity field of winds blowing over the backshore zone and this point is returned to in Chapter X.

CORAL

The factors of reef coral distribution have been discussed by a number of authors (Wells, 1957; Fairbridge, 1968; Stoddart, 1969c) and only a brief summary is given here (**Fig.**

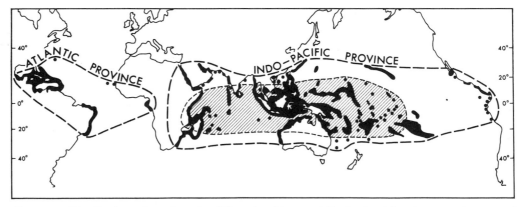

Fig. 45. Distribution of coral reefs. Many 'reefs', especially in the Atlantic, comprise a coral veneer on structures of other origin and Mabesoone (1966), for example, claimed that there are no true coral reefs in Brazil. The hatched region includes the areas of most prolific reef development and almost all oceanic atolls.

45).   Hermatypic or reef-forming corals maintain a symbiotic relationship with minute dinoflagellate algae called zooxanthellae and it is the life requirements of the zooxanthellae which are critical for reef distribution.   Other coral forms extend into cold waters but are of little geomorphic significance.

TEMPERATURE

The most important factor of horizontal distribution is temperature. Although the outside limits are from about 16°C to 36°C, the band of optimum growth is much narrower and may be taken as 25–29°C.   The mappable limits of reef occurrence are

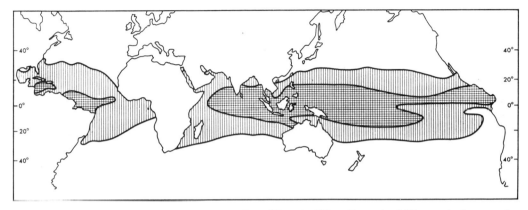

FIG. 46.   Cold month sea surface isotherms for 20°C and 26°C.   Since the fall in tropical sea surface temperatures during Pleistocene glacials was of the order of 6°C, the double hatched area gives a rough idea of the reduced availability of tropical water at such times.   Compare with Figs 45 and 47.

most generally thought of as lying close to the 20°C sea surface isotherm for the coldest month (Fig. 46).   Apart from limiting reefs to warm water areas and helping to concentrate development in the western parts of oceans, a result of the temperature factor is to separate two major distribution provinces.   As in the case of mangroves, there is an extensive Indo-Pacific province stretching from East Africa to the Pacific and a much less extensive tropical Atlantic province from the Caribbean to West Africa.   It will be seen from Fig. 45 that not only are the outside limits of reef development wider in the Indo-Pacific, but so are the limits of optimum development.   During Pleistocene glacial phases, when tropical ocean surface temperatures were reduced by something like 6°C, the distribution of reef corals was severely limited in the Atlantic province (compare Figs 45 and 46).

LIGHT

Illumination is most important in controlling vertical distribution because of the extreme phototropism of the zooxanthellae.   Limits of toleration enable living coral to reach about 90 m down, but most growth ceases at about half this depth and the 0–20 m zone can be thought of as that in which much the most vigorous reef development takes place. Although subsidence and sea level change in the past have led to a great number of situations in which reefs have been able to develop in what is now deep water, they are especially prolific in wide and relatively shallow shelf areas like those of the East Indies and the Queensland coast.

SALINITY

Salinity tolerances are from about 2·7 to 4·0 per cent and the optimum lies around 3·4–3·6 per cent. The main effect is to discourage reef building along some sections of continental coasts where freshwater outflow occurs in quantity.

SUBSTRATUM

Coral planules establish most successfully on a firm smooth substratum and, although they may colonize loose rubble and even fine sediments, they cannot initiate reef development where sediments are mobile. Within the tropics coral reefs and large sand barrier systems are more or less complementary in distribution and this may be another reason for the relative absence of reefs from the west coasts of Africa, Australia and the Americas. This well-known asymmetrical distribution within the tropical oceans is usually ascribed to upwelling of cold water, which, however, still leaves considerable stretches of coast which fulfil temperature requirements and yet do not have reefs. On many such stretches accumulation and movement of large sand masses under the influence of the dominant west coast swell is probably the prime prohibiting factor.

SEDIMENTATION

Closely linked with the last factor is that of sedimentation. Coral can tolerate a considerable amount of material in suspension, although it may limit the amount of light received, but accumulation of sediment is fatal if it is sufficiently rapid to engulf the incipient colony. Long stretches of coast in the tropics are without reefs because they are subject to extensive marine or fluvial deposition and a major reason why coral distribution in the tropical Atlantic is so minimal is that much of the coast of West Africa, the Gulf of Mexico and northern Brazil is unsuitable in terms of substratum and sedimentation regime.

AVAILABLE FAUNA

The Indo-Pacific province is notably richer in species of coral and of associated organisms than is the Atlantic province (Fig. 47) and this is reflected to some extent in the profuseness and variety of the structures which have been produced. Within the two provinces some of the east-west asymmetry in development is due to the way in which the free-swimming planules are carried in a predominantly westerly direction by the drift systems of the tropical oceans. Some species have a very short-lived larval stage but in others, which tend to be the more widely distributed, it extends for several weeks. Gardiner (1931) discussed the way in which the coral fauna increases in luxuriance and

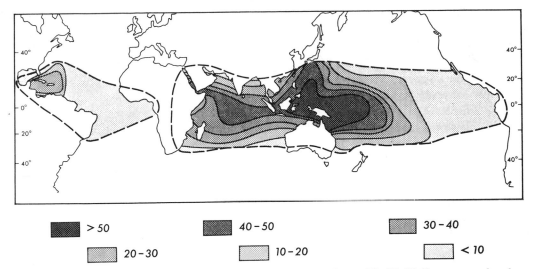

FIG. 47.   Distribution of hermatypic coral genera.   (From data of J. W. Wells put together by Stoddart, 1969c.)

diversity as one goes from east to west in the Pacific.   Reefs are absent from the Galapagos and Easter Island in what otherwise appear favourable habitats: in contrast, there is most profuse coral development in the Malaysian–Australian region in the extreme west.

WATER MOVEMENT

Continuous redistribution of the surrounding water is necessary so that temperature may be kept uniform, silting prevented, a proper oxygen-carbon dioxide balance preserved and nutrients brought within reach of the essentially sedentary reef community.   Within the tropics, where mean wave energy is generally low, it is well known that reef development is often more vigorous on the windward sides of islands.   On the other hand too much wave action may prohibit or inhibit reef development by preventing establishment of polyp planules or by destroying established coral at too high a rate.

CORAL STRUCTURES

From a geomorphological point of view the importance of reef corals lies in the way they produce structures from which landforms arise.   Sometimes these landforms are created in their virtual entirety by organic deposition, but much more commonly other marine processes are involved, so that the result is of complicated origin (see reviews by Stoddart, 1969c; Bloom, 1974).   Particularly where reef structures have become emergent because of tectonic displacement or sea level change, they have been readily cut into shore platforms and cliffs.   Reef erosion at formational and emergent levels supplies sand, pebbles and boulders from which beaches and small islands or cays are constructed.   Because fringing reefs form preferentially at salients, reef-building provides a mechanism whereby headlands may prograde instead of retreat as is required by the classical cycle of marine erosion.   They also considerably modify the offshore wave and current regime and nowhere is this more evident than on coasts sheltered by barrier reef systems.   The diversity of coral structures makes it necessary to include some discussion of their geographical relationships.

The simple breakdown into fringing reefs, barrier reefs and atolls used by Charles Darwin has stood the test of time well, but needs amplifying as a result of more modern work.   There is no generally agreed present-day system—indeed, in view of the great variation in reef form which is becoming evident such agreement may be a long way off. The simple scheme presented below will serve as a basis for discussion, bearing in mind that intermediate types occur between some categories and that the classes are descriptive and not genetic.

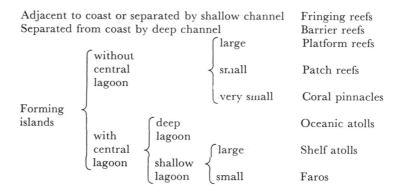

Evolutionary convergence is common so that apparently similar forms may arise in different ways.   Another difficulty of classification is that some of the larger more complex forms may incorporate examples of the smaller ones.

It may be desirable to subdivide fringing reefs on a basis of whether or not there is a shallow 'boat channel' towards the shore, or whether or not they are open to the sea or occur behind a barrier reef (Guilcher, 1958): likewise, barrier reefs may be distinguished by the degree of lateral continuity or by the degree of complexity.   Some barrier reefs are made up of more or less continuous linear or 'ribbon' reefs while others incorporate patch reefs or faros.

Fringing reefs are the most ubiquitous of coral structures.   They are found throughout the world area of reef formation, although they are generally better developed around islands because of the inhibiting effects of freshwater discharge and sediment load from the land on humid continental coasts.   All the other forms may be associated with subsidence which may, as in the case of the classical oceanic atoll, be extensive. They have in the main had more complex histories than fringing reefs and may show the effects of Pleistocene sea level changes. Perhaps it is mainly because of this that barrier reefs and the various sorts of island reefs are more or less confined to the Indo-Pacific province and are rare in the Atlantic province, where an impoverished fauna, occupying a more restricted environment, has faced much greater climatic vicissitudes through the Quaternary. Out of a world total of some 330 atolls counted by Cloud (1958), only about five are outside the Indo-Pacific province and almost all are within the area shown shaded in Fig. 45. The widespread extinction of coral which must have occurred in the Atlantic province during Pleistocene glacials must not only have limited reef building during low sea levels, but also limited the rapidity with which dead reefs were recolonized and built up with the rising, warmer postglacial sea. A study of Hogsty Reef, an atoll in the Bahamas, by Milliman (1967), for instance, suggested that the hermatypic organisms now growing on the reef are only recently introduced to a drowned Pleistocene lithified dune which appears to form the reef flat.

Since the form of many coral structures, such as the compound shelf atolls of Fairbridge (1950), owes something to subaerial karst development during Pleistocene low sea levels, it seems evident that locational differences in precipitation at these times must also have been of importance in giving rise to geographical variation. MacNeil's discussion (1954) of atoll inheritance from low sea level subaerial erosion must imply that differences exist between wet and dry oceanic areas. Again, to the extent that gaps in fringing and barrier reefs may be attributable to a lack of foundation resulting from low sea level downcutting by rivers, this factor should have operated more strongly on high rainfall coasts. The effect of subaerial erosion on reef configuration has been extensively considered by Purdy (1974).

CALCAREOUS ALGAE

A number of marine algae produce encrustations or films of carbonate material, normally calcite with a large amount of magnesium carbonate incorporated. The most prominent of these are red algae comprising the family Corallinaceae. In particular, the group which includes the genera *Lithophyllum*, *Lithothamnion* and *Porolithon* produces crusts and nodules on an extensive scale under conditions of heavy wave exposure. A conspicuous and mainly tropical family of green algae, the Codiaceae, produces lime around filaments, but is found in sheltered lagoonal situations, the best known genus being *Halimeda*.

The Codiaceae are important geomorphically for the way in which they build calcareous banks, tending to fill sheltered depressions such as those within annular reefs, but the coralline algae not only build banks and reefs in their own right but extensively build up and cement coral and other reefs. They also commonly modify the form of shore platforms in tropical seas. As a family they have much wider temperature tolerances than hermatypic corals and are distributed from the Arctic Ocean to the shores of the Antarctic. They are also able to tolerate wider ranges of salinity and turbidity and as a result occur more persistently through the tropics. Doubtless this greater ecological valency made them less susceptible to Pleistocene environmental vicissitudes, so they form reefs in, for instance, the Cape Verde Islands (Crossland, 1905), and off north-eastern Brazil (Gardiner, 1931; Mabesoone, 1966), in an oceanic zone in which corals are poorly represented, partly perhaps because of Pleistocene extinctions.

The coralline algae not only tolerate strong wave exposure but appear to be encouraged by it as long as the waves are not too effectively armed with abrasive tools. Where there is a great deal of spray from breaking waves they grow well above low water mark and this is an important factor that helps to determine the height to which coral reefs grow. In the tropical Pacific, on open coasts exposed to trade wind waves or swell from the southern storm belt, the build-up of reefs by algae is considerable (Doty, 1953): by contrast, the Indonesian reefs, in a low energy environment, carry a much more modest growth of Corallinaceae and their elevation is correspondingly less, except on the more exposed coasts of southern Java and western Sumatra (Umbgrove, 1947b). Wells (1957) commented on the contrast between Atlantic and Pacific coral reefs in this respect. In the Caribbean and tropical Atlantic, calcareous algae play a minor role in reef construction: algal ridges and pavements are poorly if at all developed and reef flats are not exposed at low tide. In this case, however, it seems unlikely that differences in wave energy are wholly or even mainly responsible and biogeographical factors are likely to be involved. It is notable, for instance, that the algal genus *Porolithon*, so prominent a contributor to reef construction in the Pacific is absent from the Atlantic.

In spite of their wide latitudinal distribution, calcareous algae are more important as constructional agents in the tropics than elsewhere. In colder regions, as off the Norwegian coast, they may form deep water banks, but they are not as effective in intertidal construction as they are in low latitudes. In high latitude regions sea ice formation keeps them at depth, but elsewhere the contrast must be due in large part to their more prolific growth in tropical seas, saturated or supersaturated with lime. Termier and Termier (1963), for instance, cite figures to show that growth rates are about five times as great in Samoa and the Maldives as on the French coast. The contrast may also reflect the greater proportion of magnesium carbonate produced by warm water forms. Within the wide ranging genus *Lithothamnion*, for example, the tropical species generate a proportionately greater magnesium carbonate content than do those from higher latitudes (Johnson, 1961). The micro-distribution of calcareous algae on shore platforms along temperate coasts such as the west coast of Britain suggests too that they do not colonize successfully those rock surfaces which suffer abrasion from pebbles and coarse sand, so that the dominance of abrasion with high wave energy and abundant tools in the storm wave environments may be yet another factor in their comparative lack of success in the temperate zone.

Because they do not suddenly cease to become of significance, it is difficult to place even approximate limits on the zone in which calcareous algae are of special geomorphic importance. However, algal terraces on shore platforms reach north to Florida and the Mediterranean and south to the extreme southwest of Australia. The zone is wider than the coral reef zone and approximates closely to that in which lithification of beaches and dunes occurs. There may well be a causal connection here because, as will be discussed in Chapter VI, part of the effect of the algae may lie in the way in which they appear to protect limestones from solution. Following this line of thought, their special geomorphic importance in the tropics may owe at least something to the widespread occurrence of tropical limestones, especially coral rocks, beach rocks and dune rocks.

INTERTIDAL ERODING ORGANISMS

While a great range of intertidal and subtidal organisms is engaged in constructive activity, an equally great range of organisms has a destructive effect. Deposition and erosion commonly proceed at the same time, so that a complex interaction arises. Either deposition or erosion may dominate, or a rough state of equilibrium may exist. There is now a large literature on rock destroying organisms—Otter (1937), Yonge (1951), Ranson (1959), Emery (1962) and McLean (1967) may be cited as examples—but no satisfactory overall geomorphological assessment yet seems possible.

The most notable plant eroders are species of blue-green algae which dissolve calcium carbonate, probably by the secretion of oxalic acid. Their most conspicuous effects are on tropical limestones, which can commonly be seen to be perforated to a depth of several millimetres. Not only do these algae erode directly but they also initiate erosion by many animal browsers, chiefly molluscs, which scrape away quantities of rock while feeding. Other invertebrates bore into rock in order to obtain food, shelter or both. Foremost among these are other molluscs, marine worms, boring sponges and a number of echinoderms such as sea urchins.

It is unlikely that fauna availability strongly influences variations in the effectiveness of eroding organisms, but in any case it is overshadowed by such factors as lithology and wave climate. Some rocks are much more susceptible to attack than others; because of their vulnerability to both biochemical and biomechanical erosion, the soft limestones and lime-cemented sandstones of the tropics are perhaps the chief of these. Although other sedimentary rocks, such as fine-grained sandstones and siltstones (Fig. 48), may also be eroded rapidly, crystalline rocks are very much less subject to organic attack. A second point is that where wave energy is high and there are abundant abrasive tools, not only will the rock area over which the organisms operate be more limited but their effects will be less visible. It is in low energy environments in the tropics where processes of weathering and solution are dominant in cliff and platform evolution that the effects of rock destroying plants and animals will be most obvious. The fact that most studies of organic erosion come from tropical and warm temperate locations can thus be taken to reflect, at least in part, the prevalence of favourable lithology and wave regime in these environments.

BIOGENOUS AND NONBIOGENOUS COASTS

Valentin's distinction between biogenous (*organisch gestaltet*) and non-biogenous coasts was based essentially on the distribution of coral reefs and mangroves, but it appears throughout the preceding discussion that there are significant differences between the tropical and temperate latitudes in the nature and effect of many other biological factors in coastal evolution. Some of these differences are directly climatic in origin.

FIG. 48.   A mollusc, *Siphurachiton*, drilling into mudstone in the intertidal zone near Kaikoura, South Island, New Zealand. (Photo by J. N. Jennings.)

The dominantly woody vegetation (Raunkaier's phanerophytic) of tropical intertidal and dune environments contrasted with the dominantly herbaceous and grassy vegetation (Raunkaier's hemicryptophytic and geophytic) of similar habitats in colder latitudes and the presence of coral reef complexes in warmer waters—these are clearly due essentially to factors of temperature.   The cold month sea surface isotherm for 20°C approximates to an extremely important divide in the distribution of marine plants and animals, and proves critical through a great range of organisms (Ekman, 1967).

However, the apparently greater part played by plants and animals in the development of warmer shorelines is due to a complex of factors, only some of which are directly climatic.   The storm wave environments of temperate latitudes, with their prevalent strong winds, commonly occurring high, steep waves and abundant coarse sediments, are not on the whole favourable to organic processes of landform development.   If many warmer shorelines can be termed biogenous, it is not just because of the greater effectiveness of plant and animal life.   In large part too it is because of the relative ineffectiveness of physical factors.

THE HUMAN FACTOR

The role of man as a factor in landform evolution has been reviewed by a number of writers (Brown, 1970, for instance).   Some human effects upon the coast are deliberate, as when sediment transport systems are modified by the building of groynes and break-waters; when cliff erosion rates are changed by the construction of wall structures at their foot; when dune morphology is altered by the planting of exotic grasses or when salt marshes are drained for agricultural and other purposes. Other effects are unintentional, as when erosion prevention methods remove a source of sediment for the downdrift coast; when removal or replacement of vegetation over a catchment area increases sediment supply from rivers; when damming of rivers decreases sediment supply, or when interference with the plant cover of coastal dunes initiates a phase of wind erosion.

On a world scale there is considerable geographical variation in the extent to which both intentional and unintentional modification has occurred along the shore. Deliberate interference especially in the form of engineering works is most characteristic of the coasts of technologically more advanced countries, whereas in 'underdeveloped' parts of the world unintentional effects such as those resulting from vegetation modification are the rule. The most spectacular example of a man-made coast must be that of the Netherlands, where the present coast has been developed in the last thousand years from a chain of barrier islands lying seaward of the Rhine–Meuse delta (see, for instance, Umbgrove, 1947a).

EROSION PROCESSES AND FORMS

Erosion along the shore produces sea cliffs and shore platforms in a wide variety of materials. Some cliffs are little more than drowned subaerial scarps or cliffs formed at Pleistocene low sea levels (Cotton, 1967), which may plunge directly into deep water without any intervening platform, but virtually all will have been modified at least in part by the action of the sea. There seem to be two basic groups of processes concerned in cliff development: on the one hand, undercutting or oversteepening by marine action and, on the other, subaerial mass movement combined with removal of waste by waves. The first is the simple case of the elementary text books in which the sea is supposed to cut into the base of the cliff and remove the material which collapses as a result (Fig. 49, 1a).

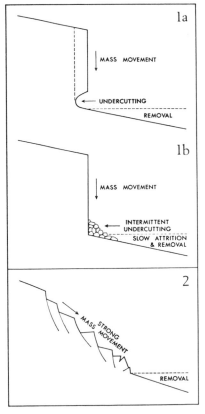

Fig. 49. Diagrammatic representation of major processes of cliff retreat and evolution.
1a: undercutting and rapid removal of collapsed material;
1b: undercutting and slow removal of collapsed material;
2: mass movement and removal of waste at various rates.

There are undoubtedly localities—particularly on unconsolidated rocks in storm wave environments—where such a simple explanation suffices, but on the vast majority of sea cliffs the sea by itself cannot cause the coast to retreat so rapidly that subaerial processes have no opportunity to contribute to morphology. The second case is that of the opposite extreme in which subaerial mass movement is so rapid in relation to wave attack that the sea has no chance of operating against the base of the cliff: its function is confined to removal with varying degrees of efficiency of what is entirely colluvial

Fig. 50. Cliffs formed by slumping and debris removal by waves, Hampshire coast of southern England. (Photo by R. J. Small.)

material (Fig. 49, 2). Examples which come to mind on a local scale are the slump cliffs of parts of the south coast of England (Fig. 50) and the mass movement dominated coast around Gisborne in the North Island of New Zealand (McLean and Davidson, 1968). The arctic coasts of Siberia, where intensive periglacial solifluction dominates, also show this condition on a large scale.

On the great majority of cliffed coasts both sets of processes operate in differing proportions, depending on the relative efficiency of subaerial and marine processes, which in turn are strongly influenced by lithology and climate.

Because most shore platforms are produced below high water mark they may be thought of as being worked on virtually entirely by marine processes. In fact, the processes that produce shore platforms are the same ones that cause undercutting of cliffs by the sea and so we can discuss them simultaneously. They may be broadly grouped into wave quarrying, wave abrasion, water layer weathering, sea water solution, frost weathering and biological erosion. The first four processes are those listed in an undeservedly neglected paper by Hoffmeister and Wentworth (1942), in which associated environmental conditions and resulting forms are set out in a table.

MARINE PROCESSES

Quarrying is the pulling away by waves of particles of material which have been prepared by some other agency.　The particles may be blocks provided by jointing or cleavage, so that closely jointed rocks like some basalts (Fig. 51) and those with pronounced cleavage such as slates and schists are especially favourable to quarrying processes. Where the sea is cutting into unconsolidated materials and directly freeing pebble and sand particles it is also quarrying (Fig. 52).　Quarrying would include the isolation of flint nodules from the chalk cliffs of England and France, the washing away of a

FIG. 51. Quarrying of closely jointed basalt in high wave energy environment; Giants Causeway, Northern Ireland.

weathered mantle of rotted granite in the tropics or even simply the erosion of a recently formed foredune.　In all these cases the sea is disaggregating rather than disintegrating.

The processes of quarrying include the exertion of shock pressures by waves breaking against the rock and enclosing pockets of air and also the direct action of water in moving previously loosened particles.　Where cliffs are cut into permafrost in the Arctic, material may be loosened by the thawing of interstitial ice (Mackay, 1963, for example).　Russian workers have described this process extensively and referred to it as 'thermoabrasion' (Are, 1968, for instance) but it is more truly 'thermoquarrying'.

We have already noted that rock type is an important factor leading to variations in quarrying efficiency from place to place, but it is clear that variations in wave regime must also be important.　The classic stories of the effects of big waves in moving around large chunks of material, such as those recorded by Johnson (1919) and frequently quoted, come from high energy coasts of temperate latitudes where big storm waves are a common and expectable experience.　It seems self-evident that in moderate and low energy environments quarrying is likely to be less effective, particularly on more massive materials.

Quarrying produces a platform with a general slope to seaward, because each quarried particle has to be higher than the particle to seaward of it in order that it may be removed. The resulting surface may be smooth if the dip of the rock strata coincides with the plane of quarrying: if not, then miniature cuesta and monoclinal forms develop. It seems probable that steeply dipping rocks are more susceptible to quarrying than

FIG. 52. Wide intertidal shore platform quarried in glacial till at Aber-aeron, west Wales. Pebbles piled into a beach at the rear of the platform appear lighter in tone as a result of reworking by waves.

those which are subhorizontal because they expose more vulnerable planes of weakness over more of the platform.

Abrasion is taken to mean the wearing away or breaking up of rock material by waves—overwhelmingly by the tools which they may carry in the form of boulders, pebbles and coarse sand. As distinct from quarrying it implies actual physical breakup of cohesive rock and includes what is usually termed attrition. This distinction between quarrying and abrasion essentially parallels that made in glacial geomorphology between glacial quarrying and glacial abrasion. In the literature on coasts 'abrasion' is commonly used in a wider sense than it is here and in glacial and fluvial geomorphology, and it seems unfortunate that there should not be uniformity between different branches of the discipline in this respect.

Abrasion at the foot of a cliff may cause notching (Fig. 53): it will also smooth the surface of shore platforms as abrasive materials are moved backwards and forwards across them (Fig. 54). A real variation in its efficiency depends essentially on wave energy and the availability of tools. In particular, effectiveness is much increased by the presence of pebbles and small boulders and the occurrence of waves large enough to throw this material against the cliff and move it repeatedly over the platform. Both these requirements are satisfied in storm wave environments of temperate latitudes, where not only is wave energy high, but shorter period waves give a greater frequency of back and fore movement and, as we have seen (Ch. II) and shall see later (Ch. VIII), pebbles are especially abundant. It should be noted too that there is a connection

FIG. 53. Formation of a high shallow notch by abrasion on a man-made cliff at Westward Ho!, southwest England, in a high wave energy environment with abundant pebble and boulder tools.

FIG. 54. Effect of abrasion on platform in steeply dipping slates near Staunton, southwest England. Wave energy is high and coarse sand and pebbles abundant.

between abrasion and quarrying in that greater quarrying means more tools for abrading waves: there are several reasons therefore why both are encouraged in the same environment.

Abrasion is associated with a general slope to seaward, which seems necessary in order that boulders, pebbles and sand may move up and down over the platform. Wave uprush pushes material upward but it returns by gravity with the help of backwash and becomes available once more as an abrading tool. On horizontal platforms, such as those produced mainly by water layer weathering and solution, loose particles tend to be pushed to the rear of the platform and to remain there in storage (Fig. 55).

FIG. 55. High tide platform near Hobart, Tasmania. The cliffs retreat by quarrying and are fronted by a narrow 'abrasion ramp' and a wide nearly horizontal surface formed by water layer weathering processes. Boulders remain on the abrasion ramp and do not move back and fore on the high tide platform proper.

Sloping platforms with strong wave backwash commonly develop rills or gullies, which in unconsolidated rocks such as glacial tills are subparallel to the direction of steepest slope but in consolidated rocks usually take advantage of structural lineations.

Abrasion and quarrying together produce the type of shore platform often called an abrasion platform or wave cut platform. In the early literature emanating from around the North Atlantic, this was the only shore platform recognized and these were virtually the only processes acknowledged. However later workers, on warmer, lower energy coasts have showed that there are other important processes and platform types.

Water layer weathering is meant to include all those weathering processes which operate when rock is alternately wetted and dried by sea water. Wentworth (1938) first used the term 'water level weathering' in relation to platform development, but Hills (1949) suggested the term 'water layer weathering' as being less ambiguous. However the same processes also seem to operate against the cliff face as a result of the action of surging waves and spray.   The effect on the cliff may be concentrated at lower levels so as to form a notch or it may be sufficiently distributed that a distinct notch does not eventuate.

Alternate wetting and drying promotes a whole complex of weathering processes. Some, such as salt crystallization pressure (Tricart, 1960) are mechanical, but the great majority are probably the result of chemical reaction between rock minerals and the periodically arriving sea water.   The zone through which these processes operate extends from the highest limit of wave spray down to a level below which the rock is permanently saturated.   Depending on lithology different varieties of pitting and fluting on lower cliff and incipient platform surfaces are produced (Fig. 56), but the

Fig. 56.   Cavernous weathering in phyllite as a result of wetting and drying by spray near high water mark south of Cairns, Queensland. (Photo by E. C. F. Bird.)

ultimate landform is a platform which is often remarkably smooth and horizontal and which lies somewhere around high tide level (Fig. 55).   This surface seems to represent the upper level of permanent rock saturation.

Water layer weathering processes vary in importance as platform producers according to rock type and structure, for they are aided by permeability of the rock and also by low angles of dip.   A low angle of dip promotes homogeneity of lithology and therefore a uniformly developing surface: high angles of dip encourage quarrying instead.   These weathering processes are also strongly influenced by climatic factors, both those controlling the wave regime and those controlling the contiguous atmosphere.   For weathering to become important in fashioning coastal landforms it seems necessary that wave energy should not be high, because big waves promote rapid quarrying and abrasion so that weathering features do not survive.   This can be demonstrated repeatedly on a small scale and there are plenty of places in Tasmania where platforms produced by weathering grade into platforms dominated by abrasion and quarrying as exposure changes and wave energy increases. On the larger scale this is undoubtedly one reason why platforms produced by water layer weathering have not been recognized from storm wave environments such as those of the North Atlantic.

The significance of the local subaerial climate lies mainly in the way in which different rates of evaporation must lead to differences in the effectiveness of wetting and drying. It is very unlikely that water layer weathering can be very effective in wet climates with low evaporation rates, particularly where the tidal type is semi-diurnal. The most effective weathering is likely to be associated with high evaporation and diurnal or mixed tides, and published records to date seem to support this deduction.

Within the tropics, where higher temperatures could be expected to encourage high weathering rates, Tricart has noted that wetting and drying effects are prominent on drier coasts, such as in Brazil near Bahia and north-east of Rio de Janeiro, but are not found in the wet tropics, such as on the Ivory Coast. In favourable environments, like southern California, rock reduction rates of about 30 cm in 600 years have been estimated (Emery, 1960).

Solution is a process which is strongly tied to lithology, because carbonate-rich rocks or those with carbonate cements are by far the most vulnerable, published rates of erosion in coastal limestones being generally in the range of 0·5 to 1·0 mm per year (Hodgkin, 1964). Solution is assisted by the considerable agitation and flow of water in the surf zone (Kaye, 1957). Any broad scale distributional factors must work by varying the dissolving capacity of seawater in various parts of the world ocean, but unfortunately we do not yet know enough of how seawater dissolves to be able to say with any certainty how this capacity varies. It has already been noted that seawater is normally saturated or supersaturated with calcium carbonate and that this supersaturation increases in the tropics (Fig. 35, p. 53). This, together with the decrease in solubility of carbon dioxide in the water of warmer seas, should lead to the deduction that solution must be most effective in colder waters and it is difficult to explain how it can take place at all in the tropics. Attempts to overcome this difficulty have been made by a number of workers. Fairbridge (1948) invoked nocturnal temperature lowering in rock pools and a resulting local short-term increase in carbon dioxide intake by seawater. Revelle and Emery (1957) also concluded that solution in the tropics must be related to local nocturnal increases in the carbon dioxide content of the water, but probably mainly associated with a surplus in the biological balance of carbon dioxide as photosynthesis by marine plants ceases during the hours of darkness. In this connection it is noteworthy that the green algae, in which photosynthesis is most rapid and which Guilcher (1953) considered particularly important in giving a high diurnal pH change, are more abundant in warmer seas. According to Guilcher and Pont (1957), above certain temperatures silica is liberated by decomposition of silicates in sand freed by solution of rock cements. This silica recombines with limestone in a silicate of calcium and liberates carbon dioxide, which attacks the remaining limestone. All these suggestions seem to require isolated or semi-isolated bodies of water in which the processes can operate and they largely envisage rock reduction by the formation and enlargement of rock pools of varying sorts (Fig. 57). Because the lower limit of such pools must lie close to low-

FIG. 57. Shore platform in limestone at Alanya, Turkey, formed by enlargement and coalescence of rock mills and solution pools (Photo by J. N. Jennings.)

water mark, this must also constitute the lower limit of these solution processes, and resulting platforms must form near this level. Revelle and Emery, for instance, considered that 'the very existence of the broad and dead reef flat just below low-tide level indicates the efficacy of erosion of limestone in the intertidal zone'. Above this ultimate low limit, solution pitting and fluting may occur to the upper level reached by wave spray.

Although it may be possible to explain how seawater solution can occur in tropical seas, it still remains probable that it is potentially more efficient in colder waters. Its apparently greater significance in the tropics stems from the much more extensive occurrence of coastal limestones, many of them poorly cemented and susceptible to disaggregation, from the lower wave energy in these latitudes which means that solution effects are not masked by those of quarrying and abrasion, from the lower rates of subaerial solution in the drier tropics, which accentuate the relative effects of marine solution, and from the greater effect of biological solution in the tropics, the results of which are difficult to separate from those of seawater. Cloud (1965), in a review of carbonate precipitation and dissolution in the marine environment, concluded that more and better evidence was required before notching and pitting features of limestones, equally well explained as the work of intertidal organisms, were attributed to seawater solution.

Frost weathering.   Some authors, for instance Aufrère (1934) seem to have thought of icebound coasts as being in a state approaching suspended development because of the absence of wave attack.   Others such as Nansen (1922) attributed to frost action along the shore the major part in the formation of the high latitude platform complex known as the strandflat.   Most present-day opinion would lie between these two extremes. Guilcher (1958) pointed to the relative lack of effectiveness of ice crystallization from seawater, because salts isolated on freezing tend to make the ice cellular and comparatively soft.   Presumably this is why those who have written on icefoot phenomena (Chapter IV) rarely seem to mention their association with platform production. Priestley (1922), for example, remarked in reference to the Antarctic that 'the chief geological effect of the icefoot is undoubtedly the cônservation of the coast to which it is attached.' However, there are many ways in which freshwater may be brought into this situation in both liquid and solid form.   Certain types of icefoot consist primarily of frozen precipitation, and Nichols (1968) recorded and illustrated 'snowdrift-ice slabs' occupying sub-cliff positions along the Antarctic coast.   He considered that their low surface slope of about 15° and lack of crevasses indicated an absence of movement and did not suggest their possible geomorphic effect, but, by analogy with what is known of the operation of subaerial transverse snowpatches, it would be surprising if they were entirely passive.   Russian writing, summarized by Zenkovich (1967) has described how blown snow may accumulate at the foot of cliffs along sections of the Siberian coast.   As reported by Zenkovich the general Russian view seems to favour the efficiency of frost action in cliff recession.

There seem to be three main factors influencing the effectiveness of freezing as a destructive agent.   One of these—that of lithology and the distribution of frost susceptible rocks—is likely to vary over short distances.   The other two are the supply of freshwater, desirable for maximum effectiveness of ice crystal growth, and the periodic wave action necessary in order that frost weathering residues may be removed.   Both of these factors are potentially of regional significance in that they are connected with climatic controls.   Perhaps this would help to explain the absence or poor development of platforms on the main coast of Antarctica, with its low precipitation, limited snow and ice melt, low wave energy and essentially marine icefoot.   In immediate contrast Fleming (1940) reported strandflat forms from the warmer, wetter and more wave susceptible west coast of the Antarctic peninsula, and Flores Silva (1952) described vertical cliffs cut in granite.

The enormous width of strandflats in some places makes it difficult to conceive of them as extraordinarily extensive shore platforms and their origin remains obscure. Tricart (1967) has noted that the Norwegian strandflat does not appear to be in process of formation today and yet was covered by glaciers during Pleistocene glacial stages. Most present-day opinion would probably be that strandflats are glacial or glacio-coastal features and Tietze (1962) has interpreted them as being due to freeze–thaw processes underneath Pleistocene shelf ice as it rose and fell with the tide.

Biological erosion.   The important part played by marine organisms in rock destruction has been referred to in Chapter V.   The efficiency of biological erosion, particularly in the tropics and on lime-rich rocks, is not in doubt and several writers, notably Emery

(1962) have considered it to be one of the most rapid ways in which the intertidal zone may be reduced, given the right conditions. A more difficult question concerns the extent to which the action of animals and plants produces recognizable landforms. The voluminous literature on intertidal zonation in marine organisms attests to the close relationship between habitat limits and levels reached by wave action, so that one would expect any topographic modification which they were able to attain also to have a zonal relationship with water level. Putting it at its simplest, a particular organism could be expected to erode down to its lowest potential level of existence and then stop. In turn this should produce notches coinciding roughly with the upper and lower limits of the eroding organism and platforms at the lower limit. One could also deduce complications due to the variety of organisms involved, each with different tolerances, and the width of the developing platform which adds another dimension to the zonation picture.

By and large such deductions are not substantiated by field observation in the high energy storm wave environment of temperate latitudes, where notches and platforms are demonstrably due to quarrying and abrasion by waves, but in the low wave energy microtidal tropics and especially on limestone or lime-cemented rocks they may have much more validity. A very good case can be made out for the contention that

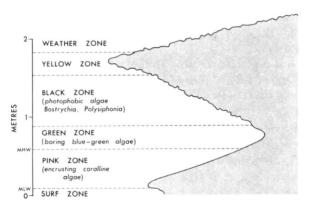

Fig. 58. Biological zonation on coral cliffs in Barbados. (After Lewis, 1960.)

'solution benches' and 'solution nips' in tropical limestones are produced not by sea-water solution but by the action of intertidal organisms (for example, Ginsburg, 1953; Newell and Imbrie, 1955). The most important organisms from the point of view of notch development in limestone are almost certainly the blue-green algae. Newell (1956) regarded notches in the Tuamotus as the result of leaching below a film of blue-green algae and mechanical rasping and boring by animals. He felt there was no compelling evidence that it is the result of solution of the rock by seawater. On coral limestone shores around Barbados blue-green algae are particularly concentrated in the major undercut approximating to high tide mark; this is the 'green zone' of Lewis (1960), usually about 15 to 45 cm wide (Fig. 58). The notch seems due to loosening of the surface rock by algae and attendant herbivorous invertebrates, coupled with removal of loosened particles by waves. That blue-green algae are also found at higher levels where cliff retreat is not so rapid suggests that their effectiveness depends in part on the quarrying action of waves on a surface prepared by the algae, and this is essentially the conclusion reached by Hodgkin (1970) from a study of notch formation on limestone coasts in Malaysia.

Whereas seawater solution may be an effective process in the development of platforms by the enlargement of tidal pools, it seems probable that where a notch occurs in relatively deep water biological agencies are mainly, if not entirely, responsible.

BIOLOGICAL CONSTRUCTION

It may seem anomalous at first sight to be discussing processes of construction in a chapter headed 'Erosion Processes', but in the tropics it is quite impossible to consider the evolution of cliffs and platforms without reference to ways in which animals and plants build or protect. Herein lies a major difference between tropical and temperate

FIG. 59. Constructional coral surface exposed by an exceptionally low spring tide on Keeper Reef, a platform reef among the Great Barrier Reefs of Queensland.

latitudes. Indeed, if the term 'shore platform' is interpreted, as it is here, in a descriptive and non-genetic way, most if not all coral reef flats must be thought of as shore platforms. Reef flats arise in a number of ways. Some appear purely constructional and represent the upper level to which the reef complex has been able to grow (Fig. 59): others seem to be the surface of agglomerations of boulders and pebbles filling what had

FIG. 60. Low-tide platform at Eclipse Island, Halifax Bay, Queensland. The platform is of complex origin; partly cut into beach conglomerate, partly cut into coral and partly built by coral into a fringing reef.

FIG. 61. Fringing reefs on the south coast of Tutuila, Samoa. The presence of the stack suggests a composite origin, due to erosion as well as construction.

previously been a depression: yet others can be shown to have been truncated near low-tide mark by some erosion process and are the end result of lowering rather than building. A clear example of this last case is that of the reef flats on Okinawa described and figured by MacNeil (1950). Many present-day reefs are shore platforms cut into older coral (Fig. 60) and on which a veneer of modern coral has accumulated (Stoddart, 1969c). Most reefs have gone through more or less complicated histories of alternate erosion and construction, so that historically and geographically, the line between eroded and constructed forms is difficult to draw (Fig. 61).

Even more difficult to separate in nature from processes of platform and cliff development are the constructional activities of calcareous algae. In warm seas where there is only a small tidal range, intergrowth of algae with marine invertebrates may build a projecting rim on vertical rock faces round about mean tide mark—the 'trottoir' of French writers who have described it from many parts of the Mediterranean. Johnson (1961) recorded having observed these features rimming narrow rock terraces on rocky coasts on Guam, Tinian and Saipan in the Mariana Islands of the western Pacific. The *trottoir* is limited in outward growth by the varying propensity of waves to break off the extremity.

Much more significant than *trottoir* building is the way in which calcareous algae modify the development of shore platforms in the tropics by the construction of algal flats and rims. Some algal flats seem almost entirely constructional and are the algal equivalents of fringing coral reefs: in other cases the algae form a crust of varying thickness on a rock platform and whether their role is predominantly constructive or protective is arguable. In either case they commonly form rimmed terracettes descending in height from the zone of greatest water supply by waves. While on narrow platforms this gives an overall slope seaward or sideways, if the platform is broad the resulting gradient may be inward.

CLIFF MORPHOLOGY

On many rocky coasts the sea has done relatively little to modify morphology. Coastal outlines have been etched by subaerial weathering, especially between 100 000 and 10 000 years ago when sea levels were low, and the waves have washed away the waste mantle to expose the weathering front. Massively jointed and impermeable crystalline rocks resistant to all processes of marine attack particularly answer this description. In other cases minor amounts of quarrying may have taken place as a result of wave action, without imposing clearly defined forms of marine origin.

Plunging cliffs have also been thought of as largely inherited and little modified by the Holocene Sea. The primarily hydrostatic forces imposed by non-breaking waves in the deep water at their foot are relatively small and much wave energy is likely to be reflected. Other cliffs have narrow, poorly defined platforms at their foot, often covered by talus which acts as an efficient absorber of wave energy.

The most spectacular free-face cliffs are generally associated with conditions of maximum marine attack with waves able to break directly on the lower face and impose dynamic forces of great intensity (Fig. 62). Free-face cliffs are also associated with easily quarried rock producing easily removed detritus, low rates of subaerial weathering and mass movement so that sloping sections are poorly developed, and landward dipping or horizontal structures (Fig. 63). Seaward dipping rocks tend to produce bare slopes. Limestones are particularly favourable for the production of free faces but horizontally bedded, strongly cemented, sandstones and coarsely jointed basalts and dolerites are also frequently associated with near-vertical cliffing.

FIG. 62. Cliffs and low-tide shore platforms in dune rock, Elliston, South Australia.

Where wave attack is weak or has been weakened by talus accumulation or platform extension, steep coastal slopes may develop and assume a cover of vegetation. In the first case the slope may have developed as the original form because of a strong

FIG. 63. Cliff and sloping shore platforms in subhorizontal flaggy sand-stones, Nash Pt, South Wales.

FIG. 64   Degraded cliff forming steep coastal slope, Sydney, New South Wales.

preponderance of mass movement over wave attack: in the second case it may have resulted from degradation of a steeper pre-existing cliff (Fig. 64).

The intimate relationship of cliff form with rock type and the frequent appearance of features inherited from past denudation systems make geographical generalizations

FIG. 65.   Tropical rain forest coming down to an almost uncliffed rocky shore south of Cairns, Queensland.   The environment is one of low wave energy and perennial rainfall of about 2500 mm a year.   (Photo by E. C. F. Bird.)

difficult and some would say impossible.   A survey, such as that for the British Isles in Chapter 5 of Steers (1953), exemplifies the way in which a large variety of forms may exist within a relatively limited area.   Even so, some broad conclusions seem possible from a consideration of the way in which the relative efficiency of mass wasting and wave attack vary in different parts of the world.   Tricart and Cailleux (1965) for instance have suggested that within the tropics a significant difference exists between humid and arid coasts.   On hot, wet shores, such as those of the Pacific coast of Colombia and the coast of Liberia, cliffs recede slowly and at relatively low angles by mass wasting.   There is almost continuous vegetation cover and only the lowest few metres are bare (Fig. 65). Landslips may produce amphitheatre-like bays as described by Tricart (1957) from the Ivory Coast of West Africa.   On hot, dry shores plant and regolith cover is limited and steeper angles are encouraged by marine attack.   This tends to be more effective than mass wasting, even though marine attack is still relatively weak and largely in the form of seawater weathering and solution.   The main lithological factor which upsets the general relationship is the occurrence of limestones, including corals and aeolianites, which tend to produce 'arid' type cliffs throughout the tropics because of their failure to generate substantial waste mantles of weathered material (Fig. 66).

FIG. 66.   Near vertical cliffs in coral limestone on the east coast of Barbados. Strong trade wind controlled waves with abundant spray produce a saline cliff top environment in which plant growth is limited.

As one moves poleward from the tropics into high wave energy latitudes where quarrying by big waves becomes proportionately more effective, marine attack tends to dominate on all rock types and to evolve steeper, more spectacular cliffs.   Further poleward still, along Arctic and Antarctic shores, wave energy decreases once more and periglacial mass movement processes maintain relatively low angle slopes.

In temperate latitudes the existence of two-cycle slope-over-wall cliffs has been

thought to reflect strong degradation of older cliffs by Pleistocene periglacial mass movement and subsequent steepening of their lower section by the postglacial sea (Cotton,
1952; Bird, 1968).   Slope-over-wall cliffs occur in many parts of the world and some of
them may result from a kind of balance between terrestrial processes acting from above
and marine processes acting from below: but in the main they probably reflect the
intervention of a low sea-level phase in which marine attack was removed and subaerial
processes held full sway.   However, where both marine and subaerial processes were in
turn particularly effective, such as in western Europe, where periglacial solifluction
extended below present sea level during glacials and wave energy was high during
interglacials, the slope-over-wall form seems especially well marked (Fig. 67).   In the

FIG. 67.   Slope-over-wall cliffs near Lynmouth, southwest England.

Southern hemisphere only relatively small sections of coast are comparable in their
Pleistocene history to those of western Britain for instance, but Fleming (1965) has
described and illustrated strongly developed slope-over-wall cliffs at the Auckland
Islands in latitude 51°S.

On cliffs where marine processes dominate, a notch may form at the base, but it is
now widely recognized that this is best developed in low energy environments where
weathering, solution and biological processes are more effective in cliff retreat than
wave quarrying and abrasion.   This is because the big waves tend to destroy the upper
limb of the notch and the varying wave height gives rise to a broad, relatively shallow
indentation.   The extreme of notch development is found on tropical limestone coasts
where exaggerated visors are produced as a result of various solution processes and
relatively weak wave attack within a limited vertical range (Figs 68 and 69).   A low
tidal range is of great importance and the best notch and visor cliffing is to be found on
microtidal coasts.

Fig. 68.   Strong notch and visor formation in an erratic coral block, east coast of Barbados.

The spectacular cliff forms, such as arches, stacks, geos and blowholes which figure prominently in elementary text books are relatively rare in nature and are largely confined to high wave energy coasts where structure and lithology are suitable for their development.   Within the tropics minor examples occur on limestone coasts and particularly in association with coral but otherwise they are uncommon.

Fig. 69.   Notch and platform in Ordovician limestone near Kua, Langkawi Island, Malaya   (Photo by J. N. Jennings.)

The form of cliffs may also owe at least something to the detailed history of sea level change along a particular stretch of coast. A number of authors (King, 1963, for instance) have concluded that a long phase of active marine erosion requires one or more periods of gradual submergence, so that the sea may continue to eat into the cliff base across a progressively wider shore platform. Cotton (1969), while agreeing with this conclusion and suggesting that existing high cliffs are probably the product of repeated periods of submergence in the Pleistocene, has pointed out that there must in fact be an optimum rate for such submergence because, if it proceeds too quickly in relation to the rate of erosion, a plunging cliff will develop, after which it will be difficult to restart erosion because of increased reflection of wave energy and a lack of tools for abrasion. If, as seems likely, the exact rate of submergence and the length of time over which it operates are of critical importance, then the factors which operate to vary such rates and times as between one coast and another must also be taken into account in explaining cliff morphology.

SHORE PLATFORM MORPHOLOGY

As in the case of cliffs, the close association between the details of platform morphology and the nature of the country rock has inhibited attempts at classification. Such attempts have also been inhibited by the apparent absence of some important types from the North Atlantic region within which earlier workers operated. The most useful simple classification may be the tripartite division by Bird (1968) into intertidal, high tide and low tide platforms (Fig. 70). These appear to represent three broad

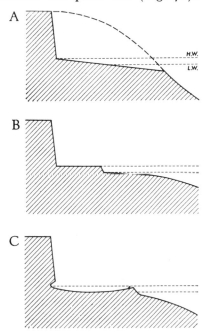

FIG. 70. The three major shore platform types of Bird (1968). A: intertidal; B: high tide; C: low tide.

themes upon which numerous variations may occur and their usefulness probably stems from the way in which they represent the basic forms which major groups of processes tend to develop.   As already indicated, quarrying and abrasion produce sloping surfaces; water layer weathering produces subhorizontal surfaces related to high tide mark; solution and biological destruction produce subhorizontal surfaces with a lower limit somewhere around low tide.   On shores where one of these groups of processes is completely dominant, platforms will approach closely one of Bird's three basic models, provided lithology is favourable.   Where process regimes are complex, intermediate or compound forms will develop, and morphology becomes further complicated where lithology and structure are complex as well, but the three models may profitably be regarded as norms from which various departures occur in different environments. The factors affecting their distribution are therefore important in any consideration of the geography of shore platforms.

Unfortunately the terminology relating to forms has become confused.   Some writers have used 'intertidal' in a different sense, not necessarily implying a slope.   The terms 'high tide' and 'low tide' also may cause uncertainty because 'high tide' platforms in particular have very varied relationships to tide levels.   In the short discussion which follows treatment is in terms of process rather than form.

PLATFORMS PRODUCED BY QUARRYING AND ABRASION

These are basically the intertidal platforms of Bird, which slope from about high water mark to somewhere below low water mark and are the traditional 'wave cut' or 'abrasion' platforms of earlier European and North American writers (Fig. 63).   The development of such platforms is encouraged by the same factors which favour maximum quarrying and abrasion—high wave energy, easily quarried rocks and an abundance of rock tools.   They are therefore virtually universal within the storm wave environments of temperate coasts, but in lower energy environments nearer the equator they occur only where local lithology or tidal conditions are especially favourable.   One of the commonest of such situations in the tropics is where deeply weathered rocks outcrop on the shore and quarrying is possible even by small waves.

The height of the inner edge of the platform is mainly related to wave exposure (Wright, 1970) and that of the outer edge to the greatest depth at which waves can quarry and abrade.   This depth is certainly less than surf base (see p. 102) and probably in most cases a great deal less.   Depending on the degree of difference between platform gradient and overall coastal ramp angle, there may be a distinguishable break of slope forming a low tide cliff, but this is submerged at most if not all stages of the tide.

In a number of studies, Trenhaile (1978) has demonstrated a relationship between platform gradient and tidal range: as tidal range decreases platform gradient also becomes lower, presumably because wave attack is concentrated on a more uniform horizontal plane.   There may be other factors operating such as the ratio of wave energy to the size of quarried particles but data relating to these are lacking up to the present.

Sloping platforms due basically to quarrying by waves may have considerable internal relief because of lithological variation and consequent resistance to erosion.

Structural lineations may lead to preferred quarrying along certain vertical planes and the excavation of gullies along which strong water and sediment movement occurs. On weaker, poorly consolidated rocks such as clays the platform is often cut by shallow semi-parallel rills down which backwash is preferentially channelled.

PLATFORMS PRODUCED BY WATER LAYER WEATHERING

The second group of platforms result from weathering processes associated with the alternate wetting and drying of rocks.   As a result they tend to develop to the highest level of permanent saturation which is most nearly related to high water mark (Fig. 71).   In practice, the height of prevailing waves may be at least as important as tidal amplitude in determining the effective level.   Rock permeability and atmospheric climate also have an effect.   The conditions which favour formation are those which favour water layer weathering—permeable, coarsely bedded rocks with low dips, high evaporation and mixed or diurnal tides to facilitate drying, high temperatures to speed chemical reaction rates and a low tidal range facilitating the maintenance of a well defined horizontal upper level of saturation.   But also important are conditions discouraging abrasion and rapid quarrying which tend to destroy the effects of weathering (Fig. 72).   To date almost all high tide platforms seem to have been recorded from low to moderate wave energy, microtidal, high evaporation regions such as Hawaii, Peru, Brazil, Madagascar, Senegal, Sicily, southern California, Australia and New Zealand.

FIG. 71.   Rear of a high tide platform cut into massively jointed basalt by water layer weathering on the north coast of Tasmania.   The modern platform is forming at the expense of older higher platforms.

FIG. 72.   Water layer weathering in massively jointed basalt with moderate
wave energy, north coast of Tasmania. The waves are too weak to quarry
the massive joint blocks (compare with Fig. 51).

There seem to be two broad subgroups of platforms produced by wetting and
drying.   In the first the platform has resulted directly from cliff retreat, with the cliff
being sapped by weathering in a narrow zone at its foot.   The 'old hat' platform of
Bartrum (1926) is a good example of this.   Such platforms are not strictly horizontal,
but have very slight slopes to seaward which may be of the same magnitude as the
flattest platforms produced by quarrying.   They do not have ramparts and their
surface is relatively continuous, but like all high tide platforms, they have well marked
low tide cliffs.

The second subgroup contains platforms produced by downwasting, probably
nearly always from older platforms (Figs 71, 72).   New platform surfaces form by
successive extension of permanently saturated level sections as rock around their edges
is alternately wetted and dried.   This is the water layer weathering process in the
strict sense and the surfaces so developed are absolutely horizontal.   Because the
process may begin at a number of levels, surfaces may develop at different heights and
be separated by minor rock dams or scarps.   Eventually however these tend to coalesce
at the lowest level.   Developing platforms may therefore have varied internal relief and
they commonly have ramparts at their outer edge.

PLATFORMS PRODUCED BY SOLUTION AND BIOLOGICAL EROSION

Bird described his low tide platforms as developed typically on the Pleistocene dune
limestones of southern and western Australia, and they seem generally to be associated

with solution or biological erosion of calcareous rocks in low wave energy, microtidal conditions.   They lie somewhat above low tide mark and the highest examples appear to approach in altitude the lowest high tide platforms.   If, as suggested previously, constructional, destructional and composite reef flats have to be considered as types of shore platforms, then it is in this category that they have to be placed, because the upper limit of coral growth and the lower limit of its destruction generally occur near to low tide level.   Platforms constructed by calcareous algae show more complicated relationships with sea level.   At one extreme they may modify low tide platforms to only a slight extent by encrustation or rim building: at the other extreme they may build massive platforms close to high water mark.   Russell (1967) has observed that the height of algal flats or reefs is strongly correlated with exposure to wave action and that they commonly reach higher elevations on headlands than in embayments.

Low tide platforms thus include a multiplicity of genetic types, but they are all overwhelmingly characteristic of warmer waters, particularly where Pleistocene beach, dune and reef rocks form the shore.

Again it seems useful to distinguish platforms produced by cliff retreat from those produced by downwasting of a pre-existing higher surface.   Examples of the first subgroup have been described and illustrated by Hills (1971).   They are commonly associated with notches and visors at their inner edge; they slope very gently and smoothly seaward; and their outer edge has no rampart but is often undercut by the sea.   As concluded earlier in this chapter, the most important formative agents are blue-green algae operating in the notch, but calcareous algae and a range of other organisms are important in protecting the developing platform.   The other subgroup is best developed on harder limestones in higher latitudes where biological erosion is relatively slow and seawater solution may be more effective.   These platforms often display complex microrelief forms such as lapies with intricate intertidal pools around which solution is presumed to take place.   Where tidal range is considerable the pools are characteristically stepped so that as they coalesce to form the ultimate smoother surface it may slope strongly seaward.   Examples of such platforms have been described by Guilcher in a number of publications and summarized in his book (Guilcher, 1958).

VII | BEACH PROCESSES

Individual beaches vary considerably in plan, profile and dynamic behaviour. Although such factors as tidal range and sediment type are important in contributing to this variation, beach morphology mainly reflects wave climate. In Chapter III an attempt was made to paint a broad general picture of world wave environments: before discussing processes operating on beaches it is necessary to look briefly at the changes which take place as waves generated on the ocean surface move to the shore. The changes can be described in terms of a number of zones, which may vary in width from place to place and may not all be present (Fig. 74).

DEEP WATER ZONE

In the open ocean, waves are basically oscillatory with individual water particles moving in almost closed, circular orbits and having negligible net forward mass transport (Fig. 73). However, the wave form travels at relatively high velocity and so

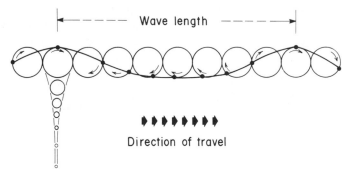

FIG. 73. Water travel in simple oscillatory wave motion.

carries potential and kinetic energy. The orbital diameter of surface water is equal to the height of the waves but this diameter decreases exponentially downwards and motion virtually ceases at a depth equal to half the wave length (Fig. 74). This depth is conventionally referred to as wave base and outside wave base the wave is in deep water. Although the concept applies strictly to a particular wave group, it is possible to think of a deep water zone off a particular coast, which is related to the general wave climate and characterized for instance by the proportion of waves which are touching

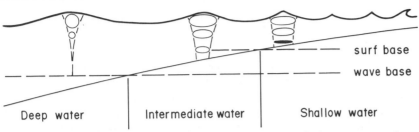

FIG. 74. Wave zones. The depiction is highly diagrammatic: in nature wave base is likely to be an order of magnitude greater than surf base.

bottom.   On some coasts with shallow shelf edges and dominated by long period swell waves, there may be very little in the way of a deep water zone on the shelf itself.

INTERMEDIATE WATER ZONE

Inside wave base, waves are in intermediate or transitional water.   As they approach the coast, wave trains travelling at a small angle to the shore tend to be filtered out and, in those that remain, changes take place as the orbital motion touches bottom. Wave velocity decreases progressively as water depth decreases and this in turn brings about a decrease in wave length.   Unequal deceleration along particular wave crests leads to refraction—a bending effect which brings them closer in plan to the submarine contours.   Wave period however remains the same.

The orbits themselves become more elliptical with their long axes parallel to the bottom and with maximum displacement taking place in fore and aft directions.   Close to the bottom, motion is essentially linear.   As wave shape becomes increasingly trochoidal, so that rather higher, narrower crests are separated by longer, flatter troughs, inequality develops between orbital velocities in the fore and aft directions. Forward movement under the crest takes place more rapidly than backward movement under the trough, giving a potential for net shoreward movement of bottom sediments, particularly those of larger particle size.

SHALLOW WATER ZONE

The changes which take place inside wave base are small at first but increase exponentially towards the breakpoint.   Closer to the shore is a zone considered by waves theorists as 'shallow water' in the strict sense and within which the sedimentological and geomorphological effects of the changes become much more pronounced. On the sea surface it is marked by a noticeable increase in refraction and in wave peakedness—especially in the case of long swell.   On the sea bottom it is related to a distinctly more powerful potential for onshore bed drift of sediment. Essentially it represents the outer zone to which material may be removed from the beach during conditions of unusually high wave energy and from which it is likely to be returned.   As a result, bottom sediments show a relationship to those on the beach and often contrast with those to seaward.

Within the shallow water zone a balance has been postulated between onshore bed drift and forces such as gravity tending to move material downslope and seaward.   For a sediment particle of given size there will be a null point where it can be assumed to be in a state of zero net movement.   A triangular relationship between wave energy, particle size and gradient is also implied by observed relationships between wave energy and offshore gradients, since wave energy and gradient vary along the coast proportionately more than does mean particle size.   If mean particle size is assumed to vary little, then larger wave energy must be balanced by a steeper gradient.   Large-scale positive relationships between offshore gradient and deep water wave energy certainly seem to occur, for example around the Australian coast (Davies, 1977, Fig. 7.2).

The shallow water zone may also be identifiable in plan as the strip within which bathymetric contours run parallel to the beach (Dietz, 1963), the implication being that where sediment is relatively mobile it will be subject to similar factors of plan distribution.

There is no term in general use to denote the division between intermediate and shallow water but many writers have followed Dietz (1963) in using 'surf base' for what appears to be essentially the same thing.   In wave theory it is generally taken to be at a depth equal to one-twentieth (sometimes one-twentyfifth) of the wave length for an individual wave group.   As judged by the sedimentological and morphological relationships suggested above its regional position seems to lie between depths of about 5 m in sheltered areas and about 20 m on the most exposed shores.   However, it may lie closer to shore on pebbly beaches and at greater depth where fine sands are found.

BREAKER ZONE

The coastward limit of the shallow water zone is marked by the breakpoint: here the waves cease to be oscillatory and form bores of water translated towards the shore. Breaking occurs when the velocity of propagation of the wave form slows to the point where it is exceeded by the orbital velocities of water in the wave crest.   The rapidity with which this point is reached determines the form of the resultant breaker.   If the offshore gradient is abnormally flat, or if the wave is already relatively steep, changes will be relatively slow and the breaking process protracted.   This could happen for instance with rock reefs offshore or in storm conditions.   Where the gradient is steep or where the incident waves are long and low, the reverse will tend to be the case.

Breaker forms constitute a continuum from spilling breakers, which break gradually and maintain a crest of white water for long distances, through plunging breakers, in which the crest curls over to plunge and reform into a bore, to surging breakers, in which the wave base rushes up the shore and the crest itself collapses.   In practice most large waves form either spilling or plunging breakers and this is the important dichotomy, described for instance by Huntley and Bowen (1975).

SURF ZONE CIRCULATION

In the surf zone, waves of translation—bores of water formed from spilling or plunging

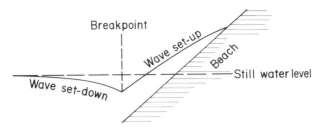

FIG. 75. Mean still water level as waves break on a beach.

breakers—are moving towards the shore. Where surging breakers occur or where plunging breakers impact directly on to steep pebble beaches, there will be no surf zone in this sense and the breaking wave metamorphoses directly into swash.

The breaking waves cause an excess flow of momentum, termed radiation stress, which produces a set-up of the mean water level towards the shore and a corresponding set-down in the breaker zone (Fig. 75). The shoreward momentum is balanced by a pressure gradient of sloping water within the surf zone. The water slope associated with wave set-up appears to be much the same for waves of differing heights but, because larger waves break further out, the resulting rise in water level on the beach may be considerably greater.

Translation of water towards the shore necessitates return flow and when waves break normal to the shore two basic sorts of flow appear to be identifiable. Under

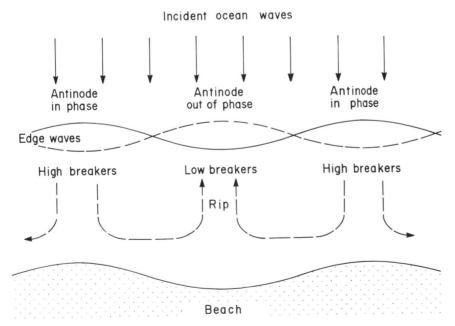

FIG. 76. Diagrammatic relationship of edge waves and rip currents. Rips are located where edge waves are out of phase with incident ocean waves.

certain equilibrium conditions or on very short beaches it may be oscillatory with negligible variation alongshore.   More commonly the return flow is channelled into rip currents of variable strength and spacing and these appear to be especially characteristic during erosional and accretionary phases.   Onshore transport takes place between the rips and offshore transport within the rips themselves, this in turn being associated with several types of rhythmic surf zone and beach topography.

Channelled return flow is the result of variations in height of the breaking waves, causing longshore variation in wave set-up.   Such variations may occur because of refraction over irregular features on the offshore bottom, but more generally because of the generation of edge waves.   These are standing waves formed by resonance between waves incident to the shore and those reflected from it, and they are observable only by the way in which they raise the height of the breakers at regular intervals (Bowen, 1969; Bowen and Inman, 1969).   Although edge waves may be generated at various harmonics, it is those at the same period as the incident waves or at multiples of that period that are important in rip generation.   Edge waves in phase with the incoming breakers cause them to increase in height at alternate edge wave antinodes and to decrease in height at other antinodes.   Shoreward translation of water and wave set-up is thus greater at the points of increased breaker height with return flow tending to be channelled into rips between (Figs. 76, 77, 78).

When waves are not breaking normal to the shore, then radiation stress has a longshore component which drives a longshore current within the surf zone.   This will also occur if there is a large-scale systematic variation in breaker height, resulting for

Fig. 77. Beach near Kiama, New South Wales, displaying conditions intermediate between the reflective and dissipative states. There is a narrow surf zone but with well marked and closely spaced bar and rip features.

Fig. 78. Dissipative type beach with wide surf zone and widely separated rip system, Muizenberg, South Africa.

instance from refraction.   The current is generated away from the direction of wave approach or away from the higher breakers.   Current velocity depends on the orbital velocity of the breakers, which will be greater for bigger and shorter waves, and on the longshore component of radiation stress, which will vary with the angle of breaker approach and longshore variation in wave height (Komar, 1975).   Velocities are highest some short distance inside the breakpoint and reduce to zero at the beach and at some short distance outside the breakpoint.   Although the speed of longshore currents may often be very low, their importance in sediment transport is accentuated by the extreme turbulence and bottom disturbance occurring in the breaker zone, causing sand particles lifted from the bottom to be readily displaced.   Maximum sediment transport is therefore likely to take place between the line of maximum current velocity and the breakpoint itself.   Superimposition of longshore currents on to the channelled return flow represented by rips may produce something in the nature of a meandering net transport system along the surf zone (Dolan, 1971; Sonu, 1972).

SURF ZONE MORPHOLOGY

Oscillatory flow with little longshore variation tends to produce an essentially planar floor below the surf zone.   In low energy conditions the sea bottom may form a surface sloping evenly seaward with minimal relief.   In high energy conditions it is marked by an elongated bar, lying parallel to the beach and located in the breaker zone—the longshore or breakpoint bar.   Between the bar and the beach is a deep trough.   The longshore bar marks the zone where seaward transport of sediment by returning oscillatory flow meets the shoreward transport system existing in the shallow water zone

outside the breakpoint.   However accumulation of sediment in this zone is limited by
the high forward velocity of water in the breakers which imposes a maximum height to
the bar.   In laboratory conditions this height has been found to be about one-third of
the initial water depth.   The existence in some cases of multiple bars has been
attributed not only to differing positions of the breakpoint over a period of time, but
also to the effect of standing or progressive edge waves (Short, 1975; Huntley, 1976).

In conditions of channelled flow the bar is modified by the existence of longshore
circulation systems.   Where onshore flow occurs the bar tends to project forward so
that various sorts of crescentic features result and these are echoed by corresponding
megacusps on the beach.   At rip locations the water is deeper and a more or less
well-defined rip channel occurs.   Although superficially alike, forms produced during
accretionary phases differ in detail from those formed during erosional phases: these are
illustrated in Fig. 85 (p. 112), which is derived from the work of Short (1979). The
effect of obliquely impinging waves is to superimpose an angled, echelon effect on the
plan form of bars and channels.

SWASH ZONE

The swash zone is that part of the beach covered and uncovered by the surf as successive
waves travel shorewards.   The swash itself contains two components of markedly
different nature: a shoreward moving component, the uprush, deriving energy from the
wave and forming a wedge of turbulent water thinning as it moves up the beach face;
and a seaward moving component, the backwash, deriving energy from gravity and
forming a thin sheet of water, with more laminar flow, percolating in varying degrees
into the beach.

The extent of backwash percolation has a controlling influence on the gradient of the
beach face.   Strong backwash from big waves and with a high proportion of surface
flow produces lower beach face angles.   Important in this is the height of the beach
water table, which in turn is strongly affected by particle size.   On fine sand beaches,
reduced pore space discourages percolation and tends to maintain a high water table.
Other factors such as rainfall and freshwater run-off from behind the beach may have a
similar result.   Tricart and Cailleux (1965) suggested that beach organisms may affect
permeability and that higher concentrations of burrowing animals on tropical beaches
may increase swash absorption.   Beach rock must have the converse effect (p. 126) and
at the other climatic extreme the frost table on high latitude beaches may reduce
permeability considerably (Owens and McCann, 1970; Harper and others, 1978).
Bigger waves, which produce greater wave set-up and larger swash volumes, and
shorter waves, which produce more interference between uprush and backwash
(Kemp, 1961) are also important in maintaining high beach water tables and low beach
face angles.

Figure 79, redrawn from Wiegel (1964) incorporates data from Bascom (1951).
Inman, Gayman and Cox (1963) have also plotted beach face angle against median
grain size for Hawaiian beaches of differing exposure.   These plots show that, while
grain size is the most important control of beach face angle because of its effect on beach

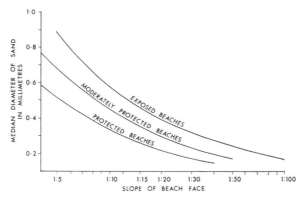

Fig. 79. The relationship between beach particle size, exposure and beach face angle on beaches in western USA. (After Wiegel, 1964.)

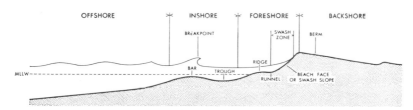

Fig. 80. Major shore zones and beach berms.

Fig. 81. Very wide, single berm beach in microtidal swell environment at Sydney, New South Wales.

water tables and the internal friction applied by constituent sediments, a secondary
effect resulting from exposure to high energy waves is also discernible.

One result of a steeper beach face is to accentuate the appearance of the beach
berm—that section of the beach above the swash limit, lying closer to the horizontal
and resulting from progradation of the beach face (Figs 80, 81). In the case of sand
beaches the height of the berm is set by the limit reached by swash uprush, but on
pebble beaches the limit is somewhat higher because of the ability of waves to throw
pebbles some distance past the swash limit. In this way storm ridges of pebbles may be
built to considerable heights above high water mark—for example 13 m at Chesil Beach
on the south coast of England according to Steers (1946). Steep pebble beaches may
often lie above a much flatter sand beach, uncovered only at low tide (Fig. 82).

The width of the berm is essentially a function of sediment supply: if more material is

FIG. 82. Very low angle sand beach backed by steep pebble ridge more
than 6 metres in height in a macrotidal storm wave environment, Newgale,
west Wales.

being added than subtracted, the berm will build out at the height and beach face angle
applying in a particular case. In a laboratory wave tank, where wave height can be
kept more or less constant while fresh beach material is being added, the backshore zone
may be quite horizontal (Bagnold, 1940). In nature, wave heights are never constant,
so that, as the berm builds out, exceptionally high uprush may carry material past the
top of the normal beach face and deposit it on the outer edge of the berm. In this way a
convex platform may be formed so that the backshore slopes inland. Repetition of this
process under conditions of extreme progradation may be one way in which ridging of
the backshore zone is effected.

Swash from waves approaching normal to the beach may be essentially planar with
little longshore variation. However it often develops small-scale circulatory patterns,

FIG. 83. Beach with strongly developed single berm near Oldenburg, Baltic Sea coast of Germany.   The cliffs are cut into glacial drift.

reminiscent of the larger-scale rip systems in the surf zone.   These appear to result from the generation of subharmonic edge waves close to the shore (Guza and Inman, 1975; Wright and others, 1977) and are reflected on the beach in the presence of beach cusps.   Uprush is strongest opposite the cusps horns where larger sediment particles accumulate with backwash concentrating in the intervening embayments where finer particles are generally to be found.

Swash from oblique waves initiates a potentially important transport process known as beach drifting, in which oblique uprush and transverse, gravity controlled backwash cause a zig-zag progression of individual sediment particles alongshore.   Although 'bulges' of material may sometimes be seen travelling along the beach as a result of this process it is generally associated with beach faces that are smooth in plan.

MACROTIDAL ENVIRONMENTS

The discussion so far in this chapter relates to the microtidal and mesotidal beaches which characterize the great majority of world coasts.   The picture is complicated by the existence of a high tidal range.

The strong tidal currents associated with macrotidal shores may affect bottom topography independently of waves (p. 52) especially in deep water and intermediate water zones where wave influence is slight.   Not only may this modify strongly the submarine morphology and sediment transport system but both the currents and their associated sea floor relief may affect wave refraction.   Closer inshore, where the effect of waves and wave induced currents is much greater, a large tidal range has the important effect of causing breaker zones, surf zones and swash zones to migrate significant distances during the tidal cycle.   Experimental work (Bagnold, 1940) and examination of the effects of the change from neap to spring tides on some beaches (Inman and Filloux, 1960) also suggest that the overall slope on beaches with large tidal ranges lies at a lower angle than that of the beach face appropriate to particle size and wave regime. In keeping with this, longshore bars and beach berms are poorly developed.

The construction of a pronouncedly convex single berm is strongly encouraged by a low tidal range and this is presumably why well-developed berms may be found on sand beaches around the Mediterranean and Baltic Seas in relatively stormy environments. Where there is a bigger tidal range, berm development tends to be more complex, with perhaps a poorly developed berm above high tide mark and one or more intertidal swash bars below. The simplest case, where the tidal range is about 2–4 m, is the double ridged beach: a ridge forms above high water mark and another just above low water mark, presumably because swash action is most prolonged at these levels. In between the two ridges is a runnel. As tidal range gets bigger, and particularly if sediments are fine and the overall beach gradient is low, multiple ridges develop and the typical ridge and runnel beach is produced.

Around British coasts, where swash bars and berms are poorly developed except in relatively low energy environments, some of the best single sand berms may be seen in Bournemouth and Christchurch Bays on the south coast, where the tidal range at spring tides is barely 2 metres. Good double ridged beaches occur on the east coast in Norfolk with a tidal range of 4 to 5 metres (Fig. 84) and multiple ridged beaches are particularly

Fig. 84. Double berm beach at low tide; Happisburgh, Norfolk coast of eastern England.

well-developed on the Irish Sea coasts of north Wales and northern England where the tidal range reaches 8 to 9 m. On southern Australian coasts, where big ocean swell provides a much more powerful constructing force and tidal ranges are little more than 1 m at spring tides, single berms are well developed and common. However, along the Bass Strait coast of Tasmania, where the range rises to 3 or 4 m, double ridged beaches appear. In Tasmania multiple ridging occurs on one group of beaches where the tide falls only about 3·5 m, but the sand here is very fine and the overall beach gradient extremely low. It is clear that factors of sediment size and wave climate have to be taken into account, especially in so far as they affect beach slopes.   At a critical tidal range it is possible for the same beach to show a single berm at one end and a double berm at the other if sand particle size changes enough along the beach.

BEACH STAGES AND CYCLES

The comparative speed with which beach and nearshore morphology changes in response to variations in wave energy level means that every beach is characterized by its particular sequential or cyclic behaviour.   There is now a large literature on the morphodynamics of beaches, recently summarized by Komar (1976).

Figure 85 represents a model developed by Short (1979) from daily observations over two years of a mesotidal sand beach in eastern Australia where waves approach normal to the shore but energy levels vary considerably.   It appears possible to place the more limited studies of other workers within this model and to apply it in both time and space.   Broadly, it suggests that two extreme equilibrium stages may be identified—a fully accretional stage (1) characterized by maximum berm development and a fully erosional stage (6) characterized by maximum bar development.   At both these stages, onshore-offshore flow is essentially planar and oscillatory but, whereas at the fully accretional stage a high proportion of the limited wave energy arrives at the beach and is reflected, at the fully erosional stage a high proportion of the much higher wave energy is dissipated in the breaker and surf zones.   The distinction between predominantly reflective and predominantly dissipative beaches was previously considered by Huntley and Bowen (1975) and extensively treated by Wright and others (1979) (Figs 77, 78, pp. 104, 105).

At intermediate stages sediment is being moved between the bar and the berm and both accretionary (5, 4, 3, 2) and erosional (2', 3', 4', 5') sequences are characterized by the establishment of channelled flow.   Sediment is moved onshore over bar segments and offshore through rip channels but the balance of effectiveness between onshore and offshore transport varies between the two sequences.   The accretionary sequence, powered by waves of declining energy, is normally distinctly slower than the erosional sequence and there is more influence of bedform on circulation so that lag effects may occur.

Cycles of cut and fill have been described widely and may be represented at their extreme by superimposing the profile for Short's full accretionary stage and that for his fully erosional stage.   This is done in Fig. 86.   Two sweep zones can be defined. Onshore sweep zones involving the beach and perhaps the outer edge of the foredune have been surveyed and described for numerous beaches in many parts of the world. However, the complementary offshore sweep zone is much less well known.   It appears to involve the longshore bar and a thin wedge out towards surf base.

It may be rare for a beach to traverse the full gamut of the sequences outlined in Fig. 85.   Many will cycle around only part of the system and perhaps oscillate between particular accretionary and erosional stages, as indicated by the arrows on the Figure. Consequently they will have smaller sweep zones.   Recurrence intervals will also vary considerably.   On some coasts there appear to be distinct annual cycles of cut and fill

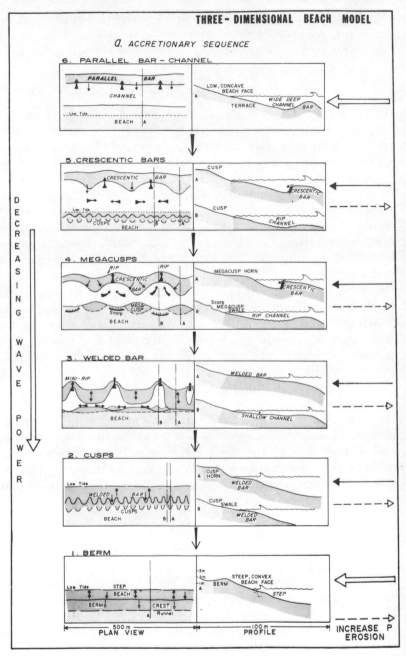

FIG. 85. Three-dimensional model of beach changes related to increasing and decreasing wave energy. Connecting arrows indicate direction of change (Reproduced with permission from Short, 1979).

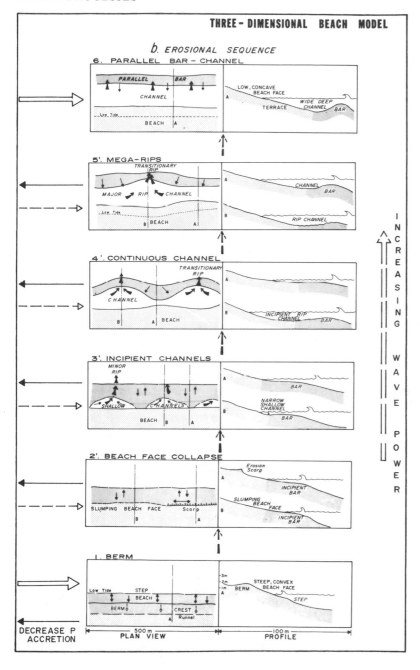

THREE - DIMENSIONAL BEACH MODEL

b. EROSIONAL SEQUENCE

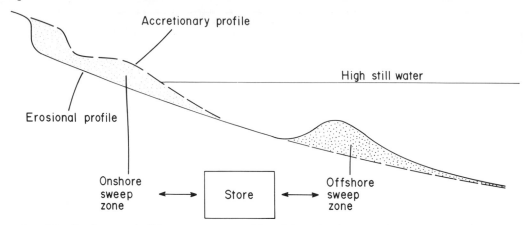

Fig. 86. Onshore and offshore sweep zones. Material moving between these constitutes the store of sediment available for redistribution under differing wave energy conditions.

giving rise to what have been called 'winter' and 'summer' profiles respectively. However, on many other coasts cycles may be less distinct and effective cycles much longer. On the east Australian coast they appear measurable in years rather than months (Thom, 1974) and more cut may take place in summer than in winter.

Sediment grain size and tidal range introduce complications. With fine sand or with a large tidal range the overall slope may be much reduced, resulting in longer edge waves and more widely spaced features of circulation along the shore. A bias towards dissipative conditions is likely, especially at low tide. Finer sediment is also liable to give more muted constituent forms because of its reduced ability to maintain steep slopes on bars and berms. On pebble beaches with steep slopes and little or no surf zone, no offshore bar occurs and varying wave energy simply has the effect of changing the beach gradient. Higher waves flatten the beach whereas lower waves steepen it.

On a global scale, Short (1979) made an attempt to indicate how the different world wave environments suggested in Chapter III might be characterized by annual beach-stage curves and these are reproduced in Fig. 87. They are intended to apply to beaches on the open coast receiving full potential wave power for the particular wave environment.

SEDIMENT TRANSPORT

The coastal sediment transport system is overwhelmingly one operating along the shore by longshore current transport and beach drifting, but there is considerable variation in the extent to which it is developed. On some coasts there is virtually uni-directional drift: on others it is bi-directional and the net movement is that which is significant in coastal form. On some coasts drift movements are strong: on others they are weak. The differences are of prime importance in the differentiation of coastal systems generally and, if they could be categorized, could form the basis of a dynamic classification of coasts. One of the inherent difficulties is that there are no really sharp dividing

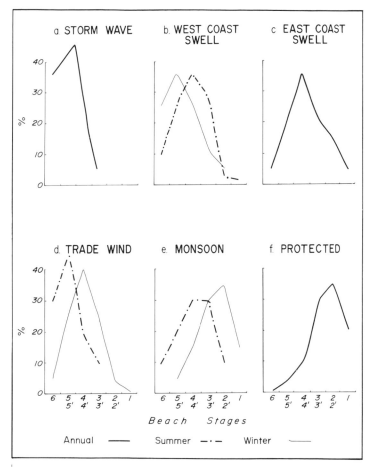

FIG. 87. Idealized beach-stage curves for the major global wave environments, based on the model in Fig. 85, assuming sand beaches receiving maximum deepwater wave power in open coast situations. (Reproduced with permission from Short, 1979.)

lines between potential categories, and a virtual continuum of types exists. In such a situation the best approach seems to be to take the extreme ends of the continuum and think in terms of two conceptual models, which can be called coasts of free and impeded transport. In the one case drift processes may proceed in uninterrupted fashion so that sediments are carried considerable distances in one direction: in the other travel is limited. In the first case sediment moves through the system so that the dynamics of a beach may be thought of very largely in terms of material entering at one end and leaving at the other: in the second, beach material is essentially entrapped. A very well documented example of a coast of free transport is that of southern California where there is a strong and largely uninterrupted movement of sediment from north-west to south-east (Handin, 1951; Trask, 1952, and many others). In strong contrast the coast of south-eastern Tasmania, with its highly complex outline and multitude of apparently isolated beaches represents a condition in which transport can occur, if at all, over only very short distances (Fig. 88).

FIG. 88. Part of the south coast of Tasmania: a coast of impeded transport dominated by heavy southwesterly swell.

A number of factors influences whether a particular coast is predominantly one of free or impeded transport.

Coastal outline. A coast which is irregular, with periodic jutting headlands will clearly impede transport in a way which a regular, smooth coast will not. The factor is well exemplified by the artificial construction of groynes on a beach, which represents an attempt to turn a coast of free transport into a coast of impeded transport by altering the degree of irregularity in plan. Other things being equal, 'Atlantic' or plate-imbedded type coasts are more likely to be associated with impeded transport than are 'Pacific' or plate-edge types.

Obliquity of wave approach. Oblique wave approach is necessary for beach drifting and the generation of longshore currents, so that on a coast where the most important sand shifting waves approach perpendicularly, longshore currents will be weak and the extent of beach drifting will be small. On its own such a factor is likely to be important only where there is a strong preponderance of wave approach from this particular direction—for instance, where considerations of fetch directions rule out all except one major angle of approach or, as on some swell dominated coasts, where only one significant wave direction exists.

Wave length. Long swell waves refract more strongly in shallow water than do shorter waves and are less likely to promote longshore movement because of their greater perpendicularity of eventual approach. Short, locally generated sea is more likely to approach obliquely.

Steepness of the offshore ramp. Shallow water offshore will encourage refraction and therefore reduce obliquity of approach of all waves. A steeper offshore ramp is more conducive to longshore movement but it cannot be too steep, otherwise there may not be sufficiently developed surf and swash zones for transport processes to operate.

Tidal range. A larger tidal range gives a larger variety of situations in which transport can occur and is therefore likely to encourage it. It is probably particularly important in promoting transport around headlands at low tide. A large tidal range also implies strong tidal currents which may provide an auxiliary mechanism for transport.

Of these suggested factors, the first two are the most significant in practice and it is the interaction between them which determines the degree of freedom of sediment transport on most coasts. These factors are difficult to separate in nature, for transport will be impeded at a larger angle of obliquity of wave approach on an irregular coast than on a comparatively smooth one. The two must therefore be considered together.

The less important factors may help to explain some apparent anomalies, such as are represented by parts of the north and east coasts of Tasmania, which are relatively smooth in outline and oblique to the important deep water swell directions, yet display minimal evidence of longshore transport. Examination of beach materials suggests strong compartmentalism between headlands. The answer may lie in the very low tidal range and very long dominant waves which refract over a relatively shallow offshore zone to break more or less parallel to the shore.

Most literature on coasts, and particularly that from the USA, seems to assume conditions of free transport—conditions approaching the infinitely long, straight beach studied under laboratory conditions by Saville (1950). Tanner (1958), for instance, in his concept of the equilibrium beach, compared the plan curve of the beach with the graded curve of a river profile and thought in terms of a stream entering at one end of the beach and leaving at the other. Emery (1960) likewise compared southern Californian beaches to stream beds.

Conditions of impeded transport seem to have been much less well appreciated, perhaps because they are most perfectly attained along irregular coasts in swell environments, where wave direction is relatively steady and refraction considerable. Such coasts have been relatively little studied. However, a section of the Californian coast north of San Francisco, reported on by Cherry (1966), can perhaps be cited as an example of marginally impeded conditions. Cherry concluded that 'the major beaches in the area are in a state of equilibrium and that their sand budgets are static. No supply of new sand is being added and these beaches are oriented to the breaking swell in a manner such that no net longshore sand movement occurs.'

VIII | BEACH SEDIMENTS

The composition of the beach, the origin and mobility of its component sediments, and the budget of sediment inputs and outputs over time all affect the responses which beaches may make to the processes discussed in the last chapter.

BEACH MATERIALS

The material making up the beach varies physically and chemically from place to place, but from a geomorphic point of view the important variations are those in particle size and lime content. Particle size influences strongly the form of the beach and the development of large scale constructional features from it. The calcareous component may influence the formation of lithified beach and dune material, the persistence of which is significant in coastal form.

PARTICLE SIZE

In the case of particle size the essential contrast is between sand and pebble, since material of granule dimension is rare around the coast. Fig. 89 represents a first attempt to map in very broad terms the varying importance of pebbles as beach constituents. It has been compiled by abstracting the frequent references to beach materials which may be found in the British Admiralty Pilot handbooks for the various coasts, and has been augmented somewhat from personal experience and coastal publications generally. It is obviously to be regarded only as a broad generalization but it does illustrate the greater importance of pebbles as beach constituents in higher latitudes and their relative absence from the tropics. This pattern parallels that shown by continental shelf sediments and brought out by the studies of Shepard (summarized 1963) and more recently by Hayes (1967a) and Emery (1968).

Rock type is an important factor in pebble distribution because, while some rocks, such as granites, are relatively rare as pebbles, such others as basalts and slates seem to form pebbles much more readily. The crucial consideration is probably the susceptibility of the rock to quarrying by waves, since rocks which are closely jointed or have a pronounced cleavage are more likely to produce the initial blocks from which pebbles are made. Along parts of the south coast of England and the north coast of France, flint nodules are readily quarried from the chalk to provide an abundant source of pebbles. But, since lithology varies relatively rapidly along most coasts and does not show broad zonal distribution patterns, it cannot explain the sort of picture which emerges from Fig. 89. The operative factors, both of which

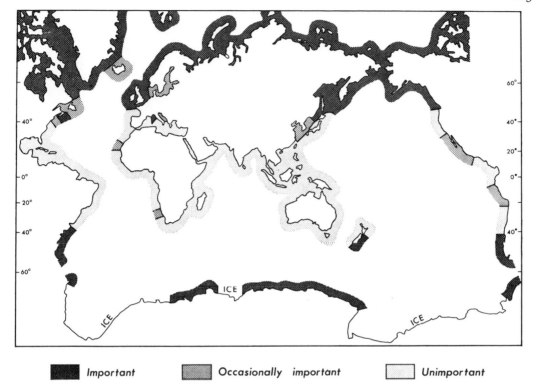

FIG. 89.   Relative importance of pebbles as beach materials on world coasts.   The categories have been subjectively estimated from references in the various British Admiralty Pilots Handbooks.

have strong climatic connotations are geographical variations in the ability of waves to quarry and in the extent to which the sea finds pebbles ready made by other agencies.

As already noted, the quarrying ability of waves is linked with their energy and therefore with their height and frequency.   Lithological factors being equal, coasts dominated by high, short period waves are more likely to produce pebbles than are those in swell environments.

On some coasts a great deal of pebble material may be derived from subaerial processes and merely concentrated by the sea to form a beach (Fig. 90).   Such concentration may be taking place today, as where waves are eroding a cliff composed of a weathered mantle or of material deposited previously by other agencies.   Concentration may also have taken place during the great postglacial rise in sea level, when, because pebbles always tend to lodge in the higher, back part of the beach, the sea would have tended to winnow particles of this size and push them gradually landward. It is possible to demonstrate direct provenance in particular instances.   The only significant pebble beaches in Tasmania, for example, are found around the mouths of the Forth and Mersey rivers on the Bass Strait coast: the upper valleys of both these

FIG. 90. Beach composed of poorly sorted glacifluvial pebbles and cobbles, delta of Hapuku River, South Island, New Zealand. (Photo by J. N. Jennings.)

streams were occupied by glaciers in the Pleistocene and they were important distributors of glacifluvial outwash. It is possible to trace lithological similarities between bedrock in the upper catchments, pebbles in fill terraces in the lower valleys, pebbles on the adjoining floor of Bass Strait and pebbles from beaches around the river mouths. Such evidence suggests strongly that pebbles brought down the rivers in glacial times were deposited in part on what is now the floor of Bass Strait and as the sea rose in postglacial times were concentrated on to the present beaches, where no local source can be found.

Something of a coincidence between beach pebbles and Pleistocene glaciation may be inferred and this closely parallels the correlation between pebbly shelf sediments and glaciation which has been noted by a number of authors (Hayes, 1967a for example). The tendency has been to invoke ice rafting as a source of shelf pebbles (Emery, 1963) but it seems probable that beach pebbles are more directly associated with morainic and outwash material deposited on what is now the inner shelf during glacial low sea levels (Fig. 91).

Perhaps an equally important correlation in the case of beach pebbles may be with those coasts where the lower limit of Pleistocene periglacial mass movement lay at or below present-day sea level. Periglacial redistribution of the regolith may well have been the most important way along some colder unglaciated coasts in which pebbles were made available for subsequent littoral concentration. A coast where this is well known to have been demonstrated is that of the English Channel, where many cliffs cut into periglacial 'head' are to be found, and where such deposits undoubtedly descended below the present level of the sea.

FIG. 91. Boulder beach of residual till boulders from which the sea has washed fines, Mourne Mountains, Northern Ireland.

Fig. 89 suggests that a second significant location for pebble beaches is along some of the drier coasts in desert or tropical seasonally dry climates (Koppen's *Aw* or *BW*) where suitable lithological and historical factors have operated.   A small section of the central coast of Queensland, too small to appear in Fig. 89 and with a strongly seasonal rainfall regime, contains what are probably the bulkiest pebble and cobble beach structures in Australia.   The biggest of these occur on the coasts of large offshore islands and have been described by Hopley (1968).   On the desert coast of Peru between Pisco and Callao, pebbles are derived by erosion of weakly cemented conglomerates deposited by Andean streams in the Pleistocene (Dresch, 1961).

On hot wet coasts (Koppen's *Af*), pebbles are rare or absent, but mud assumes an important role.   As mentioned earlier, rivers draining catchments in these regions bring down a considerable proportion of clay and silt particles and material supplied to the coasts of northern South America and monsoon Asia in particular includes a large mud fraction (Fig. 13, p. 21).   A corollary of this is that fluvially supplied sand is most abundant in the regions of seasonal rainfall further from the equator.   These relationships come out very clearly in the study of shelf sediments by Hayes (1967a) and in general his summary picture, reproduced in Fig. 92, will serve equally well to illustrate the distribution of shore materials.

The significance of Pleistocene processes in influencing the character of shelf sediments is now widely recognized (Guilcher, 1963, for instance) and in any analysis of beach particle size, similar considerations must constantly arise.

CARBONATE CONTENT

World variation in the calcium carbonate content of beaches is much harder to assess, partly because of the paucity of references in the literature and partly because variation

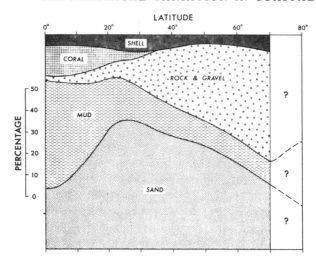

FIG. 92.   Relative frequency of occurrence of sediment
types by latitude on the continental shelves of the world.
(After Hayes, 1967a.)

over short distances may be so great as to make generalization from a few records very
dangerous.   Literature references often suggest an assumption that tropical seas
produce beaches which are more calcareous; sometimes the thought is explicitly stated,
as by Bowen and Inman (1966) for instance, who said that biogenous materials are
much more important components of beaches in the tropics than in temperate climates.
The assumption has been questioned by Keary (1968) who drew attention to the high
proportion of biogenous carbonate in some western European beaches.

From available studies such as those for the east coast of the USA (Giles and Pilkey,
1965), the Hawaiian Islands (Moberly, Baver and Morrison, 1965), Australia (Davies,
1977; Bird, 1978) and the west and south coasts of Ireland (Keary, 1968, 1969), certain
basic factors of distribution appear to emerge.   The first of these is production of
calcium carbonate, which may be found in the shore environment either as calcite or as
aragonite.   Warm tropical seas, highly supersaturated with lime, are characterized by
particularly high rates of production and low rates of dissolution.   A great range of
animals and plants of very varied phylogeny produces sheaths, spicules, segments,
branches, chambers, crusts and massive particles of calcite or aragonite (see review by
Ginsburg, Lloyd, Stockman and McCallum, 1963).   The 'coral sand' of tropical
beaches is in fact made up of the products of a great range of organisms of which coral
itself may form only a small part.

In the drier tropics in particular the relative lack of leaching of fossil calcareous
sediments, such as dune limestones, provides an additional source of lime and enables
it to circulate to some extent through successive cycles of coastal development.

Superimposed on this broad zonal variation in productivity are smaller scale local
variations depending on differences in the offshore environment or water circulation.

The second factor of distribution is the ability of waves to bring the carbonate material on to the shore and, where necessary, to break it up into sand-sized particles. It is likely that big swell with its greater depth of bottom disturbance is better able to bring material in from offshore and a high wave energy is clearly conducive to comminution and sand formation. Keary (1968, 1969) concluded that there was a significant relationship on the west and south coasts of Ireland between lime content of beach sands and the degree of exposure of the beaches, so that values are higher on the most exposed western beaches and decrease eastward towards the Irish Sea. Steers (1953) has described the carbonate rich beaches on the exposed coasts of western Scotland and high carbonate values may be obtained from the sands of many Cornish beaches. By contrast the sands of the more sheltered central and northern coasts of Wales are overwhelmingly siliceous in composition (Moore, 1968). At a larger scale still, Giles and Pilkey (1965) suggested that the pattern of carbonate distribution in the barrier beaches of eastern USA reflected the decrease in wave energy along the Georgia coast.

The third distributional factor is the extent of dilution by non-calcareous material and most commonly by quartz, principally where there is rapid shore erosion or delivery of sediment by rivers. On a small scale the dilution effect is well illustrated from the study of beach sediments on Kauai, one of the Hawaiian islands, made by Inman, Gayman and Cox (1963). Here terrigenous material is especially prominent near the mouth of the river draining the catchment with the greatest sediment yield. The highly calcareous beaches of Barbados are interrupted in the north-east of the island where the coral limestone cap has been removed and rivers are delivering siliceous material to the shore. On the coast of Israel there is a sharp contrast between the calcareous sands north of Haifa and the siliceous sands to the south supplied by the Nile and the rivers of the Sinai Peninsula (Schattner, 1967). Along the Bass Strait coast of Tasmania, the local decrease in the shell content of beach sands where rivers enter the sea seems due to additional silica supply at these points (Fig. 93). On a much larger scale, the well-known contrast between the calcareous sands of the west and south coasts of Australia and the siliceous sands of the east coast must be due primarily to the relative absence of rivers entering the seas contiguous with the drier parts of the continent (Davies, 1977). A similar relationship appears to occur in South Africa, where Logan (1960) commented on the shelly nature of sand on the western Namib coast and Russell and McIntire (1965) remarked on the essentially siliceous nature of sediments along the east coast. The consistently low proportion of carbonate material in beach sediments along the west coast of USA seems to be correlated with the importance of rivers as sources of supply for littoral sands (Twenhofel, 1946; Handin, 1951, for instance).

In all three factors—productivity, transport and dilution—climate plays an important part. The most important non-climatic determinants are probably terrestrial relief and lithology. High relief, as along the young fold mountain coasts of Pacific America, encourages dilution, while the presence of a rock particularly rich in silica in the land catchment or along the coast has a similar effect. The pattern of carbonate distribution along Tasmanian beaches, for instance, correlates with the occurrence of quartzites and granites.

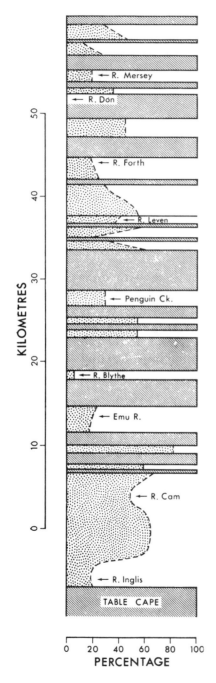

In terms of broad world patterns then we could expect the productivity factor to favour lime-rich beaches in the tropics and the transport factor to encourage high values for carbonate along west coasts exposed to big waves. But these are counterbalanced to a large extent by the dilution factor which will tend towards decreased carbonate where rainfall is higher, relief is greater or rocks are particularly siliceous.

LITHIFIED BEACHES

On warmer coasts the form of the shore may be affected by the occurrence of lithified beach and dune material. Aeolianites will be discussed in connection with dune formation, but it is appropriate to say something at this stage of what have been termed beach rocks, the distribution of which (Fig. 94) appears to be influenced by climate. Beach rocks are beach sands and pebbles cemented sometimes with calcite and sometimes with aragonite. They are exposed, normally by beach retreat, in the intertidal zone; usually projecting from the unconsolidated beach, sometimes forming reefs, and sometimes being refashioned by the sea into what may clearly be called shore platforms (Fig. 95).

The nature and origin of beach rocks have been reviewed by Guilcher (1961), Russell (1963a) and Stoddart and Cann (1965). It seems likely that there is not just one process of lithification but perhaps several tending to produce materials at least superficially similar. Beach rocks with calcite cement may be formed along the water table as a result of precipitation of calcite from groundwater: they appear characteristic of high coasts where a freshwater body is present. Beach rocks with aragonite cement, however, are likely to have been produced as a result of deposition of aragonite from seawater and are characteristic of low reef coasts

FIG. 93.   Percentage calcium carbonate in beach sands on the north coast of Tasmania between Table Cape and Point Sorell. Hatched blocks represent hard rock sections. Note the reduction in carbonate near river mouths.

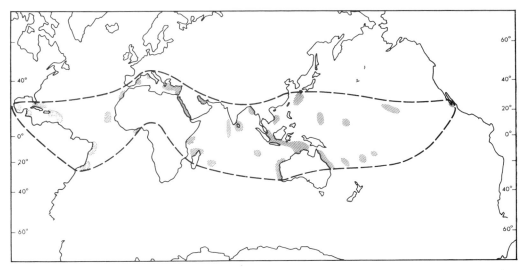

FIG. 94.   Recorded distribution of modern beach rocks.   The map gives only a general impression because of variations in interpretation and identification by different authors.

and islets where the presence of a groundwater body is unlikely or impossible. The situation is complicated further by the way in which recrystallization of aragonite to calcite may occur after a lapse of time. In addition to these physical processes the possible role of beach micro-organisms in precipitating the cement has been mooted by a number of authors (Nesteroff, 1956, for instance).

FIG. 95.   Beach rock at Port Hedland, northwestern Australia.

Climatic control of beach rock cementation probably operates through the availability of both warm seawater or groundwater, supersaturated with calcium carbonate, and high rates of evaporation and upward capillary movement through the sand. It is particularly characteristic of tropical climates with a well marked dry season. Although the distribution of beach rocks may coincide roughly with the region in which carbonate-rich beaches are particularly prevalent, the connection is not necessarily a causal one, since beach rock cements are precipitated from water and the cemented particles may be of very varied nature.

Since some degree of internal stability of beach sediments seems necessary for cementation to occur, beach rocks are less likely to be found where there is a significant degree of sediment movement either transverse or parallel to the shore. It seems probable that, where they do occur, their exposure stems partly from the way in which cementation reduces or prevents percolation of wave swash and so encourages removal of overlying non-cemented sand. However, in the longer term, they have an undoubted protective effect and many shores where beach rock occurs have an 'armour-plated' appearance. Many coral cays are partly anchored to the underlying reef by development and exposure of beach rock on their windward ends. On some coasts subject to tropical cyclones—parts of north-west Australia for example—beach rock slabs may be broken up and piled into beaches of enormous angular boulders.

SEDIMENT SOURCES

In the classical cycle of marine erosion, particularly as it was enunciated in many earlier texts, material is eroded from the headlands and moved up into the bays so that coastal outlines gradually become regularized. In nature there are probably few coasts where such a simple system is of significance and the true situation is almost invariably more complex or even quite different. There are important location differences in the sources of sediments, the nature of transport systems and the types of sediment sinks and traps.

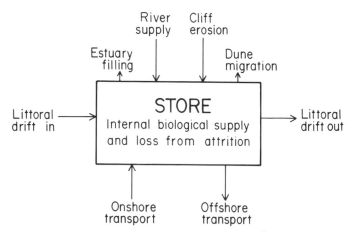

Fig. 96. Diagrammatic representation of shore sediment budget.

If, for the time being, we ignore the effects of longshore transport, there are three immediate sources of beach sediment (Fig. 96). These are the coast itself where the development of cliffs and platforms implies a transportable residue, the land behind the coast which may have provided the products of subaerial denudation, and the sea floor in front of the coast from which material may have been derived by onshore transport.

MARINE EROSION

There is great variation in the extent to which marine erosion is quantitatively significant as a source of sediment. In the storm wave environment, with high energy wave attack on unconsolidated or otherwise easily quarried material, the supply of sediment from this quarter may be locally abundant: in moderate or low energy environments and on massive rocks everywhere it is likely to be very small. Many predominantly argillaceous rocks produce particles too tiny to be retained in the shore transport system while rocks like sandstones and granites which are potential sources of quartz sands are among those which erode most slowly. Along very long sections of the world's coasts, especially within about 40 degrees of the equator, bedrock reaches the shore along very limited stretches or not at all.

In very few published coastal studies has cliff erosion proved a significant source of sediment. Shepard and Grant (1947) in a study of wave erosion effects on the southern Californian coast showed that retreat of rocky shores had been negligible over a period of fifty years, even on relatively soft shales: however, on some unconsolidated rocks, retreat had been of the order of 30 cm a year. The best known examples of rapid cliff erosion come from storm wave environments, especially where cliffs are cut in unconsolidated materials such as the Pleistocene glacial and periglacial deposits of north-western Europe (for instance the well documented case of the Holderness coast of eastern England considered by Valentin, 1954).

Older unconsolidated marine deposits—old beaches and dunes in the main—can be an important source of modern coastal sediment where they are undergoing erosion. On some parts of the New South Wales coast of Australia, old Pleistocene barrier systems are being cut into by the present sea and their sands recycled into the present coastal system (Thom, 1965). A similar sort of situation exists on the coast of India south of Cochin where old barriers are being eroded at rates of about 5 or 6 metres a year (Manohar, 1961) and such examples could be multiplied by reference to other coasts.

TERRESTRIAL EROSION

Sediment is brought to the coast by a number of land agencies. Mass movement in its various forms delivers some material along virtually all erosional coasts, but is particularly important along those such as the Arctic coast of Russia where active periglacial solifluction occurs down to sea level. Where glaciers reach the sea, as described in Spitzbergen by Moigu and Guilcher (1967) for example, they too may bring material directly into the coastal transport system or, as in Iceland (King, 1956), it may be derived from glacial outwash. By far the most important agents on a world scale, however, are rivers, and Kuenen (1950) calculated that globally they contribute something of the order of one hundred times more sediment to the sea than does marine erosion.

The ratio between river supply and cliff supply of coastal sediments varies geographically. As discussed in Chapter II, in the tropics sediment supply by rivers is particularly strong and here also marine erosion is least efficient. In higher latitudes, where bigger wave energies and smaller river loads are the rule, cliff erosion may be proportionately more important. Even so, Inman (1960) considered that most temperate beaches probably contain no more than about five per cent of material originating in cliff erosion. The latitudinal variation is complicated by the fact that predominant grain size of river loads is a disturbing factor as far as supply of beach sediments is concerned. In parts of the perennially wet tropics, such as Malaya, where rivers bring down little sand but much mud, beaches may be nourished by a relatively bigger contribution from eroding cliffs (Nossin, 1965). Lithological factors intervene on a small scale, but large-scale structural patterns disturb the potential climatic zonation considerably. Plate-edge (collision) coasts and those associated with zones of crustal spreading, which have steep tectonically active hinterlands, tend to be well supplied with river sediments everywhere. Along the whole of the west coast of USA (Bowen and Inman, 1966), and perhaps along the whole of the west coast of the Americas, much the greatest proportion of coastal sediments comes from this source.

ONSHORE TRANSPORT

The tendency for onshore movement of bed particles to occur in the intermediate and shallow water offshore zones was referred to in the last chapter. It would seem to imply that the adjacent sea floor is a potential source of sediment and indeed sediment supply to beaches from relatively short distances is normal. Thus sand removed from the beach beyond the breakpoint by storms may be replaced by shoreward transport and river sediments commonly find their way on to beaches after first having been carried into the immediate offshore zone. Beaches in the USA and elsewhere have been artificially nourished by the dumping of sand at calculated distances offshore. The calcareous and siliceous remains of marine organisms are added to the beach in the same way.

Some authors however, working on open, oceanic shores and on coasts where occasional tropical cyclones occur, seem to have envisaged much greater distances of onshore transport by waves. As an example, Pierce (1969), in a quantitative study of the sediment budget of an isolated section of the North Carolina coast, found it impossible to explain the net accretion occurring over the last century without postulating a shoreward movement of material from the continental shelf. Swift (1970), in discussing problems of grading of shelf sediments, summarized evidence for shoreward movement of sand along the eastern coast of the USA, where the 'near-shore modern sand prism' is being supplied from the 'shelf relict sand blanket'. Supplies from cliffs are unimportant here and, in contrast to the west coast of the USA, there is little accretion from rivers. Many beach sediment characteristics are matched by shelf phenomena rather than by those of the hinterland.

There seems to be a growing consensus of opinion that an important proportion of sea-derived non-biogenic sediment along the present coast was emplaced during or immediately after the great postglacial marine transgression and is not being brought in in significant quantities under present conditions.   This material consists of sands and pebbles deposited on the exposed inner continental shelf by various agencies and moved up to the present shoreline by the sea, either as it rose during the period of transgression or afterwards as the offshore ramp was adjusted to the prevalent wave regime and surplus material carried shoreward.   Many of our 'modern' constructional shore features were probably built at this time of excess offshore sediment and it is now widely suspected that subsequent erosion may largely reflect the cutting off of this supply after the equilibrium ramp was attained (Russell, 1967; Thom, 1968).

Mid-Holocene onshore movement from what is now the sea floor has been suggested for a variety of coasts—for instance from the Ivory Coast of West Africa by Le Bourdiec (1958), the Brazilian coast by Tricart (1959), western France by Gabis (1955) and Bourcart (1958) and south-eastern Australia by Bird (1963).   It will probably prove to have been of major significance in most parts of the world.

The implication is that a very large proportion of sediment supplied to the shore by terrestrial agencies gets there as a result of initial deposition on the present shelf and subsequent concentration on the shore.   However, because it is fossil and no longer being supplied, material derived in this way will only have remained important where it has been retained by some means or other and not moved laterally elsewhere.

Regarded in this light, modern sediment supply from the sea floor could be seen as occurring where some sort of equilibrium has not yet been attained or where it has been disturbed by the accumulation of further sediment as a result of river deposition, the death of marine organisms, the dumping of sand for beach nourishment and so forth.

TRANSPORT SYSTEMS

Beach sediment moving along the coast in conditions of impeded transport will be trapped most commonly in a bay or other re-entrant where it is prevented from moving along the coast by land jutting seaward.   Bay head beaches are the landforms which normally result, but many barrier systems have also formed in re-entrants, which are sometimes of enormous size.   On coasts of free transport on the other hand a common situation where sediment is lost is where the coast suddenly trends landward. Sediment may continue to be deposited more or less along the line of the first stretch of coast, so producing a spit extending into deep water.   These two sorts of traps may be called re-entrant and salient traps respectively.

Coasts of free transport must have an active source of beach sediment or they would run out of material.   In effect this means there must be vigorously eroding cliffs or a sufficient supply from rivers.   On the southern coast of California the damming of rivers which previously brought the largest proportion of sediments into the coastal system has caused a reduction in the coastal sediment stream (Norris, 1964). Sediments brought from seaward during and immediately after the postglacial marine transgression are unlikely to be present along coasts of free transport, except where they have been deposited in local re-entrant traps and displaced inland by wind or by rapid progradation of the shore.

In contrast, coasts of impeded transport need not be actively supplied with sediment and in any case may be characterized by very little transport at all. If eroding cliffs form a source, then transport is only to the next re-entrant, but this situation is difficult to envisage because cliffs eroding at a rate sufficient to produce significant amounts of sediment are unlikely to form strong headlands and therefore unlikely to be associated with impeded transport. If rivers are a source of sediment then they will almost always enter the sea directly at a re-entrant trap and the sediments will not therefore travel far if at all. If the sea floor has been a source then the resulting sediments are likely to have been more or less stationary for thousands of years since they were first entrapped near the end of the postglacial sea level rise. Such 'fossil' sediments are much more likely to be associated with conditions of impeded transport than with conditions of free transport.

Coasts of free transport are likely to lose sediment in salient traps: coasts of impeded transport, virtually by definition, are likely to lose sediment in re-entrant traps. In the chapter which follows it will be suggested that there are differences in the ways in which beach plans tend to evolve under the two sets of transport conditions, so that what are termed 'swash alignments' are associated usually with re-entrant traps and impeded transport, while 'drift alignments' are typical of salient traps and free transport. Another difference which may be foreshadowed, but which is enlarged upon in the next chapter, concerns the direction of inlet deflection. Under conditions of free transport, gaps in coastal barriers tend to form near the downdrift end because of 'drift deflection': under conditions of impeded transport they tend to be 'swash deflected' and occur near the point of minimum wave energy, which is usually towards the direction of deep water wave approach.

SEDIMENT SINKS

The term 'sink' now seems to be achieving general acceptance, especially among coastal engineers, to cover all those processes whereby sediment is lost to the coastal system. Omitting again the possible effects of longshore transport, they may be considered under three main heads. The first sink is represented by the migration of dunes inland where they can no longer be acted on by waves at times of storm, the second by the filling of estuaries and coastal lagoons by material coming from seaward, and the third by transport offshore on to the sea floor.

It is noteworthy that all three groups of processes apply to sand but rarely to pebbles. Pebbles are not moved by wind, move reluctantly into estuaries or offshore and are retained more readily in beach situations.

DUNE MIGRATION

On many coasts of the world, transgressive dunes extending inland from the shore and resulting from erosion of original frontal dune systems (see Chapter XI) represent the most important way in which sediment is lost. This is especially true of coasts that experience strong onshore winds or where protective plant cover has been reduced. Less commonly, as on the Oregon coast of USA, there is no original frontal dune stage and large masses of sand move inland from the beginning. Generally speaking dune migration is of little importance in the tropics, the main exceptions being where extraordinarily large quantities of sand have been available locally along the shore.

ESTUARY FILLING

As will be discussed more fully in Chapter XII, estuaries are filled predominantly from seaward and coastal lagoons behind barriers must be virtually entirely filled by material which would otherwise be available on the shore. Particularly on coasts where deep estuaries resulted from postglacial drowning by the sea this has represented, and may continue to represent, a significant loss. In most cases of active filling, the major morphological expression of the process is the flood tidal delta, a channelled mass of sand intruding landward; but, in the case of lagoons behind narrow barriers, filling may take place by high waves moving sediment right over the barrier in the form of washover fans. Both flood tide deltas and washover fans are common for example along the barrier systems of the east coast of USA.

The importance of estuary filling as a sink will vary with the history of the estuary in that it may be expected to be more important at earlier stages of development. Tidal range is a major distributional factor. Macrotidal estuaries appear generally to be full and not likely to be subtracting more sediment whereas mesotidal and microtidal estuaries and lagoons often contain residual holes indicating that filling is still going on.

OFFSHORE TRANSPORT

Sediment may be lost to the sea floor when the recurrence interval of storms is such that the much slower onshore bed transport by ordinary waves is unable to return it to the shore or that it comes under the influence of other bottom currents. This may be an important way in which increased storminess can change budget trends and initiate shore retreat.

Removal of sediment also occurs in salient traps where the downdrift ends of spits and barrier islands are adjacent to deep water. Sandy Hook in New Jersey and Fraser Island in Queensland are good examples.

Inshore depressions on the shelf may have a similar effect. Well-documented examples are those of the La Jolla submarine canyon off southern California and the submarine canyon at the tip of the Cape Lopez spit on the Gabon coast (Bourgoin and others, 1963), both of which swallow some of the sand moving along the coast. The 'swatch of no ground' at the head of the Bay of Bengal is said to have a similar effect in relation to sediments from the Ganges delta (Nagaraja, 1966).

SEDIMENT COMPARTMENTS

On a coast of completely impeded transport, such as that figured in Fig. 88, individual beaches are likely to represent discrete compartments within which sediments move only to a limited extent in a more or less closed system.   On a coast of completely free transport no natural compartments may exist at all.   The majority of coasts are in some intermediate condition with identifiable compartments comprising a number of beaches and the size of compartments, their degree of exclusiveness and the extent of internal sediment movement varying considerably.

In recent years a start has been made in developing the concept of the coastal sediment compartment because of a growing interest in the question of sediment budgets (Johnson, 1959; Bowen and Inman, 1966; Pierce, 1969; Vallianos, 1970).   In many ways the coastal compartment is the equivalent of the drainage basin in terrestrial geomorphology—a unit within which it is theoretically possible to compute sediment gains and losses and so arrive at a quantitative budget statement.   On coasts of relatively free transport where natural 'sediment-tight' compartments do not exist it is necessary to define notional compartment or longshore drift cells, the boundaries of which may be placed where transport rates are reduced, change significantly or are more easily measured (Bowen and Inman, 1966).

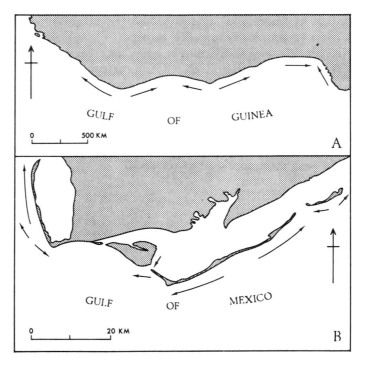

FIG. 97.   Sediment compartments at two scales: (A) on the Guinea coast of Africa (after Tricart, 1957; Sitarz, 1960 and others) and (B) on the coast of southwest Florida. (After Stapor, 1971.)

Hierarchies of compartments may be identified where large exclusive compartments may contain smaller non-exclusive subcompartments. Again the analogy is with different orders of drainage basins in the terrestrial situation.

The landward and seaward boundaries of the sediment compartment lie respectively at the landward edge of the onshore sweep zone and the seaward edge of the offshore sweep zone (Fig. 86).

SEDIMENT BUDGETS

The various inputs and outputs of the sediment budget can be represented by Fig. 96. What is there termed 'the store' is the sediment which oscillates between the onshore and offshore sweep zones and is therefore available to enable the shore to respond to temporal variations in wave energy. The amount of material in the store is related to particle size and wave climate (Chapter VII). If the sediment budget is a positive one it is displaced seaward and the shore progrades: if it is a negative one it is displaced landward and the shore recedes. In either event the volume of the store will tend to remain the same, the major exception being where, in the case of a negative budget, erosion does not provide material of a size suitable for replenishment. Most commonly this occurs where protective engineering works have been inserted in the subaerial sweep zone by man.

A rise in sea level will also produce a negative budget and a landward displacement of the store with recession of erodible coasts in the general manner suggested by Bruun (1962). This is because a rising sea level changes the balance between onshore and offshore transport so that more sediment is taken out more often to depths from which it is unlikely to return.

Calcareous sand may be generated within the store from the remains of animals and plants, and in some tropical seas by the precipitation of oceanic calcium carbonate to form oolitic particles. Sediment may also be lost internally by attrition—especially in the case of pebble beaches where the products may be too small to be retained. With these exceptions, the inputs and outputs are the sources and sinks described earlier in this chapter, always remembering that littoral drift may have to be taken into account.

A survey, recently organized by a Working Party of the International Geographical Union and reported by Bird (1976) indicated that comparatively few of the world's coasts are prograding at present. Those with apparently positive budgets tend to be in tectonically active areas like Japan and New Zealand. Most shorelines are stable or in retreat and this probably reflects the large proportion of modern beach and dune sediment that was supplied at and immediately after the end of the postglacial marine transgression. Through much of the world loss of this material into the various sediment sinks is barely or inadequately being counterbalanced by supply from present day sources.

The study of sediment compartments and sediment budgets is in its infancy but is likely to develop considerably over the next couple of decades. As it does, an enormous geographical variation will be revealed and an important and meaningful technique for differentiating coasts will be developed.

IX | WAVE CONSTRUCTION FORMS

On a world scale, wave constructed coastal landforms are not evenly distributed. Several authors, including Tricart and Cailleux (1965), have remarked on the greater frequency of such forms, and particularly of immense barrier systems, at low latitudes. In mid-latitudes, smaller mainland beaches are the rule. This they correlate with the relatively large quantities of fine material being supplied by rivers, because it is here that the largest sediment loads are being brought to the sea. However, the optimum zone is that of the seasonally dry and semi-arid tropics, where sand is in best supply (Fig. 92, p. 122). In hot wet regions, sand masses are smaller and tend to be developed in conjunction with great mud deposits, often in the form of chenier systems (for example, in Surinam as described by Brouwer, 1953). So the biggest barrier systems are associated with Koppen's *Aw* and *Am* climates and not with his *Af*.

In addition to this factor of sediment supply, it seems likely that factors of wave climate are involved. Low latitude coasts as a rule are dominated by long low waves, which tend to concentrate material towards the shore and to build stronger swash bars and berms, which in turn provide the nuclei for larger features. The abundant sand not only provides material for the above water sections but also produces shallow offshore ramps on which barriers are built as a result of a suitable wave climate combined with generally low tidal range. Gierloff-Emden (1961), stressed the geographical association of barrier systems with small tidal ranges—an association valid also in polar latitudes where barriers are usually of pebble. Very few barrier systems occur where tidal range exceeds 3 metres, and off the best developed sand barriers the range is generally less than 2 metres. Arctic Ocean shores appear to represent a second maximum zone of barrier development as a result of the relatively large supply of pebbles in periglacial environments and the low wave energy microtidal conditions.

Tidal range also affects the extent to which a barrier completely encloses a lagoon, by controlling the degree to which gaps in the evolving barrier system are kept open by the action of tidal currents. Johnson (1919) long ago noted how the barrier system of the eastern USA becomes increasingly interrupted by inlets as the tidal range increases towards the coast of Georgia, although this is certainly not the only factor. The classic example, however, is the contrast between the '*Haff und Nehrung*' of the almost tideless Baltic coast of Germany and Poland and the '*Watt und Nehrung*' of the North Sea coast of Germany and Holland.

ORIGIN OF BARRIER BEACHES

Distributional relationships suggest that barrier beach construction is encouraged by low tidal range, abundance of sediments, a shallow shelf and moderate wave energy, although only some of these factors may operate in a particular case. However, the question of the origin of barriers—or more strictly the lagoon behind the barrier—remains contentious.

It is possible to build a barrier beach in a wave basin under laboratory conditions (see Fig. 99, p. 137, for example) as a swash bar is formed on a relatively flat and shallow offshore bottom to the highest level of wave uprush. Some smaller barrier beaches in nature may be built in a similar way with periodic deflation added to their height as dunes are constructed. This is essentially the process suggested by Elie de Beaumont (1845) and Johnson (1919). Another widely supported mode of origin is that of longshore extension: the barriers were built across embayments by littoral drift along the coast. On coasts of free transport it is often undoubtedly at least a partial explanation.

However, stratigraphic exploration of massive sand barriers in several parts of the world in recent years—for example Holland (Van Straaten, 1965), eastern USA (Kraft, 1971), Gulf of Mexico (Otvos, 1970) and eastern Australia (Thom, 1978) has shown that they have had a long and sometimes complex history antedating the end of the postglacial submergence. Since they reached their present position, some have built upward, some have built outward by progradation and some have retreated over the lagoon sediments behind (Thom, 1974). At least some may have originated at times of lower sea level on the continental shelf and been translated landward with the rising postglacial sea. Swift (1975) arrived at this conclusion for some eastern USA barriers and postulated detachment of mainland beaches by flooding of lowlying areas behind when submergence was initiated. Hoyt (1967) also proposed a process of mainland beach detachment but around the time of maximum submergence. Other variations on these hypotheses seem possible.

BEACH PLANS

There has not been a great deal of explicit discussion of factors determining the plan form of beaches and the most extensive treatment is that by Zenkovich (1967), to whom the reader is referred for detailed discussion. Here it is suggested that two general equilibrium cases, which may be called swash and drift alignments, appear definable (Fig. 98).

SWASH ALIGNMENTS

The first and simpler case is where net lateral sediment movement is at a minimum and the beach tends to be built parallel to the crests of the constructing waves. Any temporary divergence of plan between wave crests and the shore produces local beach drifting which quickly restores equilibrium. This condition is the one described by Davies (1958) and is commonest where the coast is irregular and/or where the

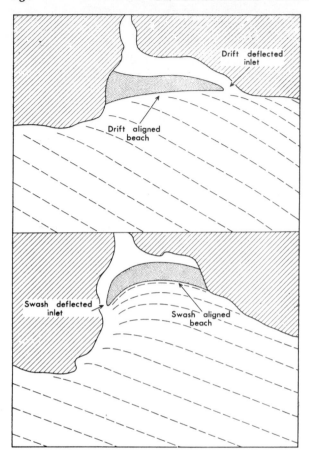

Fig. 98.   Beach alignment and inlet deflection under conditions of free transport (*top*) and impeded transport (*bottom*).

important wave trains come in close to the perpendicular.   It is associated therefore with coasts of impeded transport.

DRIFT ALIGNMENTS

The second case is where the beach tends to be built parallel to the line of maximum drift, which lies in the region of about 40° to 50° to the direction of wave approach.   Any increase in the angle causes a slackening of drift potential and therefore of deposition, so that the alignment is restored: any decrease in the angle causes deposition for the same reason but in this case a change to a swash alignment occurs.   Complications introduced by variations in sediment supply and erosion of the coast to which the beach is attached are dealt with in the discussion by Zenkovich.   The drift alignment is the condition which was produced experimentally by Sauvage de Saint Marc and Vincent (1955), for example, and it is associated with coasts of free transport, where initial outlines are comparatively regular or important sediment moving waves come in at an angle.

It is possible to create these two fundamental alignment conditions experimentally, and Fig. 99 illustrates two model examples constructed in a 20 by 40 m wave basin kindly loaned for the occasion by the Hobart Marine Board in Tasmania. A moderately well sorted quartz sand was used with 63 per cent of grains in the fine class of the

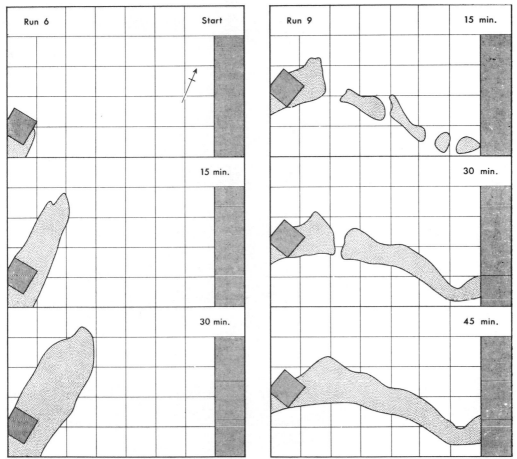

FIG. 99. Development of drift aligned (Run 6) and swash aligned (Run 9) shore features produced in a large wave basin. For further explanation, see text.

Wentworth scale. Wave period was 1·5 seconds and height before breaking 2·5 cm. In Run 6 a spit was built out into deeper water from a concrete block 'headland' by waves approaching obliquely from southward. Sand was added continuously at a point to the south of the headland and this was drifted by wave swash to form the spit which lay at an angle of about 50° to the wave crests. In Run 9 shallow water conditions were created in the re-entrant by the building of a sandy bottom at depths of only 0·5 to 1 cm, sloping southward at a gradient of about 1:150. Every effort was made to eliminate possible sources of sand supply from along shore. Under these conditions the same waves used in Run 6 built a swash bar parallel to their refracted crests and this developed into a model barrier with apparently perfect swash alignment.

Complex constructional forms such as cuspate forelands and angled spits may incorporate both swash aligned and drift aligned beaches.   Escoffier (1954) interpreted some 'travelling' forelands as comprising one drift aligned side and one swash aligned side: material moves from the drift aligned side around the apex and is added to the swash aligned edge so that the foreland as a whole moves in a downdrift direction.   On the other hand Williams (1956) described forelands travelling updrift, and Russell (in discussion) suggested that an accreting edge facing the approaching waves (swash aligned) could be contrasted with an eroding edge where material was being removed by strong littoral drift (drift aligned).   Other variations on this theme occur and await investigation.   When the constructional feature changes from a drift alignment to a swash alignment during the course of its existence, a 'fulcrum' effect is created. The swivelling of spits due to accretion distally and erosion proximally is well known and Guilcher and King (1961), for example, have pointed out how frequently spits are

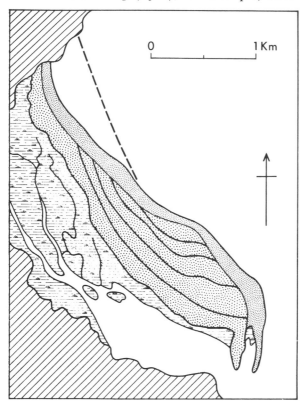

Fig. 100.   Rheban Spit, eastern Tasmania.   An older segment (open stipple) shows a drift alignment reconstructed by the broken line: a newer segment (close stipple) shows a swash alignment.   Wave approach is restricted to the northeast by coastal configuration.   A good example of spit swivelling giving rise to narrow proximal and broad distal ends.

narrow proximally and broad distally.   They may even be broken through at the proximal end.   It is clear from the discussions of Lewis (1932) and Steers (1946) that the Dungeness foreland on the south coast of England provides what is perhaps the best documented instance of this effect.   A much less well known example is that of a spit on the east coast of Tasmania illustrated in Fig. 100.   Swash alignments are to be regarded as the ultimate equilibrium condition towards which all beaches tend: given the right environment some will reach it virtually instantaneously; some others reach it through an intermediate drift alignment; others again will probably never reach it.

In environments where the wave regime is a relatively simple one, it may be possible to show reasonable correlation between beach alignments and putative single wave trains. This may happen where coastal configuration cuts out all except one major wave direction or where the wave climate itself revolves around waves from one major source. A good example of the latter situation is provided by south-eastern Australia, where southern swell of consistent direction and consistent optimum wave period is known to be completely dominant, and relatively simple fits between beach plans and swell crests have been postulated (Davies, 1958, 1960; Bird, 1961). On other coasts where the wave regime is a complex one, both swash and drift alignments are likely to represent resultants of multiple energy sources. In general, it is reasonable to deduce simpler conditions in swell environments, where wave directions and periods are more consistent than on stormy coasts.

BEACH FABRICS

Relatively little work has been done on the organization of the constituent particles in beaches in relation to environments and there may well be a fruitful field for inquiry here. Longitudinal grading for instance, so notoriously well developed on the pebble barrier at Chesil on the south coast of England, is the rule rather than the exception on sand beaches which I have sampled in Tasmania and other parts of south-eastern Australia. As indicated by King (1959) in the case of Chesil, it seems to be a response to energy variation along the beach where there is no strong unidirectional movement of material in either direction so that bigger particles accumulate where energy is highest. It is strongly correlated with other energy dependent variables such as berm height, and at Chesil for instance, energy, pebble size and berm height increase towards the south-east. A similar sort of relationship was discovered in sand by Bascom (1951) at Half Moon Bay in California. It will be obvious that this condition is favoured by, and may be quite characteristic of, swash aligned beaches on coasts of impeded transport. Chesil appears to be a swash aligned feature formed under conditions of locally impeded transport, and the much more extensive occurrence of this phenomenon in south-eastern Australia, for example, probably reflects the general occurrence of swash aligned beaches along these coasts.

On drift aligned beaches, good longitudinal grading has been attributed to increasing attrition of further travelled particles and to a tendency for smaller particles to travel further in any case. It is generally postulated, therefore, that particle size will tend to decrease in a downdrift direction. In some cases, such as those described by Kidson (1960) from Bridgewater Bay in western England and by Muraour (1953) on the Algerian coast, this condition can be shown to exist, but it does seem to demand one, or at most only a few, points of origin for the beach material. Judge (1971) has shown that, along the southern Californian coast where there is a number of well marked fluvial sources, it is possible to distinguish repeated patterns of mean particle size diminution downdrift: where supply sources are more complex it is hard to see how this condition could arise, especially as day-to-day variations in the competence of the system would mean that different sized particles could be transported at different times.   In such circumstances beaches are likely to be more akin to stream beds as far as grading characteristics are concerned.

Several workers have found a strong correlation between mean particle size and sorting of beach sediments, with poorer sorting associated with larger mean size (for instance, Folk and Ward, 1957), but there is some indication that greater wave energy may also be conducive to better sorting.   Giles and Pilkey (1965) found that beach sands along the east coast of the USA were better sorted in higher energy environments.   Arctic beaches, formed where wave energy is low and available particles large, seem to incorporate particularly poorly sorted sediments (Fig. 36, p. 54, and King, 1969).   It seems likely that more extensive accumulation of data would show wider geographical relationships of a range of sedimentary parameters, and that the establishment of such relationships would provide useful keys in genetic interpretation of constructional coastal landforms.

INLET DEFLECTION BY BEACHES

One effect of beach construction by waves is to deflect the discharge of water from the landward direction, whether it be river flow or tidal ebb, so that the resulting coastal inlet commonly occurs at one end of the beach or the other.   On drift aligned beaches the direction of deflection is virtually always downdrift and this is the usual situation assumed by older writers on coasts.   The second condition, which may be termed 'swash deflection' in contradistinction to the 'drift deflection' of the first condition, does not seem to have been described until 1954, when Bascom wrote a short paper recognizing it from a section of the Californian coast.   On beaches where drift is minimal – that is generally swash aligned beaches on coasts of impeded transport—the inlet position is determined by the height of the berm, which in turn is determined by the distribution of wave energy along the beach.   Where refraction is greatest the berm is lowest and it is here that the breach in the barrier is most likely to occur.   It is worth noting also that, as discussed above, it is here that particle size is least and sediment is thus most easily moved by outflowing currents.   If waves approach an embayment obliquely they tend to refract most around the nearest headland (Fig. 98, p.136) and so the position of the inlet will usually be in an upwave direction.

Swash deflection is the norm in Tasmania and probably in south-eastern Australia generally, and may occur more widely than is commonly supposed, because of a tendency in the past to assume both a drift deflected condition and drift directions from the position of inlets.   Discussion of apparently anomalous inlet locations on British coasts for instance, (Robinson, 1955; Kidson, 1963), may possibly have been clouded by lack of consideration of the swash deflection process.   Swash deflection is likely where there is relatively impeded transport and beaches tend to assume swash alignments, but it does seem to require strong berm construction.   It is therefore most characteristic of swell wave environments, and is to be expected in the storm wave environment mainly where pebble structures exist.   An example of its operation in eastern Australia is given later in this chapter in the discussion of zetaform bays.

RECURVATURE OF SPITS AND
BARRIER ISLANDS

A distinct geographical variation seems to exist in the degree to which the distal ends of spits and the ends of barrier islands adjacent to inlets are recurved landward.   Bird (1968) described spits as 'usually ending in one or more landward hooks or recurves' and this view is certainly reflected in most writings from North Atlantic shores.   Johnson (1919, 1925) gave numerous examples of spit convexities from north-eastern North America, and British texts continue to cite Hurst Castle spit, Blakeney Point and Scolt Head Island.   However, out of what might be regarded as nineteen major spit features around the Tasmanian coast, only two show traces of recurvature and one of these is strongly concave for most of its length.   In fact in southern Australia generally, spits are normally concave and hooked features are rare.

The reasons for this seem to lie in the two major factors conducive to spit recurvature. The first of these is the presence of subsidiary waves from different directions acting occasionally on the distal end of the spit in the manner postulated by, for example, Steers (1953, p. 21), to explain the plan form of some spits on the east coast of England. The process works best where the end of the spit projects into exposed waters and where the waves are multi-directional.   On southern Australian coasts very few spits project into exposed situations because coasts are dominantly characterized by impeded transport: most spits represent re-entrant traps and salient traps are rare.   The strong concavity reflects the prevalence of swash rather than drift alignments.   In this environment too, waves are typically unidirectional, with strong swell maintaining very consistent angles of approach right through the year.   The whole spit is moulded by one major set of waves.

The second explanation is that put forward by Evans (1942) in which recurving is seen as a normal accompaniment of spit building, and is due simply to deflection of the constructing waves around the tip of the spit, and the consequent smoothing landward of material transported by beach drifting and longshore current movement.   The idea was presented in greater detail by Schou (1945) and has been widely accepted.   This process requires relatively deep water off the end of the spit in order that the waves may refract around into the inlet.   Again, these conditions are not common in southern Australia, partly because spits tend to terminate in sheltered situations, partly because river flow is often deficient or intermittent and partly because low amplitude, mixed or diurnal tides increase water depth only slightly at high tide and promote only feeble current action.   A large tidal range is conducive to spit recurvature because it ensures deep water while the high tide plan of the shore is being determined.   This can be demonstrated from many spits where low tide features are concave and high tide features convex.   Although exceptional in its regional context because of its very local four metre tidal range, a spit in north-western Tasmania illustrates this well (Fig. 101).

In summary then, spit recurvature is most inhibited in microtidal, swell environments with conditions of predominantly impeded transport and swash aligned constructional forms.   It is most characteristic of macrotidal, storm wave environments with predominantly free transport and drift aligned spits and barriers.

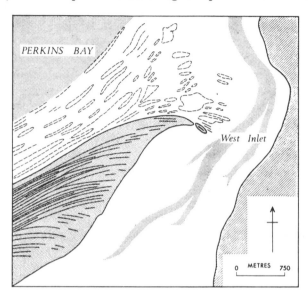

FIG. 101.   Spit at eastern end of Perkins Bay, northwest Tasmania where tidal range is 4 metres.   Intertidal ridge and runnel are concave seaward but grade into convex (recurved) high tide alignments.

ZETAFORM BAYS AND OFFSET COASTS

Along the east coast of Australia from south of Sydney to Fraser Island extends an almost continuous series of asymmetrically curved bays joining one headland to the next.   The southern section of every bay curves more sharply than the northern section. These were called 'zeta curve' bays by Halligan (1906) who noted their resemblance in plan to the Greek letter zeta.   They seem to result from the movement of sediment from one side of the bay to the other under the influence of a predominant drift, but appear to be basically swash aligned features with their shape reflecting the wave crests of south-easterly swell as it refracts around each headland.   They were described by, for instance, Langford-Smith and Thom (1969), and have been reproduced experimentally in a wave tank by Silvester (1960).   Silvester produced zetaform beaches by sending waves at an angle of 45° towards a straight stretch of model shore where three concrete sections simulated headlands.   The resulting beach curves resembled those occurring in nature with the sharply curved end upwave and a quasi-permanent stage was reached when the waves broke simultaneously around each bay.   Although Silvester called his equilibrium form a 'half-heart shaped bay' it is clearly the same thing as Halligan's zeta curve.   The term 'zetaform' may be preferable because along many coasts long sections of such beaches appear actually rectilinear with only a limited curved section.

Yasso (1965) also recognized such forms and called them 'headland bay beaches'. He confirmed the suggestion of Krumbein (1947) that some examples from the USA gave a good approximation in plan to a logarithmic spiral.   Subsequently, Silvester (1970) established a direct statistical relationship between the logarithmic spiral constant and the angle of wave obliquity and found that in model experiments this was the sole determinant of shape.

Field survey of Australian zetaform beaches shows that their curved southern ends display lower berms with finer sand particle size and less steep beach faces than their straighter and more exposed northern ends.   The greater berm height and larger particle size towards the northern end is a response to increasing wave energy in this direction in a condition of largely impeded transport, and the steeper beach face results from the coarser sediment.   The systematic variation in berm height has an effect on the position of stream outlets which tend to be swash deflected and occur, as described in the last chapter, where berm construction is weakest.   Thus, along the east Australian coast from Norah Head to Sandy Cape, of twenty-nine zetaform bays identified, twenty-three have stream outlets in the south, in spite of the fact that prevailing longshore current movement and beach drifting is to the north under the influence of the southerly swell.   In Australia at least, the sands of zetaform beaches are well graded longitudinally, which is expectable in the case of what seems to be an essentially swash aligned feature.   Bascom (1951) demonstrated a similar grading, and similar changes in beach characters at Half Moon Bay in California, which also seems to be a zetaform bay with its strongly curved end towards the prevailing north-westerly swell.

A coast which is composed of a series of zetaform bays takes on a characteristic appearance in plan since each successive bay is recessed behind its neighbour.   Gulliver (1899) and Johnson (1919) used the term 'offset' for a condition of successive recession and this seems appropriate in a wide context.   According to Gulliver, 'one shore curve offsets another when the curve itself, or the continuation of the same, passes to seaward of the next succeeding shore curve'.   From comparison of map evidence with available knowledge of dominant longshore currents, he arrived at a general law that 'the current flows from the outer curve toward the inner one,' or from the more sharply curved section of each beach towards the less sharply curved.   Neither Gulliver nor Johnson (1919), who noted once again the connection between current direction and offsetting, attempted an explanation, although they seem to have implied a causal connection. In fact, the two phenomena are the result of a common cause rather than being themselves cause and effect.   On the New South Wales coast which has been taken as an example, the southerly swell which gives rise to successive offsetting of a series of zeta-form bays with more sharply curved southern ends also tends to set up longshore currents from south to north.   Much more recently, and apparently independently, Silvester (1962) has realized the significance of the correlation between offsetting and

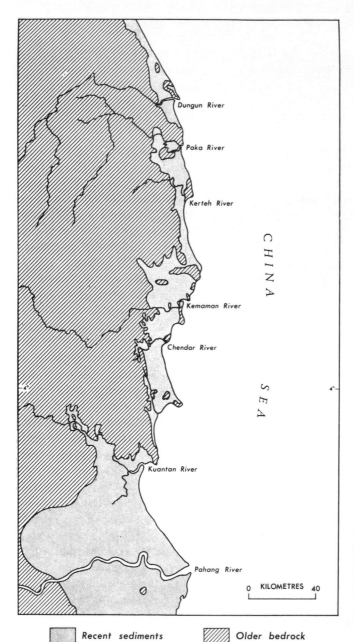

FIG. 102. Zetaform bays on the offset coast of eastern Malaya where major wave approach is from the northeast. Note the position of river outlets at the more strongly curved northern ends of beaches.

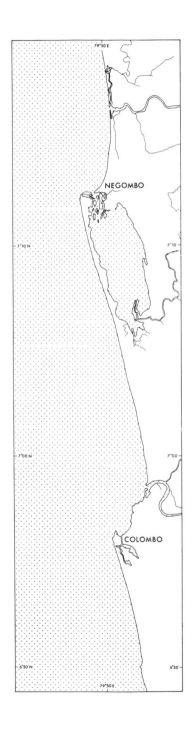

the direction of dominant overall longshore drift, and has used it in an attempt to deduce large scale world systems of coastal sediment movement.

Offset coasts are of very wide distribution. They are particularly evident in low latitudes where depositional features are more continuously distributed and there is a very consistent direction of approach of the constructing waves. Good examples are to be found on the east coast of Malaya (Fig. 102), the west coast of Sri Lanka (Fig. 103), on the west coast of Africa north from the mouth of the Zaïre to Cap Lopez, and between Cape Lucia and Delagoa Bay on the coast of natal. The angle of offset (Fig. 104), which may be taken as that between a line through successive headlands and one parallel to the straighter section of the zetaform beach, varies from about 35° downward. As the angle becomes small, the zeta form flattens, offsetting becomes progressively less obvious until it is almost imperceptible and, as Gulliver suggested, 'it may be perceived by looking along the shore curve putting the eye close to the map'.

Normally, offset coasts comprise alternate beach sections and hard rock headlands, but they may also be formed solely in sediments and even solely in bed rock. Where sediments only are involved, as for instance along sections of the west coast of Sri Lanka (Fig. 103), the place of the usual hard rock headland appears to be taken by a river mouth from which relatively large sediment loads are periodically discharged. A strong oblique wave attack causes deflection of the river mouths in a downdrift direction and the outlet therefore occurs at the updrift end of each zetaform bay, as it does in the more usual case discussed earlier: the outlets are in fact both drift and swash deflected. It will be noted that in the case illustrated in Fig. 103 each stream comes from behind the previous updrift bay, whereas in the normal case with hardrock headlands this is not so. Offset coasts formed substantially of bedrock, such as that between Cape Agulhas and Port Alfred in South Africa, and that represented by Bournemouth and Christchurch

FIG. 103. Depositional offset coast in western Sri Lanka where the most important waves approach from the southwest.

Bays on the south coast of England, form where bands of rock of unequal resistance intersect the coast at an angle. In these cases the general outlines must owe much to the drowning of a subaerially eroded landscape and it seems better to consider them as separate phenomena, even though they obey the general rule of having their more sharply curved sections towards the direction of approach of important waves.

In general, offset coasts appear to represent a condition in between completely free and completely impeded transport, their exact position probably depending on the

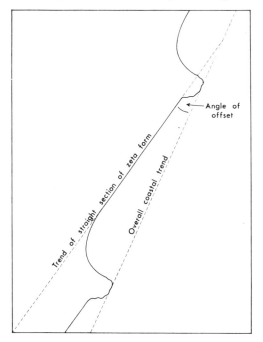

FIG. 104. The angle of offset.

angle of offset. It may be argued that longshore movement is limited since the zeta-form is an adjustment to the refraction of constructing waves and this is supported by the lack of inlet deflection downdrift, but there are also indications that slow but steady undirectional drift proceeds, with leakage of sediment around headlands, from one zetaform beach to the next.

WORLD ORIENTATION OF
CONSTRUCTIONAL FORMS

Figure 105 illustrates major world trends in beach orientation. Attention has been confined to open oceanic coasts in order to avoid local factors of coastal alignment and fetch direction, such as apply for instance in the more or less enclosed seas of western Europe. The map is based mainly on a study over a period of years of a great number of large scale maps and charts from multitudinous sources, and essentially it records instances or groups of instances where spits, barriers and even bayhead beaches depart from the main coastal trend and take up independent alignments. Sometimes these are the straighter sections of zetaform beaches. Although it would clearly be dangerous to argue too closely from the picture which thus emerges, the directions indicated do seem to have a regional significance which helps to support their validity.

On the west coast of the Americas there is a tendency for beaches to face north-westerly from Oregon south to Baja California, but from Baja California to south

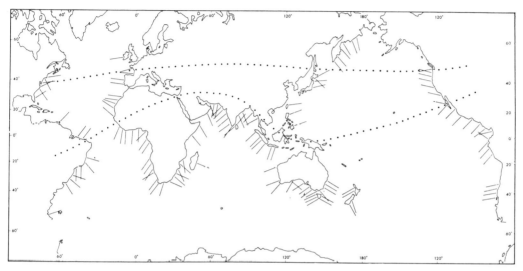

Fig. 105. General world trends in orientation of constructional shore forms. For explanation see text. The dotted lines mark locations of major trend changes.

central Chile they tend to face the south-west. On the east coast, beaches south of the Rio de la Plata are rather indeterminate in alignment but from here to the north-east tip of Brazil a south-easterly facing trend is evident. From north-east Brazil to Massa-chusetts the tendency is to face north-east.

On the west coast of Europe and Africa south-westerly facing trends appear in Ireland and northern France, but these are replaced between the mouth of the Gironde and Cape Verde by north-westerly facing trends. From Cape Verde to the southern tip of Africa a south-westerly facing trend is evident. On the east coast of Africa beaches tend to face a south-easterly direction everywhere. On the southern and wes-tern coasts of Asia and Australia a south-westerly facing tendency is equally present, and it appears again in New Zealand; but along the east coast of Australia from Tasmania to Fraser Island beaches tend to face south-eastward. From the Phillippines to Hokkaido they tend to face north-eastward but in Kamchatka they tend to face south-eastward again.

It might be argued that these trends simply reflect the overall trends of the con-tinental coasts themselves and clearly there is some relationship because the distribution of land and sea limits the directions from which constructing waves can approach. This is the fetch factor on a global scale. But the coincidence is not as great as might appear at first sight.   Thus beaches between Oregon and Baja California show a tendency to face north-westward even though the continental coast faces south-westward.   The beaches of Chile tend to face south-westward though the coast as a whole faces slightly north of west.   The general alignment of the Portuguese coast does not favour a north-westerly facing tendency more than a south-westerly facing one.   Nor is the coast of Baluchistan aligned in such a way that beaches are likely to face south-westerly rather than south-easterly.   In detail it is usual to find that constructional shore features are not aligned completely parallel to the lie of the hardrock coast and it is the nature of this departure which is mapped in Fig. 105.

The very distribution in detail of major depositional coasts reinforces the evidence provided by their alignment, for on any coast which shows a tendency for beaches to be aligned in a certain direction, there is also a marked tendency for beaches to occur most commonly in locations which enable this alignment to be achieved.   The east coast of South America can be used to illustrate this: from Rio de la Plata to north-east Brazil it is the more southerly facing sections which carry the big barrier systems, and on the sections facing more to the east they are absent or weakly developed.

The evidence of barriers flying at an angle to the main coastal trend is also pertinent. The mirror image 'wings' formed on either side of the Australian continent by Fraser Island and Dirk Hartog Island have their counterpart in the large depositional complex of Point Aguja north of Chiclayo in Peru (the Sechura Desert), at Sherbro Island in Sierra Leone and to some extent Cap Blanc in Morocco.   All show a tendency for large constructional forms to perpetuate an alignment trend past the point where the continental coast takes a marked change in direction and other trends become possible. They are salient traps on the largest scale.   Taken as a whole the evidence suggests that, although the shape of the continents and oceans is a major factor in deciding possible directions of wave approach and of beach alignment, there are other factors at work. By far the most important of these are the global wave generation pattern and the overall directions of significant ocean wave approach discussed in Chapter III.   Comparison of Fig. 105 with Figs 27 (p. 43) and 106 shows a very strong relationship which must be a causal one.   It suggests that the principle developed by Lewis (1938), that beaches tend to be built up transverse to the direction of approach of the most important beach constructing waves, is applicable on a global scale as well as on a local one.   In the terminology used here whether the trend of a wave-constructed shore tends to follow a swash alignment or a drift alignment, that shore will turn partly or completely towards the direction of approach of the constructing wave.

WORLD MOVEMENT OF
COASTAL SEDIMENTS

If, as is concluded above, it is possible to identify overall world trends of direction of wave approach and related constructional shore alignment, some interesting questions regarding sediment movement are posed.   The deflection of global wave energy equator-ward, by swell from the regions of temperate frontal activity and waves generated by the tropical easterlies, must tend to induce longshore drift in a similar

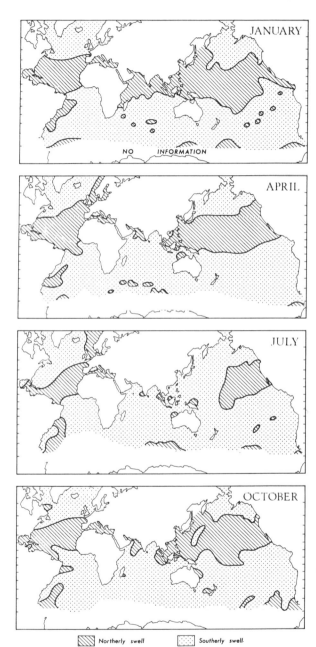

JANUARY

NO INFORMATION

APRIL

JULY

OCTOBER

FIG. 106. Predominant direction of swell in January, April, July and October from shipboard records accumulated in British Meteorological Office Monthly Meteorological Charts of the Oceans.

Northerly swell   Southerly swell

direction.   There are strong *a priori* grounds for thinking that sediment should move dominantly from temperate regions towards the equator.   This movement should be more evident in the southern hemisphere because of the greater regularity of coastal outline and because of the generally bigger and more regular waves generated in the more oceanic hemisphere.

Silvester (1962) made an independent approach to this question by using the evidence of zetaform bays and offset coasts.   If we accept Gulliver's rule that 'the current flows from the outer curve towards the inner one', then by examining the distribution of offset features it should be possible to reconstruct the direction of major overall

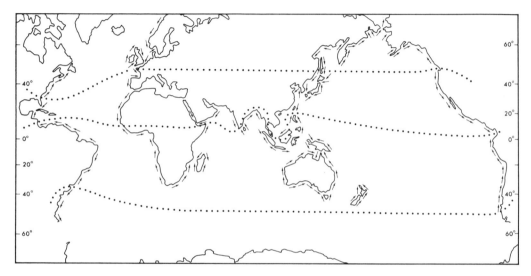

FIG. 107.   Major overall trends of net sediment movement around world coasts as deduced by Silvester (1962).   The dotted lines indicate major changes in trend (compare with Figs 105 and 106).

directions of net drift.   Silvester attempted to do this and his resulting maps are reproduced in generalized form in Fig. 107.   Comparison of this with Figs 105 and 106 again shows a large measure of agreement.   There are some coasts where Silvester's interpretation differs from that offered in Fig. 105.   Most of these are coasts, such as the west coast of India, where there is strong seasonal reversal of longshore sediment movement and the evidence of offsetting appears somewhat equivocal and difficult to interpret.   However, in spite of some disagreement in interpretation, there is general accord between the results of the two exercises.

The *a priori* deduction that net long-term drift should tend to be from temperate latitudes towards the equator is supported by Silvester's line of reasoning, but also by such direct evidence as is available.   As forecast, this evidence is perhaps clearest from southern hemisphere coasts.   There are abundant indications that net sediment movement on the east Australian coast is from south to north and every likelihood that Fraser Island represents a gigantic salient trap in which huge amounts of sand have been accumulating through the Quaternary (Coaldrake, 1962). On the other side of the Australian continent, Logan and others (1970) have described the large barrier complex of Shark Bay, built up by northward movement of sand over long periods of time. The powerful northerly drift of material along the west coast of southern Africa is stressed by Tricart and Cailleux (1965), who quote the work of Abecasis on the Lobito spit in Angola. Logan (1960) described the effect of powerful northward drift on the coast of South West Africa and Paterson (1956) concludes that dominant drift on the south-eastern coast of the continent is towards the north. On the South American coast Ottman (1965) records that material is moved from Patagonia as far as the Rio de la Plata.

Earlier in this chapter the apparent prevalence in the tropics of large-scale constructional shore features such as barrier systems was attributed to the relatively large supply of material by rivers and the favourable wave climate. It may be, however, that a general movement of shore sediments equator-ward over long periods of time and different sea levels during the Quaternary has contributed something to this phenomenon.

X | COASTAL DUNES

Coastal dunes vary considerably in size and form, and also in occurrence. On some coasts in the tropics where their existence might be expected, they are completely absent. Although their form depends on other factors such as the nature of the back-shore zone and the effect of vegetation, their presence or absence, and size, depend essentially on the rate of abstraction of sand from its source on the beach.

FACTORS OF SAND TRANSPORT FROM THE BEACH

SAND SUPPLY

An abundant supply of sand of suitable grain size is an obvious necessity for a large dune system and, in most cases, this in turn requires active injection into the coastal transport system—normally from rivers. The enormous dune complexes of the Oregon and Washington coasts, described by Cooper (1958), are associated with a ready supply of sand from rivers draining wet steep catchments. Cooper noted also that whereas 44 per cent of the Oregon coast north of Cape Blanco is dune bordered, only 21 per cent is so bordered to the south. He attributed this to a contrast in the degrees of piling up of sand against the coast. To the north of Cape Blanco littoral sediment movement is more impeded and, with an abundant sand supply, beaches prograde.

On coasts where retrogression is the rule, new dunes are commonly being built by a process of 'cannibalization' of older eroding dunes.

WIND VELOCITY

Given a supply of sand on the beach, the next requirement is the sufficiently common occurrence of winds, blowing at speeds above the threshold velocity necessary to move the particular sand which is present. Because it is the shear velocity along the sand surface which is critical, the microclimatic wind is the operative factor. Unfortunately, there is very little data available on shear velocities on actual beaches, and the general practice is to gain some relative appreciation of their strength by assessing the resultant of strong onshore macroclimatic winds (Jennings, 1957).

The overall importance of wind velocity in the evolution of large dune systems is attested by such things as the occurrence of almost all the biggest systems in the temperate zones of intense frontal activity, the larger dune complexes of windward coasts as compared with leeward coasts and the virtual absence of dunes from the doldrum areas of the tropics. The velocity of the microclimatic wind may be affected towards the rear of the beach by the nature of the backshore zone and particularly by any obstacles to air flow which might increase turbulence and reduce shear strength on the sand surface. Cliffs or steep slopes at the rear of the beach may have this effect and so, perhaps, may tall trees.

HUMIDITY

Belly (1964) confirmed earlier work by showing experimentally that an increase in the humidity of the air stream slightly increases the threshold velocity for any particular particle size. The presence of sand moisture increases threshold velocities very considerably and the increase is particularly marked for the first 2 per cent of sand moisture content, apparently because it causes the sand to present a smoother surface to the wind. The dampness of sand grains has been suggested as a possible reason for poor dune development in the wet tropics and, from the work of Belly and others, it seems fair to deduce that, on coasts subject to heavy precipitation and high atmospheric humidity, significantly higher shear velocities are needed to move equivalent sand grains than on drier coasts.

SAND GRAIN CHARACTERISTICS

Sand grains with the approximate density of quartz are most readily set in motion as their diameter decreases down to about 0·1 mm, below which they are unlikely to be found on beaches. Bagnold (1941) found experimentally that rates of transport of sand by wind increased where it was more poorly sorted initially, but more recent work has suggested that this may only be the case at higher wind speeds. More spherical material has been found to move at a greater rate with high velocity winds and the fact that dune sands seem normally to be more spherical and more rounded than those of the adjacent beach has commonly been attributed to selective wind transport. It seems clear that the nature of beach sand, which in turn is related to provenance and wave action, may have a detectable effect on the rate of dune building.

TIDAL RANGE AND TYPE

Beaches with a large tidal range expose a larger sand expanse to wind action and, other things being equal, can therefore be expected to suffer greater sand removal by wind. Diurnal tides and, to a lesser extent, mixed tides enable beach sediments to dry out for a longer period than do semi-diurnal tides. However, in nature, diurnal and mixed tidal types tend to be associated with small tidal ranges and semi-diurnal tides with large tidal ranges so it is unlikely that this factor is a very significant one.

DUNE DISTRIBUTION IN
RELATION TO FACTORS OF
SAND TRANSPORT

From this summary of factors we can conclude that large dune complexes are likely to occur where there is active sand supply, impeded littoral transport, strong onshore winds, low precipitation and humidity, low beach face angles and large tidal ranges. The important factors of high wind velocity and flat, wide beaches are strongly characteristic of what was called, in Chapter III, the storm wave environment and it is here in such areas as north-west Europe and north-west USA, wherever sand supply is sufficiently abundant, that by far the largest number of big dune systems is to be found. The exceptions, such as the very massive dunes of Fraser Island in Queensland mentioned in the last chapter, arise from peculiarly large supplies of sand over a long period of time.

The opposite condition occurs on coasts in the humid tropics, where, as in Sri Lanka and Malaya and along the Guinea coast of West Africa, long stretches of sandy beach may be completely devoid of dunes (Fig. 108).   The question of why dunes are largely absent from hot, wet coasts has received some attention in the literature and was

Fig. 108.   Beach with wide berm and no apparent dune development typical of wet tropics at Negombo, west coast of Sri Lanka.

reviewed by Jennings (1964, 1965).   All the factors affecting beach deflation militate against dune development under such conditions.   As we have seen, sand supply tends to be limited in the wet tropics, where rivers supply much mud.   The coasts concerned lie generally in regions of low wind velocities and largely within the doldrums.   Where strong monsoon winds are experienced seasonally, as in Sri Lanka and Malaya, these may blow at around 10 m/sec^{-1}, which is above the threshold velocity for dry sand of all expectable particle sizes.   However, sand transport varies as the cube of the excess of velocity over this threshold (Bagnold, 1954), and apart perhaps from rare tropical cyclones, it is the absence of winds blowing at well above threshold velocities which seems to be crucial (Fig. 109). Jennings (1965) analysed wind data for coastal stations within and without the tropics in Australia by summing onshore vectors of the cubed velocity above an assumed threshold of 4·4 m/sec^{-1} (10 m.p.h.) and found that values varied from 305 to 1511 (mean 794, median 757) outside the tropics, and from 424 to 1 (mean 90, median 23) inside.

The effectiveness of winds which do occur may be reduced by the common presence

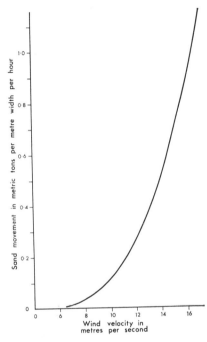

FIG. 109. Relation between wind velocity and rate of sand transport according to Bagnold (1954).

of high trees at the rear of the beach and the consistent high humidity and heavy rainfall which considerably increases threshold velocities by wetting the sand (Figs. 110 and 111). These are also coasts where waves are normally low and flat, so that beach face angles are steep and, with few exceptions, where tidal range is slight so that only a relatively narrow strip of beach is ever exposed to wind action. Another factor which has been suggested as inhibiting sand movement by wind on tropical beaches is that of sand binding by salt from evaporated seawater or spray (Morton, 1957). Boughey (1957) described how a thin crust of salt and sand is formed on the surface of fine sand beaches in Ghana and movement is inhibited so that bare sand well above high water mark does not move in years, even when onshore winds are of a force he judged sufficient to transport sand on temperate coasts. The rare instances of sand blowing which were observed occurred in the rainy season when leaching of salt is predictable. More recent writers have tended to ignore or be sceptical of this factor but it should not be

FIG. 110. *Cocos* and *Hippomane* forming tree wall behind microtidal low energy beach at Holetown, west coast of Barbados.

FIG. 111. Narrow, steep duneless beach on microtidal north coast of Oahu, Hawaii subject to moist northeast trade wind attack.

dismissed entirely. On the trade wind coast of Barbados, where Gooding (1947) measured soil water salt content in the backshore zone at about 5 per cent, spray evaporates on the warm sand surface to form what is sometimes a visible encrustation. Winds of around 10 m/sec^{-1} appear ineffective as sand shifters and the few low dunes may mainly be activated at the passage of infrequent tropical cyclones.

DUNE CLASSIFICATION

Any discussion of geographical variation in the form of coastal dunes would seem to require some sort of classification and uniform terminology, but no really satisfactory comprehensive scheme appears to exist. The older European attempts, such as the very detailed one of van Dieren (1934), are limited in that they do not accommodate many forms found outside that continent. Overall schemes covering desert dunes as well, such as that of Melton (1940), are not sufficiently explicit as they stand. The most complete list is probably that of Smith (1954), and the scheme which is used as a basis for discussion here incorporates the Smith categories in a classification bearing some resemblance to that of Melton and owing some inspiration to the writings of Cooper (1958, 1967). It may be set out as follows:

A.   Primary dunes (derived from the beach)
  (*i*)   Free dunes with vegetation unimportant (transverse ridges, barchans, oblique ridges, precipitation ridges and so on). Wind oriented and generally lying perpendicular to the direction of constructing winds.
  (*ii*) Impeded dunes with vegetation important (frontal dunes, sand beach ridges, dune platforms, etc.). Nucleus oriented and generally parallel to the rear of the source beach.

B.   Secondary dunes (derived from erosion of A(*ii*))
  (*i*)   Transgressive dunes (blow-out dunes, parabolic dunes, longitudinal dunes, transgressive sheets, etc.) Wind oriented and generally lying parallel to the direction of constructing winds.
  (*ii*) Remnant dunes (remanié dunes), eroded remnants of vegetated primary dunes.

  This scheme is not completely satisfactory, if only because the categories are not always as fully separate as it suggests. Transgressive dunes for example, although initiated by erosion of vegetated primary dunes, may later in their history derive sand directly from the beach and many primary dunes on desert coasts are intermediate between the free and impeded state. However, the broad outline seems to work well as a framework for discussion. A great deal of work is still needed on the taxonomy of individual dune forms: it is fair to say that coastal dunes have been studied extensively as plant habitats but have been relatively neglected as landforms.

FREE PRIMARY DUNES

Primary dunes in which vegetation is unimportant as a factor of dune form occur in two main sorts of situation: along desert coasts where there is insufficient moisture for vigorous plant growth and in more humid regions where a suitable sand binding flora is not available.

The first situation occurs along parts of the coast of Baja California, the Peruvian coast, the Namib coast of south-western Africa, the Atlantic coast of Morocco, coasts of the Red Sea and northern Arabian Sea and some southern and western coasts of Australia (Fig. 112). Dresch (1961) has described free dunes moving inland from the Atacama coast, where vegetation is scarce. The most common dune is a small barchan about 2 to 6 m high and 10 to 15 m across. On parts of the desert coast of Baja California fields of free barchan dunes averaging 6 m high form transverse ridges moving

Fig. 112. Barchan dunes of calcareous sand moving inland from the shore; near Eucla, Western Australia. (Photo by J. N. Jennings.)

inland from the shore. The barchans arise immediately from the beach in major re-entrant traps along this coast (Inman, Ewing and Corliss, 1966). On the Namib coast, plants such as *Mesembryanthemum* may fix small patches between which the sand continues to move (Logan, 1960), and near Suakin on the Sudanese coast Kassas (1957) mentioned both free barchans and very low vegetation fixed mounds. On the most arid sections of the Australian coast, the grass *Triodia* extensively fixes dune systems (Burbidge, 1944), and may be unusually successful by general world standards for such an environment.

Much the best documented example of the second situation is that of the west coast of the USA, described in the monographs of Cooper (1958, 1967). Particularly in Washington and Oregon, large sand masses move inland from the shore with little hindrance from vegetation. It is important to remember that the effectiveness of a sand binding flora is relative to that of the sand moving forces. Cooper noted that, although native strand plants such as the grass *Elymus* were generally inefficient under rigorous conditions of massive sand emplacement by wind in Oregon, in limited, more favourable situations they were able to establish themselves and produce characteristic impeded primary dunes. The importance of species availability is well illustrated by the way in which marram grass, introduced to the west coast of the USA within the last hundred years, has already established frontal dune systems where the native flora had previously failed.   There are other coasts, in southern Australia, for example, where marram has been introduced and has supplanted apparently less effective native species and thereby altered dune morphology.

Except for the tip of the Antarctic Peninsula, flowering plants are absent from Antarctica so that any dunes there are vegetation free.   The dominant offshore wind regime, relative lack of source material and low tidal range inhibit dune development, but from the McMurdo Sound coast Nichols (1968) has described low dune sheets about one metre thick on which sand shadows and sand drifts develop behind physical obstacles.   In other parts of the world, even in wet areas where potentially effective plants are present, excessive sand supply coupled with strong wind movement may result in essentially free dunes.   On the south coast of Java rapid erosion of young volcanoes provides particularly abundant sand, which may be blown from the beach by monsoon winds before it can be adequately fixed by *Spinifex* and *Ipomoea* (Verstappen, 1957). In this and other cases, human destruction of vegetation may be an important contributing factor.

The characteristic free primary dune is the transverse dune, forming at right angles to the direction of strong winds, and moving gradually downwind.   Individual barchans may also occur.   A much rarer form described by Cooper is the oblique dune which is stable in position, very much larger than other forms and apparently due to interaction between two seasonally alternating winds.   It requires not only rather special wind conditions but also a large amount of sand, and the only other possible examples Cooper was able to cite are some dunes in Portugal which are now largely modified by planting.   However, more recently, oblique dunes have been described from the Indian coast of Orissa by Siddiquie (1966).   Sand moving northward from the Mahanadi delta, at a net rate according to Manohar (1961) of 1·5 million tons per year, is blown into free dunes 4 to 6 metres high.   Although a few barchans were seen, most of the dunes were thought to be comparable to Cooper's oblique form.

Cooper's precipitation ridge occurs where transverse dunes are halted by meeting a forest edge.   It is similar in form to the transverse dune but its orientation is mainly determined by the alignment of the forest edge.   In these ways it obviously represents a transition form between free and impeded primary dunes and, because it demands the existence of trees, it can only occur where free dunes result from the absence of a suitable sand binding flora.

IMPEDED PRIMARY DUNES

Dunes formed from the beach as a result of the interaction of wind and vegetation are the traditional coastal dunes of most text books.   They are produced in humid areas and, less characteristically, in semi-arid areas wherever there is sufficient sand supply from the beach and a sand binding flora competent in relation to wind strength and sediment supply.   Their greatest development is achieved in temperate humid areas, where high winds pile up great quantities of sand and moisture promotes vigorous vegetative growth. As climates get drier the effect of vegetation becomes less evident and, as they get less windy, sand transport decreases.

The typical impeded primary dune is the frontal dune, or foredune, lying more or less parallel to the rear of the beach (Fig. 113). Its normally close approximation in plan to the beach is brought about partly by the way in which the back of the berm acts as a nucleus for sand accumulation, and partly by the way in which high waves periodically trim the front of the growing ridge. Accordance in plan appears closest in microtidal swell environments, where beaches are swash aligned, and this reflects stronger berm development and greater regularity of wave crest approach. It appears to diverge

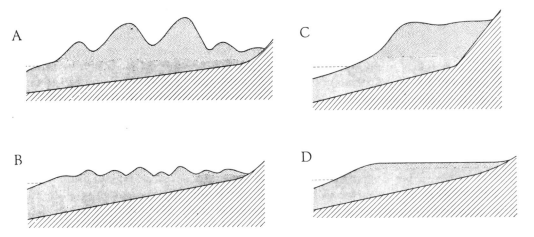

FIG. 113. Four types of impeded primary dune in diagrammatic profile. (A) frontal dune ridges; (B) sand beach ridges; (C) high dune platform; (D) low dune platform.

most in macrotidal storm wave environments with drift aligned beaches where the opposite conditions apply. In this latter case frontal dune alignment may owe more to the direction of sand moving winds and it is perhaps no coincidence that some European writers have thought of foredunes as being 'transverse' to the wind (Steers, 1946, for example).

A rather similar contrast exists in the extent to which foredunes are ridged. Some frontal dunes form a well marked ridge or a whole system of ridges: others are massive and unridged forming a dune platform or dune plateau: yet others display a jumble of hillocks without discernible pattern. The last case usually results from the partial development of secondary dunes and the essential distinction is between the first two. Strong ridging seems to be associated with strong sand berm development so that sand beach ridge systems, which may be regarded as the ultimate in ridging, are found where tidal range is small and where long, low waves are dominant. The extensive sand beach ridge systems of south-eastern Australia, illustrated in Fig. 114 for instance, have no true counterpart in the British Isles, where many frontal dunes have a foundation of pebbles (see Steers, 1946, for examples). On coasts such as some of those in north-west Europe, where beach profiles are perennially rectilinear or somewhat concave, sand removed from the beach just piles up against the foot of the existing foredune so that, if progradation takes place, a high unridged dune platform is formed. Good examples occur on the Picardy and Vendée coasts of France.

Extensive low sand 'plateaux' with level surfaces about 1·5 m above high water mark have been described from the Seychelles by Russell and McIntire (1965), and Sauer (1967). These are thought to represent enormously wide berm platforms built up simply by wave action on a prograding shore, but in other parts of the tropics

FIG. 114. **Closely spaced and regularly ridged low foredunes (sand beach ridges) at Bakers Beach, north coast of Tasmania.** They are cut by transgressive secondary dunes initiated by European settlement and burning in the late nineteenth century.

apparently similar features seem to have a limited amount of wind-blown sand as a capping (Fig. 115). Nossin (1965) described and illustrated vegetated unridged sand flats, above high water mark and 0·5 to 1 m thick, on the east Malayan coast, and thought them likely to be due to wind accumulation. Swan (1967) noted that, although there are no large dunes on the monsoon-exposed south-west coast of Sri Lanka, some wind sorted beach sands veneer the landward margin of the berm. He found that such sand was usually fine and well sorted, but otherwise resembled wave worked sand. Sometimes, as along the west coast of Barbados, such low platforms are faintly ridged, but often seem quite amorphous. They frequently support littoral woodlands such as the *Barringtonia* formation of Asian coasts and the *Coccoloba-Hippomane*

FIG. 115. *Ipomoea* and *Spinifex* covering the outer edge of a low dune platform behind a beach north of Townsville, Queensland.

FIG. 116. Biabou Bay, east coast of St Vincent, West Indies. A black sand beach strewn with coconut husks is invaded at the rear by shrubby *Coccoloba* and creeping *Canavalia*.

formation of the West Indies.   Commonly they are so low as to give the initial impression that the shore is completely duneless.

The development of these low, unridged dune platforms may be related to very low rates of sand accretion under conditions of beach progradation and effectively low wind velocities with rapid plant colonization.   However, another factor worth considering is the effect of the characteristic trailing habit of the most important tropical shore plants.   The *Ipomoea-Canavalia* community in particular is of outstanding significance as a sand colonizer throughout the tropical zone (Fig. 116).   The long trailing shoots sent out by its constituent plants tend to cover the sand in a sheet of vegetation and in this way promote a surface which shows minimum ridging and minimum hummock development.   The typical low, flattish beach ridges formed under the influence of colonizing *Ipomoea* are well illustrated for instance by Hill (1966) from the east coast of Malaya.

Something of this effect can be seen along the east coast of Australia in the contrast between embryo foredunes colonized by the native *Spinifex hirsutus* and those colonized by the introduced *Ammophila arenaria*.   *Ammophila*, although rhizomatous, grows in strong compact tufts which encourage sand accumulation in the form of hummocks: *Spinifex* is strongly creeping and its long horizontal surface runners tend to promote more uniform accumulation of sand.   In the first case the new foredune tends to be hummocky and ridge-like: in the second it has much more of the appearance of a low platform (Fig. 117).

The height attained by foredunes, whether ridged or not, depends essentially on the rate of beach progradation and the prevailing onshore wind velocities.   On the broad geographical scale it is the second factor that is more important and leads to a prevalence of high dunes on temperate west coasts.

FIG. 117. Platform-like embryo dune colonized by *Spinifex hirsutus* at Barragga Bay, southern New South Wales.

SECONDARY DUNES

By definition, secondary dunes have a similar distribution to the impeded primary dunes from which they are derived and they occur in such diverse localities as southern Greenland (Bellknap, 1928) and tropical Queensland in Australia (Bird, 1965). For fullest development they require strong winds but smaller examples may be found in some of the more modestly developed dune areas of the comparatively windless tropics, where sand supply is sufficient (Fig. 118).

FIG. 118. Transgressive dunes on the Burmese coast near the Irawaddy delta viewed from about 12 000 metres up. The axes parallel the direction of the southwest monsoon.

Transgressive dunes are aligned in the direction of the most effective sand moving winds and a good approximation to this can be obtained from the resultant of onshore winds blowing at Beaufort Scale 3 and over (Jennings, 1957). Particularly where the direction of strong winds is relatively constant, transgressive dunes are often markedly linear (Fig. 119a) but greater variation in wind direction or lateral coalescence of the sand bodies may create transgressive sheets (Fig. 119b) of considerable width. Parabolic or 'hairpin' dunes seem to develop especially when the dune is no longer receiving new sand and begins to wander inland. As the dune travels, the sand body at the head is progressively exhausted and the two trailing edges develop into long slightly converging ridges (Fig. 119e). The development of such a sequence requires not only time but also the frequent occurrence of high velocity winds from one major direction. It also requires a large flattish area to the rear over which the sand can be moved. If the coastal zone is steep and particularly if there is great variation in

FIG. 119. Forms of transgressive dunes: (a) linear dunes, (b) transgressive sheet, (c) (d) (e) parabolic dunes, (f) wandering transgressive sheet.

approach direction of strong sand moving winds, then the parabolic dunes remain massive with a high ratio of width to length and the sequence leading to longitudinal dunes does not materialize. On the west coast of Tasmania, exposed to gales from both western quarters, parabolic dunes remain massive and wide. On the eastern part of the north coast, where strong winds come only from the north-west, there is a fine assortment of blowout, hairpin and longitudinal dunes in an association initiated in the Pleistocene. Some of the longitudinal arms are over fifteen kilometres long.

In conditions of relatively impotent plant growth the transgressive dunes may be barchans instead of parabolics. Snead (1967) described sparsely vegetated eroding beach ridge systems on the dry coast of Baluchistan being transgressed by massive barchans moving inland. One of these was a kilometre in width and had smaller barchans on top.

Where sufficient sand has been freed for blowouts to coalesce, and especially where a secondary dune system begins to tap a sand source on the beach, a large transgressive sheet may be generated and there is convergence towards the forms of free primary dunes, with small transverse dunes and barchans possibly being produced on the surface of the large transgressive sheet.

LITHIFIED DUNES

Processes of dune lithification which occur along some coasts are important from a geomorphic point of view, not only because they tend to preserve the dune form from further modification by wind and initiate something of a karst landscape, but also because they provide a limestone or lime-cemented sandstone rock which the sea fashions into cliffs, platforms and other shoreline features. Old lithified barrier systems, comprising dune and sometimes beach rocks may, with sea level change, form drowned or truncated offshore reefs as in the Bahamas (Newell and others, 1951), Brazil (Branner, 1904), Western Australia (Clarke and Phillips, 1953) and Sri Lanka (Swan, 1963). Many of these have subsequently been modified by the superimposition of coral and algal growth. In Australia there is a well-known contrast between the south and west coasts, where Pleistocene dune rocks are an important coastal element, and the east and north coasts, where more or less continuous leaching is the rule and old dunes develop advanced podsolized profiles, often with humus rich hardpans (Fig. 120).

Although both beach rocks and dune rocks are found along the warmer coasts of the world, their distribution is by no means coincident (Fig. 121). The development of

FIG. 120.   Pleistocene dunes with humate eroded at Evans Head, New
South Wales.

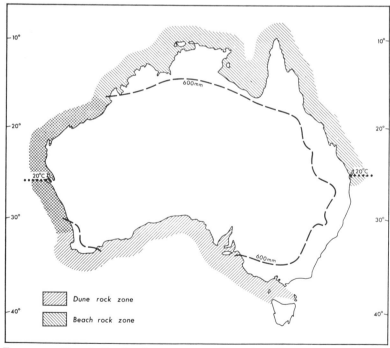

FIG. 121.   Broad distribution patterns of beach rocks and dune rocks in
Australia.   The 600 mm annual isohyet and 20°C cold month sea surface
isotherm are indicated. Beach rocks tend to occur on the warmer coast:
dune rocks on the drier coasts.

lithified dunes appears to demand a climate moist enough periodically to dissolve the calcium carbonate fraction in the sand but with a sufficiently high evaporation rate at other times to cause it to be retained in the profile and to reform as cement. It is characteristic therefore, of warm, seasonally wet and dry, climates of a variety of types and has been recorded for example, from the Mediterranean, Morocco, South Africa, Australia, Mauritius, Bermuda, The Bahamas, Madeira, Ecuador, Brazil, Hawaii, southern Arabia and western India. In general, dune rocks extend further into high latitudes than do beach rocks, but it is difficult to make meaningful deductions from this because of the frequent occurrence of Pleistocene fossil examples.

Lithification obviously requires an initial lime content but this need not be very high provided the climatic factors are favourable. On the coast of Israel, Yaalon (1967) found that carbonate values as low as about 8 per cent were sufficient to initiate cementation, although there is a very strong correlation within one environment between carbonate content and degree of lithification. The cliffed aeolianites illustrated in Fig. 122 have a carbonate content of around 50 per cent. It seems likely that, on coasts

FIG. 122. Cliffs of dune rock with basal notch; near Middleton, South Australia.

which are marginal climatically, a higher initial lime content becomes increasingly essential, but no work on this question has been reported. However it is clear that dune rocks include limestones or calcarenites with high carbonate contents and also lime cemented sandstones. Their degree of lithification varies enormously.

Where it occurs the influence of dune lithification on coastal evolution is considerable. The preservation of old dune fields and old barrier systems in this way ensures a greater degree of Pleistocene inheritance than occurs normally in the case of depositional forms. Drowned or truncated barriers formed at lower sea levels modify the coastal wave regime and the nature of sediment transport. Dune systems intersected by the present coast form cliffs and headlands which perpetuate coastal alignments from previous phases of the Pleistocene (Fig. 62, p. 90).

XI | TIDAL FLATS

There are three basic kinds of shoreline—the rocky shores described in Chapter VI, the beach and dune shores described in Chapters VII to X, and a third kind which are here called tidal flat shores. Rocky shores are generally associated with high levels of wave energy and, except where biological construction is important, are erosional and in retreat. Beach shores are found in association with a greater variety of energy levels spatially and temporally; they may vary all the way from being strongly progradational to strongly erosional. Tidal flat shores are confined to low energy environments. They may occupy very low energy sections of oceanic coast, such as western Florida, Sierra Leone and Exmouth Gulf in northwest Australia but on higher energy coasts they are confined to sheltered situations such as coastal lagoons, estuaries and deltas. Like beaches they may be prograding or eroding but, because of the low energy environment, changes take place much more slowly and less obviously. Lower energy and finer sediments also lead to more muted and less clearly defined landforms. Of the three kinds of shoreline, beach shores have been much the most studied and are much the most strongly represented in scientific journals and textbooks.

On tidal flats patterns of deposition and erosion are strongly influenced by tidal currents and only to a minor extent by waves. Much deposition is envisaged as taking place at times of slack water around high tide: it may take place with or without the assistance of plants. The role of plants on tidal flats is analogous to that on coastal dunes. Deposition may take place without them and both tidal flats and coastal dunes may be virtually plantless. The effect of vegetation is not so much on the total amount of sedimentation taking place as on the location of sedimentation. In both cases plants tend to reduce the shear velocity of the transporting medium over the ground surface and so encourage selective deposition.

By far the greatest proportion of literature on tidal flats relates to botanical and sedimentological aspects and there has been relatively little consideration of geomorphology. One result is that there are no generally agreed terms for recognizable landforms. Van Straaten (1954) distinguished three main zones on Dutch tidal flats and his division has been widely used since, at least within temperate regions. Somewhat above mean high water mark is the salt marsh, covered with vegetation, almost flat and more or less dissected by creeks. Between high water and mean low water are the tidal flats, normally bare of vegetation except perhaps for algae, and dissected by channel floors. Thirdly the channel floors themselves lie below low water mark. Thompson (1968) also recognized these three units, but since he was working in the very arid, saline environment of the Colorado delta where plant growth is extremely limited, he used the physiognomic terms 'high flat', 'intertidal flat' or 'intertidal zone' and 'subtidal mudflats' or 'subtidal zone'. Allen (1970) has used 'salt marsh', 'intertidal flat' and 'subtidal zone' for these same basic units. Most recently the contributors to a review volume on tidal deposits (Ginsburg, 1975) appear to recognize the same three zones but tend to refer to them as 'supratidal', 'intertidal' and 'subtidal'. Characteristically the terminology relates strongly to vegetation and tidal datum.

It seems clear that as morphological units Van Straaten's three basic zones can be extended into other environments, but in order to do this some revision of terminology is necessary so that landform names can be used independently of the vegetation types (Fig. 123). Since the highest unit lies somewhere near high water mark and is

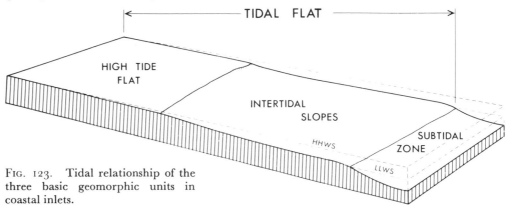

Fig. 123. Tidal relationship of the three basic geomorphic units in coastal inlets.

subhorizontal, the term 'high tide flat' seems appropriate. It may represent what is elsewhere called 'salt marsh', 'mangrove swamp', 'high flat' and 'supratidal zone'. The second unit seems most expressively referred to under the term 'intertidal slopes'. These are commonly referred to as 'intertidal flats' but by definition they slope between high and low water mark even though the slope may be extremely gentle. The term 'tidal flat' has been used not only in the broader sense in which it is used here but also for the intertidal slopes and for the lower part of very wide macrotidal beaches (Russell and McIntire, 1966; Komar, 1976 for instance). The third zone, the 'subtidal zone', suffers from much less terminological confusion and may be represented by a range of morphological features such as 'inshore bottom', 'flood channel', 'ebb channel' and 'river channel'.

That these three basic units may be identified through a wide range of climatic and vegetational environments (Fig. 124) reflects the azonal nature of their relationship to depositional controls. Thus the high tide flats are near high tide because, apart from organic accumulation, the extreme limit of deposition is provided by the level of the very highest tides: they are more or less flat because the water surface is more or less flat. Their surface is relatively stable and vegetated, and represents within limits an ultimate form. The morphology of the subtidal zone is clearly related to the hydrodynamic regime in the inlet. Although channels may change in form and position, such changes normally occur slowly and over a long period of time. The third

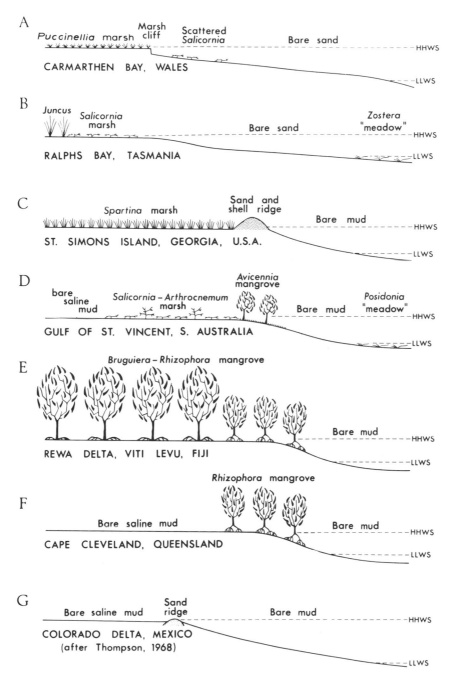

A
Puccinellia marsh Marsh cliff Scattered Salicornia Bare sand
CARMARTHEN BAY, WALES

B
Juncus Salicornia marsh Bare sand Zostera "meadow"
RALPHS BAY, TASMANIA

C
Spartina marsh Sand and shell ridge Bare mud
ST. SIMONS ISLAND, GEORGIA, U.S.A.

D
bare saline mud Salicornia – Arthrocnemum marsh Avicennia mangrove Bare mud Posidonia "meadow"
GULF OF ST. VINCENT, S. AUSTRALIA

E
Bruguiera – Rhizophora mangrove Bare mud
REWA DELTA, VITI LEVU, FIJI

F
Rhizophora mangrove Bare saline mud Bare mud
CAPE CLEVELAND, QUEENSLAND

G
Bare saline mud Sand ridge Bare mud
COLORADO DELTA, MEXICO
(after Thompson, 1968)

FIG. 124. Relationship of vegetation zones to geomorphic zones in a variety of environments. Profiles are diagrammatic and not to scale.

unit—that of the intertidal slopes—is usually one of considerable instability, where alternate deposition and erosion creates a substratum unfavourable to plant growth. In many cases, and particularly on temperate coasts, this zone is consequently bare or only partly vegetated.   Whereas the high tide flat represents a zone of predominantly vertical deposition in the discussion of inlet sedimentation by Van Straaten (1954), on the intertidal slopes deposition is predominantly lateral.   Allen (1970) has also outlined basic differences in sedimentation between all three zones.

The relationship between the high tide flat and the intertidal slope has many similarities to that between the river flood plain and the point bar, but most importantly in the present context it is strongly similar to that between the beach berm and the beach face.   Like the beach berm, the high tide flat must extend seaward as a result of successive deposition on the intertidal slope, but deposition continues to take place slowly on the flat itself as a result of 'overbank flow' at the highest tides.   In some situations, and especially perhaps where mangroves are present, deposition may occur preferentially on the outer edge of the high tide flat so giving a levee effect and a landward slope (see for instance Thom and others, 1975).   If erosion is occurring then the high tide flat may be cliffed, just as the beach berm may be cliffed.

The relative distinctness of the two upper zones is affected by a number of factors of which tidal range is probably the most important.   On coasts which are more or less tideless, the high tide flat is constructed by relatively irregular wind-induced tides—for example, in the Red Sea (Vesey-Fitzgerald, 1957) and Gulf of Mexico (Hayes, 1967b). Price (1954b) called these 'wind-tide flats'.   Under such conditions, particularly with high salinities and little or no plant colonization, the break between the high tide flat and intertidal slopes may be very difficult to determine.

At the other extreme on macrotidal coasts high tide flats and intertidal slopes may be so wide that they have a considerable amount of internal relief, especially because of the development of channel systems.   It is on sandy substrates in the mesotidal environment that similarities between beaches and tidal plains are most obvious to the eye.

HIGH TIDE FLATS

In contrast to the many intertidal slopes that are commonly called 'tidal flats', most high tide flats really do approach flatness.   They are usually more or less completely covered by mangrove woodlands or by salt marsh—the high marsh of many authors.   In temperate latitudes bare areas are normally confined to pans, produced from sections of dismembered creeks or residual from plant colonization.   In both cases the high salinity of the resulting depression is the main factor which enables it to persist.   In the tropics bare areas may be quite a lot more extensive, especially where rainfall is slight or seasonal.   Fosberg (1961) drew attention to vegetation free zones behind mangroves on the coasts of Nicaragua and Ecuador, and on the Queensland coast of Australia.   In these three instances the tidal range is high and the suggestion was that the bare zone represented the area inundated by high spring tides and dried out with resulting salt concentration between inundations.   That the same kind of phenomenon may occur with a small tidal range is demonstrated by the existence of similar but smaller areas behind mangrove and salt marsh communities in southern Australia.   On desert coasts saline flats may occur without associated vegetation as in the Colorado delta (Thompson, 1968; Fig. 124, p. 171) or with a few shrubby mangroves as along the coasts of the Red Sea (Vesey-Fitzgerald, 1955, 1957).   In such cases mats of algal growth, which occur on all coasts, may be particularly well developed and a rather extreme example of this phenomenon has been described by Kendall and Skipwith (1968) from the Persian Gulf.   One of the best illustrations of the effect of climate on the development of saline flats comes from the Queensland coast, where Macnae (1967) has described how the gap between the mangrove fringe and the inner edge of the bare saline flat increases with the increasingly dry seasonal climate between Innisfail and Townsville (Fig. 125).

FIG. 125.   Broad mangrove belts backed by small areas of salt marsh and bare saline patches on the coast of Upstart Bay, Queensland.   (Photo by D. Hopley.)

Whereas on temperate coasts the high tide flat is covered with salt marsh and on tropical humid coasts usually supports mangrove, there are many shores on which salt marsh and mangrove occur side by side.   Normally the mangrove trees form a fringe along the outer edge of the high tide flat and along the channels.   Chapman, in discussion on Fosberg (1966), has suggested that this pattern and juxtaposition occur where salinity becomes too high or water supply too deficient for mangroves to compete away from the most favourable situations.   In line with this suggestion, mangrove and salt marsh do occur together on coasts such as those of India where there is at least seasonal aridity, and it is noteworthy that in Sri Lanka salt marsh occurs only on the drier coasts. They may also occur together, as in southern Australia and northern New Zealand, where mangrove species are approaching their latitudinal limits.   Although these variations in the pattern of plant cover are striking to the eye, a great deal of work remains to be done in comparing the morphological consequences.

At the junction between the high tide flat and the intertidal slope there is a convexity, sometimes so gradual as to be difficult to distinguish but often quite sharp and even marked by a miniature cliff.   Where mangroves are dominant the break of slope is perhaps more often gradual and this may be related to the way in which the trees normally grow right across it (Fig. 126).   In temperate salt marshes however, a well-marked marsh cliff may separate 'high marsh' from 'low marsh' or the '*schorre*' from the '*slikke*'.   Chapman (1960) has associated marsh cliffs with rising coasts, and contrasted the emerging marshes of the Solway in Scotland, where multiple cliffs can be found, with the subsiding marshes of much of the east coast of the USA, where they are poorly developed or absent.   Guilcher (1958, p. 109) also suggests that marsh cliffing in Brittany may be connected with a recent lowering of sea level, but points out that the high marsh is still being slowly built up by deposition at the same time that it is being eroded laterally, and he leaves open the possibility that it results from a normal cycle.

Fig. 126.   Stilt-root mangroves, *Rhizophora*, growing on narrow intertidal slope north of Townsville, Queensland.

Observations in a large number of cases suggest to me that the cliff is largely, if not mainly, a function of the efficiency of wave attack.   It is certainly particularly evident in open estuaries on high wave energy coasts and its association with higher wave energy may be one reason why it is so often found in salt marsh and less often in mangrove.   Because the intertidal slope must slope between tide marks while the high tide flat is virtually horizontal, there must be a convex break of slope between them.   It seems that where wave attack is sufficient this break is sharpened into a tiny cliff, which, if there is sand available, often has a miniature beach piled up against it.

The most conspicuous geomorphic feature of most high tide flats is the system of tidal channels or creeks, which, as we have seen, may extend across the intertidal slopes with varying degrees of obviousness.   The three main distributional factors are the nature of the substratum, the type of plant cover and the tidal range.

A clay or silty-clay substratum is most conducive to channel development because the fine sediments encourage runoff and are cohesive enough to ensure that channel banks can maintain a steep slope. On sandy substrata channels are fewer and more poorly defined. This general effect of the substratum factor is well known and, as Chapman (1960) has pointed out, is exemplified by the contrast between marshes on the west and east coasts of Britain. The predominantly sandy marshes of the Irish Sea coast have more rudimentary channel systems than the predominantly muddy marshes of the North Sea coast.

The effect of vegetation is more problematical. In San Francisco Bay, Pestrong (1965) noted that *Salicornia*, with its more intricate and extensive root systems, maintained steep and often undercut banks, in contrast to *Spartina*, which maintained sloping banks. He concluded that asymmetry of cross profile was related to the vegetation on the banks rather than to the meander pattern. Chapman (1960, 1964) has suggested that the clump-like growth habit of some marsh plants—notably *Spartina* may favour the development of exceptionally intricate and tortuous meanders. Some plants are more effective than others in blocking and perhaps extinguishing channels: Thom (1967) concluded that *Rhizophora* mangroves caused non-tidal channels on the Mexican coast to silt at an accelerated rate, and also thought that they assisted levee building to some extent.

Tidal range has an obvious effect in controlling the extent of channel development through its influence on ebb discharge: it is also the major control of the channel depth. On microtidal coasts channels may be absent, and where they exist are commonly less than a metre in depth, whereas on macrotidal coasts they may be several metres deep and represent considerable features. As pointed out by Chapman (1964), tidal range also appears to influence the drainage pattern. In *Spartina* marshes along the Bristol Channel coast of Britain, where the range is over 12 m, relatively simple systems occur with small branched parallel channels at right angles to the main shoreline. In contrast, *Spartina* marshes in Poole Harbour on the south coast of England, where the tidal range at springs is only about 1·5 m, have more complex dendritic systems with much more tortuous meander patterns. It seems that the overall slope of the channel system is the direct influence and this is reflected in the way in which more tortuous systems on the high tide flat often develop more parallel patterns as they cross the intertidal slopes. The most striking parallel patterns (the candelabra pattern of Chapman) seem to evolve, as in Bridgewater Bay, south-west England, on muddy intertidal slopes with a large semidiurnal tide.

INTERTIDAL SLOPES

A complex channel system produces an equally complex agglomeration of slopes in the intertidal zone. Usually these slopes are bare muddy or sandy expanses, sometimes dissected by shallow creeks emanating from the high tide flats above but normally typified by smooth even outlines (Fig. 127). Exceptionally, the typical smoothness may be disrupted by microrelief forms, as in environments where the sea is seasonally frozen. Dionne (1968) has described pitted and boulder-strewn intertidal slopes from muddy shores of the St Lawrence estuary in Canada and also long grooves ploughing

FIG. 127.   **High tide flats covered with** *Spartina*, **intertidal slopes in mud and channel system at Sapelo Island, Georgia.**

the surface (Dionne, 1969).   All these effects are attributable to the varying action of blocks of ice.

The lower part of the intertidal slope, rarely uncovered at low tide, may extend into the habitat of 'sea-grasses' (*Zostera, Posidonia, Thalassia* and so on).   In temperate climates the upper part may carry 'low marsh' with plants such as *Puccinellia, Salicornia* or *Spartina*.   According to Chapman (1960), the low marsh lies at about mean high water and commonly undergoes more than 360 submergences a year: it is separated from the 'sea-grasses' by a bare zone, so that in discussions of classical successional concepts it has been doubted whether for instance, *Salicornia* may be thought of as truly succeeding *Zostera*.   In the tropics and on many warm temperate shores mangrove species may grow directly from low water mark so that the intertidal slopes may be largely vegetated and trees grow adjacent to 'sea-grasses' (Fig. 128).   The ability of mangroves to grow in the intertidal zone is probably due in part to the greater stature of the plants as compared with salt marsh herbs and grasses.   Fosberg (1966) suggested that this greater ability to maintain growth in periodically deeper water might be one way in which mangroves are particularly adapted to tropical deltas where deep flooding is a normal feature.   The same argument would seem to apply to their success on the lower intertidal slopes.   Another factor is the greater ability of viviparous mangrove species to establish themselves in spite of tide-induced water movements.   Wiehe (1935), in an investigation of the establishment of *Salicornia*, obtained data suggesting that the lower limit of successful growth may be set by physical removal of seedlings by the tide.   However the intertidal slopes remain a relatively unstable zone and mangrove establishment is often spasmodic, particularly where there is exposure to occasional strong wave attack.   In such circumstances their seaward edge is typically trimmed to form a sharp 'vegetational bluff' (West, 1956).

FIG. 128.   **Young** *Avicennia* **mangroves establishing themselves among 'sea-grasses'** *Ruppia* **and** *Posidonia* **on the lower intertidal slopes; Gulf of St Vincent, South Australia.**

Where tidal range is sufficient and the substratum is mainly of fine material, well defined channels, usually referred to as creeks, may extend from the high tide flat across the intertidal slopes.   Pestrong (1965) described how this happens on the mud flats of southern San Francisco Bay and contrasted this situation with that in the Dutch Wadden Sea, where the predominantly sandy sediments do not encourage the maintenance of clearly defined channel banks.

ESTUARIES AND LAGOONS

There are three broad classes of coastal inlet—lagoons, estuaries and deltas—which form a continuum and are difficult to define as entities (Fig. 129).   At one end of the continuum are lagoons produced solely by marine action and lying between some sort of barrier feature and the original coast.   Then come estuarine lagoons where a river emerges into a lagoon which still owes most of its form to the sea.   In the middle of the continuum are estuaries which are essentially the lower courses of rivers more or less invaded by the sea and which may or may not be partly blocked by marine barriers. Further along still are estuarine deltas in which there has been appreciable infilling of the estuary and the river bifurcates around the fill.   Finally at the other end of the continuum come deltas in which river action is so strong that it causes progradation in one of many forms.   Deltas themselves were arranged by Gulliver (1899) into a series in which river action becomes increasingly effective in relation to the forces of the sea.

A useful general review of these forms was provided by Emery and Stevenson

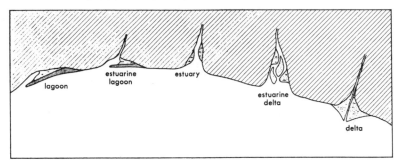

Fig. 129.   Diagrammatic representation of main inlet types, forming a continuum from coastal lagoons to deltas.

(1957).   The volumes edited by Ippen (1966), Lauff (1967) and Cronin (1975) and the extensive treatment of Samojlov (1956) are also particularly pertinent.

The apparent existence of a continuum of inlets, from the simple barrier-blocked lagoon owing all its form to marine processes to the birdsfoot delta formed virtually entirely by a river, emphasizes the way in which all such features may profitably be considered as resultants of marine and fluvial processes.   The most important way in which inlets vary geographically is in the relative size and differing nature of the contributions made by the two groups of processes.

FACTORS OF GEOGRAPHICAL VARIATION

FORM OF ORIGINAL INLET

The history of all inlets associated with rivers, begins with subaerial erosion at times of Pleistocene low sea level or even earlier (Galloway, 1970), and the drowning of this landscape by the postglacial marine transgression.   Although a legacy of multiple river downcutting is commonly decipherable, the results of the last sea level swing make the essential contribution to present inlet form.   Two factors in particular may be of special importance in influencing width and depth.

On coasts with a steep offshore ramp, downcutting during the low sea level phase would be greater than on coasts where there is a wide gently sloping shelf.   In the latter case a lowering of the fluvial base level would make little difference to the river gradient and the minimum of incision would be expected.   The effect would be accentuated if the hypothesis of differential isostatic movement of deep and shallow shelves, put forward by Bloom (1967) and mentioned in Chapter II, proves valid.   Other things being equal then the deepest inlets are likely to be along the steepest coasts.

The other major factor is the volume and periodicity of river discharge at the time of low sea level.   Along the most arid coasts discharge was generally non-existent except where exotic rivers such as the Nile and Colorado reached the sea and where short heavily loaded streams came from steep hinterlands, as along much of the Peruvian coast.   One of the most striking characteristics of coasts in dry regions is, as a result, an almost complete lack of inlets other than wave created lagoons.   On those coasts where runoff to the sea was significant, this is generally assumed to have been greater in volume during glacial low sea level phases, if only because of the reduced evaporation to be associated with colder periods.   In some regions it is also assumed to have been more episodic because of the contribution made by seasonal snowmelt and glacial meltwater. The effectiveness of river incision will have varied as a result.

SUPPLY OF RIVER SEDIMENT

The amount and character of sediments carried down the river in postglacial time has had an obvious effect on the extent to which the initial inlet has been filled.   Russell (1967) commented on the ephemeral nature of estuaries where rivers carry heavy loads of sediment and cited in particular the case of Mobile Bay in Alabama, now about 40 km long and almost filled, but originally extending inland for about 140 km.   The effect has probably been most marked in tectonically active areas of the wet tropics where extremely rapid fluvial progradation has been recorded.

The dominant particle size is also important.   Normally, as river influence increases, particle size decreases.   So non-estuarine lagoons are usually sandy, estuaries muddier and deltas muddiest, but much individual variation occurs.   Rivers draining an area with mainly siliceous rocks may carry great quantities of sand to the coast whereas others may transport loads in the finer grade sizes.   The contrast between muddy and sandy inlets is an important one, not only because it affects the development of constituent forms such as channel systems, and influences colonization by geomorphically important vegetation, but also because it has an effect on the extent to which marine influence may be exerted.   A river bringing down large quantities of coarser materials is supplying sediment which can be piled into barrier features by waves: a river carrying mostly or entirely mud is not.

On a global scale we have seen that fluvial influence is at its greatest in low latitudes: it is here that the filling of postglacial inlets has proceeded most rapidly and the building of deltas and alluvial plains has been most marked.   We have already noted too a broad contrast between on the one hand the wet tropics, where sediments are largely muddy and fluvial construction tends to dominate so that marine barriers are commonly perched in chenier fashion on a basement of fines, and on the other hand the semi-arid or seasonally wet tropics, where sand has been or is being brought down in greatest quantity and wave built barrier systems tend to contrast with relatively unfilled lagoonal environments to landward.   Tricart and Cailleux (1965) contrast the coast of Rio Grande do Sul in southern Brazil, where there is strong sand supply and big barriers behind which little silting has occurred, with the Guiana coast, which is practically destitute of lagoons, and beaches may form on or even behind mudflats as described by Vann (1959).

WAVE INFLUENCES

Where there is a sufficiency of material capable of being built into beaches the most fundamental effect of waves is to construct barriers.   These create lagoons in their entirety and affect the general configuration of estuaries. The extent of barrier construction, and especially the extent to which inlets may be closed by barriers, control the degree to which tidal influences may be experienced in the lagoon or estuary.

Waves generated within the enclosed body of water may erode its shores and cause sediment to be internally redistributed. However, wave influences are relatively small and the most important marine processes are those associated with the tides.

TIDAL INFLUENCES

In tidal situations a body of water—the tidal prism—enters and leaves the lagoon or estuary during the six hourly or twelve hourly tidal cycle. Where tides are mixed there are corresponding asymmetries in the tidal prism. At the entrance the height of the tidal prism is close to the tidal range in the adjoining ocean but it changes landward according to the configuration of the lagoon or estuary basin. In funnel-shaped estuaries which converge landward, tidal amplitude tends to increase, often with the occurrence of a tidal bore. In parallel sided estuaries and in lagoons, tidal amplitude tends to diminish landward.

Lagoons into which no fresh-water flows may have water characteristics essentially similar to those of the adjoining ocean. However, on coasts where evaporation rates are high and especially along desert coasts, salinities may be notably higher within the inlet than outside. One of the most intensively studied of such hypersaline inlets is the Laguna Madre on the south Texas coast (Fisk, 1959; Hedgpeth, 1967), where low rainfall, high evaporation, a shallow lagoon basin, general lack of stream inflow and scarcity of oceanic connections produces salinities averaging about three times greater than those in the open waters of the Gulf of Mexico. Notable features of the lagoon floor include gypsum precipitation and the formation of algal mats.

If there is a significant fresh-water inflow as in normal estuaries and deltas, the sedimentation pattern is influenced by the extent of mixing which occurs between fresh-water and salt (Fig. 130). Simmons (1966) suggested that the likelihood of mixing could be estimated by dividing the volume of fresh-water entering the estuary during a tidal cycle by the tidal prism. If the ratio is 1·0 or more, the estuary is likely to be of a highly stratified type, characterized by an invading salt wedge at the bottom moving in and out with the tide and from which there is negligible diffusion to the strong fresh-water outflow at the surface. Under these conditions sedimentation tends to take place at the tip of the salt water wedge. A ratio in the range of 0·2 to 0·5 would be

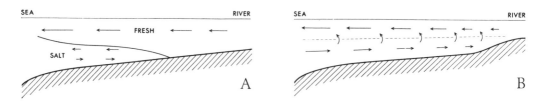

FIG. 130. Diagrammatic sections to show water mixing characteristics in (a) stratified (salt wedge) and (b) mixed types of estuaries. (After Bowden in Lauff, 1967.)

associated with a partly mixed, two layer flow type, in which there is a certain amount of entrainment of bottom salt water into the outflowing fresh-water higher up. Sedimentation in this case usually tends to be at a maximum near the nodal point or points for bottom flow predominance. With a ratio of 0·1 or less the estuary is likely to be of the well-mixed, vertically homogeneous, type where salinities vary little from surface to bottom over the entire distance of tidal intrusion. In this condition it is doubtful whether the vertical circulation pattern has a dominating effect on the locus of deposition, which is more likely to be influenced by inlet configuration. In general, therefore, increased mixing promotes more dispersed sedimentation, but also increases flocculation of fines, which is the process which enables most clay material to be deposited. Estuaries where there is a marked seasonal or ephemeral change in river discharge will change concurrently in mixing type, so that sedimentation conditions vary accordingly.

A far-reaching effect of the water mixing process is the production of gravitational currents that are superimposed on the tidal ebb and flood. Upward entrainment of salt water causes landward flow to be augmented and results in bottom currents flowing for longer periods and at higher velocities in a landward direction, whereas surface currents flow more strongly seaward. In lagoons and parallel sided estuaries the landward decrease in tidal amplitude means that water surface gradients and flood tide currents are strongest at high water. Conversely ebb tide currents are strongest at low water. One result is that intertidal sediments are transported landward by flood currents but are subaerially exposed at low water when maximum ebb velocities occur (Hines, 1975).

All this results in an overall tendency for coarser sediments, transported as bed load, to move landward rather than seaward. It is easier for such sediments to enter estuaries from seaward and correspondingly difficult for any material supplied by rivers to pass out to sea. Work in tidal estuaries in many parts of the world in recent years has confirmed the overall tendency for them to fill from seaward. For instance the predominantly landward travel of bottom sediments in east-coast estuaries of USA was described by Meade (1969) and Moore (1968) concluded that estuaries in Cardigan Bay in Wales were being filled from the sea. On the other hand the predominance of outward flow near the surface enables fine suspended sediments to move seaward and in highly stratified conditions a strong surface stream of fresh-water may carry fine material out beyond the coast for enormous distances. The work of de Groot (summarized 1966) in tracing muds from the Amazon and from the Chao-Phya in Thailand gives some indication of the distances which may be involved. Although there do not seem to be many data relating to the question, it seems probable that the ability of rivers to move sand-sized material through their estuaries at times of flood is related to a greater proportion of sand going into suspension at such times.

Principally because tidal flood currents begin to flow before the ebb has finished and vice versa, ebb and flood currents are mutually evasive and tend to follow different paths through the estuary or lagoon. Flood channels, tending to deepen seaward, and ebb channels, tending to deepen landward, may normally be identified. In macrotidal

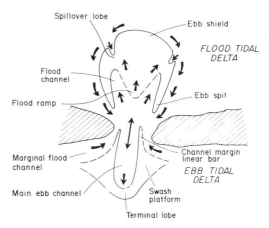

FIG. 131. Diagrammatic inlet threshold with flood tidal and ebb tidal deltas and terminology after Hayes (1975). In nature flood tidal deltas are normally significantly bigger than ebb tidal deltas the form of which may be strongly modified by wave attack.

environments these channels are strongly linear and parallel: in mesotidal and microtidal situations they are more horseshoe-like in plan.

Particularly in mesotidal environments, well-marked ebb and flood tidal deltas form on either side of the inlet. The flood tidal delta tends to be much larger because of the dominantly inward movement of sand. It may entirely fill the estuary or, as in southern New South Wales (Bird, 1967), form a threshold, prograding upstream into a residual deep water reach. Higher up the estuary the ebb flow tends to be confined to the main river channel, while flood channels cross the point bars as described by Van Veen (1950). A terminology of ebb and flood tidal deltas has been formulated by Hayes and his co-workers (Hayes, 1975) and is given in Fig. 131.

EFFECT OF TIDAL RANGE

In practice tidal range appears much the biggest single factor influencing variations in the form and sedimentary character of lagoons and estuaries. With few exceptions such as the Amazon and the Mississippi, river flow tends to play a very minor role in determining water circulation compared with the size of the tidal prism. As discussed earlier (p. 109) tidal range is also an important determinant of the significance of wave action, with barrier construction being strongly encouraged in microtidal and mesotidal environments. This has a fundamental effect on the form of estuaries and the existence of lagoons.

Resulting from this, Hayes (1975) has proposed general depositional models for estuaries on microtidal, mesotidal and macrotidal coasts. Microtidal estuaries are dominated by river and wave action so that characteristic features are small river deltas and small wave constructed features occurring internally, washover fans where barriers occur, and minor development of tidal deltas. In mesotidal estuaries, tidal action predominates and results in large tidal deltas whereas in macrotidal estuaries tidal dominance is so great that the characteristic depositional forms are linear banks in the centre of what is usually a broad-mouthed, funnel-shaped re-entrant.

DELTA FORMS

Gulliver's (1899) classification of deltas took account only of the actual coastal outline, which was conceived as the result of the balance between fluvial and marine forces

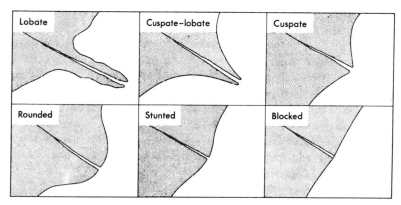

FIG. 132. The delta outline types of Gulliver (1899). The 'rounded' type is now more usually termed 'arcuate'.

(Fig. 132). So he proposed a series—lobate, cuspate-lobate, cuspate, rounded, stunted and blocked—in increasing order of marine influence, although, following the suggestion of Johnson (1919), the rounded type has more usually been termed arcuate. Where there are two or more distributaries the outline may be more complex so that, for example, the Mississippi delta is multi-lobate and the Nile multi-cuspate (or multi-cuspate-lobate according to Gulliver). Arcuate deltas such as that of the Niger retain their smooth outlines irrespective of the number of distributaries. In spite of the difficulty of fitting in some indeterminate examples, Gulliver's terminology remains useful for gross description. More important from the point of view of the present discussion, it does appear to some extent to reflect variation in the relative efficiency of river deposition and wave attack. Some of the most typical lobate deltas have formed in lagoons, estuaries and lakes where wave energy is minimal and the Mississippi delta, which is the supreme example of an open sea lobate delta, has developed in relation to high rates of fluvial deposition and low wave energy. Conversely, the Niger, with a much smaller sediment load than the Mississippi and entering the South Atlantic in opposition to prevailing big swell from the south, has produced one of the most perfect of arcuate deltas.

Contrasts appear also when the component sections of deltas are examined. If we

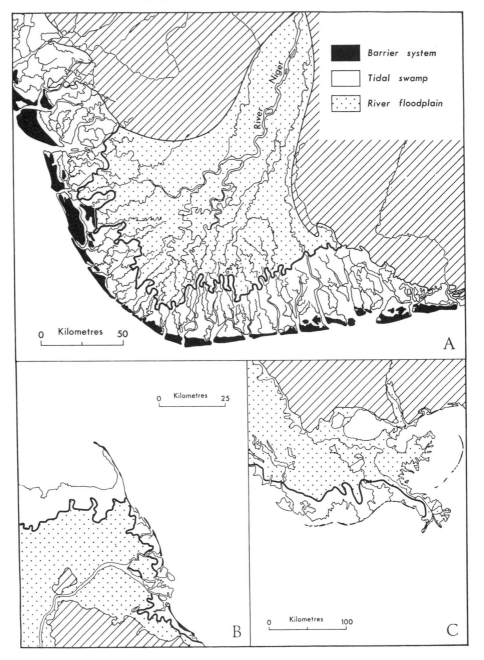

FIG. 133.   Disposition and extent of the three major delta zones in (A) the Niger delta (after Allen, 1965); (B) the Burdekin delta (after Hopley, 1970); (C) the Mississippi delta (mainly after Fisk, 1944).   Note that the scale varies between maps.

take the simplest division between fluvially built plains and levees, wave built barrier systems and intervening zones of tidal sedimentation, the relative size and disposition of these varies considerably from delta to delta with factors which have already been listed.   Figure 133 shows the Niger delta with strongly developed symmetrical barrier systems, the Burdekin with more weakly developed asymmetrical barriers resulting from a southerly wave regime, and the Mississippi where barriers are less important still in relation to the fluvial forms.   The weaker and less extensive barrier systems tend to be associated with less extensive tidal plains, since generally these arise in the shelter of the barrier.   In deltas like the Ganges with a large tidal range, barriers are very poorly developed or non-existent: on the other hand the neighbouring delta of the Mahanadi, where tidal range is less and sand supply by littoral drift from the south is strong, incorporates relatively large barrier systems.

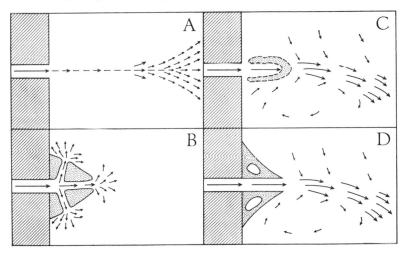

FIG. 134.   Flow types of Bates (1963) with associated deltaic patterns. (A): hyperpycnal flow and submarine delta; (B): homopycnal flow and Gilbert-type delta with topset, foreset and bottomset beds; (C): hypopycnal flow with limited sediment supply produces a lunate bar; (D): hypopycnal flow with moderate sediment supply produces a typical marine littoral delta of cuspate, arcuate or birdsfoot type.

However, these simple correlations can not be taken too far because other factors are involved.   Many deltas have undergone a history of construction and destruction in which major distributaries have changed position several times.   As in the Mississippi and Burdekin deltas, this is an important cause of asymmetry and the resulting form is impossible to analyse genetically without detailed stratigraphic work.

In recent years more sophisticated systems of delta classification have been attempted incorporating geomorphic features other than just simple plan outline.   Bates (1953) suggested a breakdown according to the ratio between density of river water and density of water in the accommodating basin, since this affects the types of flow pattern.   He distinguished three types(Fig. 134).

Hyperpycnal flow (inflow more dense) is associated with a plane jet pattern. Sediment is carried considerable distances at depth by turbidity currents.

Homopycnal flow (inflow equally dense) is associated with an axial jet pattern. Considerable mixing takes place and a system of shoals and banks is formed.

Hypopycnal flow (inflow less dense) is associated with a plane jet pattern, but in contrast to the first case the river water tends to float on top of the seawater and deposition takes place at a considerable distance in the form of horseshoe shoals.

The first two cases are very largely confined to lakes, a major exception being the Hwang-Ho, which has by far the greatest load to discharge ratio of any major river and which is apparently characterised by hyperpycnal flow. The vast majority of deltas come under the third heading and the Bates categories are thus limited in usefulness for the present discussion.

A much more comprehensive classification of estuaries and deltas was put forward in the book by Samojlov (1952 in Russian, translated into German 1956). The classification itself was reproduced by Volker (1966) and is essentially descriptive in nature, relying on the number and distance apart of distributaries and the character of tidal flats and the offshore zone. However, Volker has pointed out the way in which many of the characters used by Samojlov appear to be related to the overall slope of a delta from apex to sea. Variation in slope is considerable, so that while the overall gradient of the Colorado delta is around 1:3500 that of the Mississippi delta is about 1:50000 and that of the Lena delta about 1:100000. Steeper overall slopes are associated with fewer distributaries, relatively high level interdistributary areas and poor levee development. Conversely, deltas with a low overall gradient from the apex to the sea tend to have many distributaries with well marked levees and the interdistributary areas are low and swampy. Steep deltas tend to occur in arid and semi-arid areas and at the mouths of steeper, shorter rivers, and figures presented by Volker strongly suggest that the connecting factor is relative coarseness of the sediments making up the fluvial load. Although other genetic factors and perhaps also the complicated history of many deltas prevent a close correlation, Volker's data do show that the steepest deltas are those with the coarsest sediments.

An important factor which also affects overall gradient and has an effect on the height and form of the seaward section of relatively flat deltas is the tidal range. Where this is appreciable, as in the Ganges and Irrawaddy (range over 5 m), tidal action may be more successful than that of the river in building levees. The result is that the coastal strip tends to be higher than inland parts and, as the delta progrades, chains of depressions are produced parallel to the coast, like the bhils of the Ganges described by Strickland (1940). Vegetation is probably an important factor in this and, as noted by Allen (1965), the production of channels parallel to the coast in tropical deltas with a relatively large tidal range is aided by the stronger growth of plants, especially mangroves, in the zone of periodic inundation (Fig. 135). It may also be aided by headward erosion of channels and by channel capture in deltas with strong tides (Santema, 1966).

More recently Silvester and de la Cruz (1970) have attempted a quantitative approach to the isolation of delta forming forces by regression analysis of delta para-

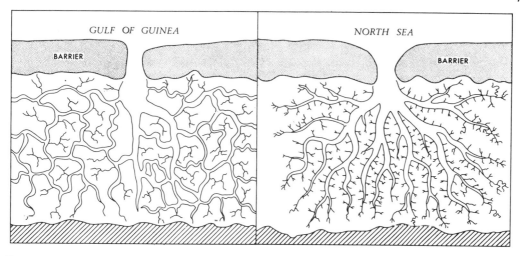

FIG. 135. Typical channel patterns in tidal plains of Niger delta and Dutch wadden. (After. Allen, 1965.) The dendritic pattern of temperate latitudes is contrasted with a reticulate pattern where mangroves are able to colonise much of the zone inundated by the tide. However, as noted by Bird (1968), many Australian mangrove swamps display more dendritic channel patterns and other factors must be involved.

meters against values for presumed factors. They found that the apex to sea dimension varied directly with river discharge and inversely with river gradient inland, continental slope offshore, sediment particle size and tidal range. Delta width also varied inversely with river gradient and tidal range, but was also strongly related to the wave climate, in that wider deltas tend to be associated with strong oblique swell. These authors concluded that temperature is an important ultimate control of many aspects of delta formation. High average air temperatures tend to lead to the drying out of sediments and so allow them to be fixed before subsequent floods or high tides, and they promote quicker plant growth on land and in the water. High sea temperatures promote the precipitation of carbonates and provide high salinity values which cause flocculation and deposition of bed load well upstream of delta mouths.

Wright and Coleman (1973) have examined the relative contribution of fluvial and marine processes in influencing the morphology and sedimentology of a number of major deltas. They concluded that the balance between nearshore wave power and the discharge effectiveness of the river is critical. The main way in which the river opposes the sea is by construction of a shallow offshore profile which attenuates waves coming in from deep water.

XII | CONCLUSION

From the preceding discussion there emerge three broad latitudinal zones, between which important shore processes display significant differences, and these may be referred to as low-latitude, mid-latitude and high-latitude. Each of them may be subdivided in less clear, more arguable, but apparently valid ways. Within each of the three broad zones it is possible to suggest a conceptual model of shoreline evolution which could be made to incorporate variations in such additional factors as structure and tidal regime. What is much more difficult is to attempt to portray such zones on a map. Mainly this is because of the azonal effect of non-climatic factors: because the climatic factors themselves operate in complex fashion and it is difficult to isolate single parameters: because of the appreciable effect of historical inheritance on many coasts—especially those which are climatically marginal—and because of the inherent difficulty anyway of drawing lines on maps where none exist in nature.

With these reservations in mind, the lines drawn in Fig. 136 are a subjective approximation to the zonal boundaries. It will be seen that the line between low-latitude and mid-latitude zones comes very close to 40° North and South, but, because the line bounding high-latitude coasts is taken as the general limit of shore ice, its course in the northern hemisphere is considerably more erratic than in the south. In this scheme there are very few mid-latitude coasts in the southern hemisphere and their particularly great extent in western Europe is very evident.

I conclude that the most important latitudinal distinction is between cool temperate coasts and those which are warm temperate or warmer, and not between non-tropical and tropical nor between non-biogenous and biogenous coasts.

LOW-LATITUDE COASTS

The major characteristics of low-latitude coasts are reduced wave energy and a relatively consistent direction of wave approach in swell and trade wind environments: geomorphically significant construction by algae and in some areas by corals: lithification of beaches and dunes: abundant coastal sediments, partly built into massive barrier systems and rarely containing pebbles: relatively few rocky coasts with weak cliff and shore platform development, mainly by processes of weathering, solution and biological erosion, so that platforms tend to be horizontal: poor development of coastal dunes, and, except in some peripheral sections, occurrence of tidal woodlands.

Discernible large scale variations exist among these coasts, related in the main to the rainfall regime. On perennially wet, hot coasts there is a particular abundance of mud

188

and it is here that mangrove reaches its ultimate development.   Dunes are especially poorly represented and often quite lacking.   Mass movement is of major importance in cliff evolution and near-vertical profiles are not much in evidence.   Seasonally dry coasts are those where coastal sands are especially abundant and pebbles may make an appearance along the shore.   Wetting and drying processes of rock weathering are potent, and dune rocks reach their greatest development.   Perennially dry coasts also show effects of wetting and drying processes, but mass movement is so minimal that where cliffs occur they commonly approach the vertical.   Free primary dunes are to be found—though of no great dimension.   Estuaries and deltas are extremely scarce and, where tidal plains occur in lagoons, they exhibit extensive bare saline areas, sometimes abundantly colonized by algae.

MID-LATITUDE COASTS

Mid-latitude coasts form a zone of high wave energy, where frontal storm activity is at a maximum.   Hard rock coasts are more extensive than in low-latitudes and cliffs are relatively strongly developed under the influence of more intensive quarrying and abrasion processes.   These processes also produce typical sloping intertidal shore platforms.   Beaches are correspondingly less in evidence, barrier systems relatively weak and often capped by pebbles, but where sand beaches do occur, they give rise to what in general are the world's most massive coastal dunes.   Except for the influence of vegetation on the evolution of dunes and tidal plains, biogenic effects are insignificant and the natural cycling of carbonates is not an appreciable factor.

The most important sub-division of this zone may be that between those sections which were glaciated in Pleistocene times and those which were not.   Glaciation left a legacy, not only of drowned landforms but of great bodies of sediment which have been reworked by later seas.

HIGH-LATITUDE COASTS

The shores of high-latitude coasts are frozen for at least part of the year and wave energy levels are low.   Coarse sediments, especially in the pebble grade, are relatively abundant and barrier construction is well in evidence.   In detail, beaches show forms resulting from seasonal ice action.   Coastal dunes are very limited and tidal flats are dominated by grassy vegetation.   Cliff morphology is often strongly influenced by the effects of mass movement, both past and present, but there is considerable divergence of opinion on the extent to which retreat of hard rock cliffs may result from various freeze–thaw processes.

The most important intrazonal differences result from the varying length of the season of marine freeze-up.   The longer the sea freezes over, the less obvious are the effects of what are regarded elsewhere as normal shore processes.

OTHER BASES OF DIFFERENTIATION

The broad zones that have been defined are basically climatic in origin, either directly or indirectly.   Factors of coastal variation which are not climatically controlled, cannot, with perhaps one major exception, be considered in terms of such broad world distribution patterns, but this does not necessarily make them less important.   There are three major controls of coastal differentiation which cut across latitudinal zones and tend towards convergence of form in contrasting climates—tidal regime, structure and sediment transport system.

TIDAL REGIME

Neither tidal type nor tidal range are significantly related to the latitudinal zones delimited here, although an analysis of average tidal range per unit length of coast in

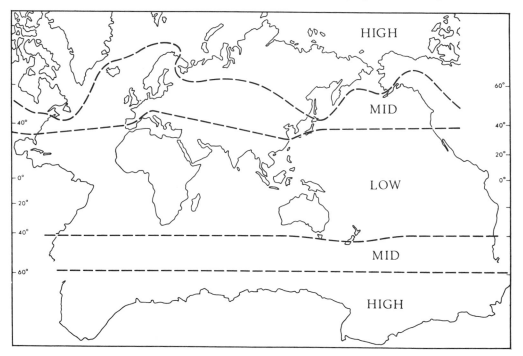

FIG. 136. Major shore process zones of the world.

the three zones shows that high-latitude coasts are strongly microtidal and the mid-latitude zone contains the highest proportion of macrotidal coasts.   Examination of Fig. 136 and of Fig. 33 (p. 51) will show, however that there are some striking exceptions.

We have seen that by controlling the width of the zone of wave attack and by influencing the strength of tidal currents and estuarine water systems, tidal range in particular has a vital effect on such things as beach profiles, barrier building effectiveness, dune development, shore platform evolution and tidal plain sedimentation.   Macrotidal coasts everywhere will tend therefore, to have some features in common: the extraordinarily wide lower beach zone of the macrotidal Australian tropics, for instance, has morphological counterparts on macrotidal coasts in western Europe. In a similar way, barrier beaches in the tropics and in the arctic have both come into being at least in part because of low tidal ranges.

STRUCTURE

More important still is the effect of variation in structure. The distinction on a world scale between plate-edge (Pacific) coasts and the various types of plate-imbedded (Atlantic) coasts is a fundamental one, with many repercussions on such factors as rock type and attitude, tectonic stability and sediment supply. This dichotomy cuts right across the climatically controlled latitudinal zones and creates some striking contrasts, as between the west and east coasts of the Americas, or between South America and Africa. In terms of coastal classification the most rewarding overall scheme may eventually result from superimposition of a latitudinal zonation, reflecting shore processes and second and third order landforms, on to a predominantly longitudinal scheme, mainly reflecting geophysical processes and first order landforms.

More local structural variations are obviously less significant in terms of world-wide differentiation, but in earlier discussion the effects of many climatically controlled factors have had to be circumscribed in terms of structure. On rocky coasts in particular, landform evolution is controlled by a complex interaction of climatically and structurally based factors and, while such variables as wave energy and air temperature may primarily decide the potential processes, the actual processes which are able to operate depend in large part on structure. The distinctive appearance in all parts of the world of granite coasts, for instance, has already been noted.

SEDIMENT TRANSPORT SYSTEM

The study of transport systems in the broadest sense is central to an understanding of coastlines. Erosional landforms produce sediment which is transported and deposited to create constructional forms. In addition much sediment is introduced from other sources. Chapter VII attempted to review variations in the nature of sediment sources and sediment traps and to suggest something of the significance of degrees of freedom of transport. It is rather surprising that so little explicit discussion of these topics is to be found in the literature on coasts and especially that they have not been considered as possible criteria in classification. The basic difficulty is that the necessary data must result in the main from detailed field study, but, as knowledge of world coasts increases, such information holds promise of providing the foundation for a dynamic classification, at least of depositional shores, full of practical as well as academic implications.

There are some latitudinal connotations in relation to transport systems, and sediment source in particular varies significantly in this sense, but there are so many other factors involved, such as structure and continental orientation, that the final picture must be very complex.

It has already been postulated that, on low-latitude coasts, littoral transport is generally more uni-directional and forms large-scale patterns in response to the comparatively steady approach of trade wind waves and swell from higher latitudes. This situation may prove eventually to contrast significantly with the mid-latitude zone, where transport systems are probably more complicated.

THE SIGNIFICANCE OF VARIATION

Having summarized very briefly the main conclusions of this study, it may be appropriate to end with some discussion of the utility of the findings.   There would appear to be five main reasons why it is important to study locational variation in coastal process and form.

THE GEOGRAPHICAL APPROACH

The first, and probably most important reason is that the geographer's approach to the study of phenomena by examining the way in which they vary in space is, or at least ought to be, a fundamental scientific method.   The more we can find out about why a process or a form varies from place to place and occurs or does not occur, the more we know of how the process operates and how the form evolves.   This statement is so self-evident as to appear trite but perhaps it is not unfair to say that geographer-geomorphologists generally have not pursued this line of approach with enough vigour.   In coastal geomorphology, the study of coastal variation will continue to be a most rewarding way in which we will find out more about the coastal system.

ECONOMY OF ARGUMENT

It would be easy, but doubtless invidious, to give examples of arguments which have arisen in geomorphology because workers in different parts of the world thought that conclusions reached by their studies were correct and those reached by others somewhere else were wrong, although all were correct for their particular environments.   This sort of argument at cross purposes has gone on in several fields of coastal geomorphology and has proved very wasteful of effort.   It is clear that an appreciation of the nature and extent of the variation of coastal phenomena between different environments will do much to avoid such waste.

HISTORICAL EXTRAPOLATION

One of the criticisms most often levelled against attempts to delineate morphogenic regions or systems is due to the fact that the present environment is a comparatively recent one.   The coastal complex includes features inherited in varying degree from the past and particularly from the relatively violent climatic and sea level oscillations of the Pleistocene.   So one cannot always argue directly from present process to present form.   The criticism is a cogent one, but one could reason in reverse with equal cogency. If the present is the key to the past (and there seems general agreement that, however imperfect, it is the only key we have) then we must understand the effect of environments varying geographically today before we can understand the effects of environments varying historically in the past. Attempts to identify old shorelines and to deduce old sea levels, for instance, must rely on an appreciation of the environmental conditions operating at the time and the nature and effect of likely processes.

ENGINEERING PROBLEMS

Civil engineers have made enormous contributions to our knowledge of the coast, but this knowledge has been gained mostly in the mid-latitude zone and there has been a tendency to extrapolate directly into other environments. Differences in the littoral transport system are of special importance here and many engineering manuals and rules of thumb reflect experience on shores of free transport. Thus whereas the most important sediment movements along most coasts of the USA are alongshore, experience in Tasmania suggests strongly that the most important movements there are transverse to the shore and this may be true of much of the coast of south-eastern Australia. Where consultant engineers are able to carry out adequate preliminary surveys to establish the nature of the environment, the problem does not arise and a valuable new set of data becomes available to fill out the total picture: but there is an obvious danger attached to any attempt to proceed from a tacit assumption that problems in one environment can be solved by rules of thumb developed in others.

IDENTIFICATION OF SYSTEMS

The most important contribution which coastal engineers have made to shoreline studies is in the development of theoretical relationships which potentially enable accumulated data to be fed into a quantified system. If, as seems likely, the future of coastal geomorphology lies in the increasing quantification of the inputs and outputs of coastal systems, then the geographical approach of identifying and explaining variations from place to place has an important part to play in defining the systems. We have some distance to go yet before this stage is reached, and coastal geomorphology lags behind some other branches of geomorphology in this respect, but it is a goal worth striving for.

BIBLIOGRAPHY

ALLEN, J. R. L. 1965. Coastal geomorphology of eastern Nigeria: beach ridge barrier islands and vegetated tidal flats, *Geologie en Mijnbouw*, **44**, 1–21.

ALLEN, J. R. L. 1970. *Physical processes of sedimentation*. Allen and Unwin, London.

ARE, F. E. 1968. Development of the relief of thermoabrasive coasts, *Izv Akad. Nauk SSSR, ser. geogr, geofiz.*, **1**, 92–100. (In Russian.)

ARTHUR, R. S. 1949. Variability in direction of wave travel. *Ann. N.Y. Acad. Sci.*, **51**, 511–22.

AUFRÈRE, L. 1936. Le rôle du climat dans l'activité morphologique littorale. *C. r. 14th Congr. internat. géogr.*, 1934, **2**, Warsaw.

BAGNOLD, R. A. 1940. Beach formation by waves: some model experiments in a wave tank. *J. Inst. Civ. Eng.*, **15**, 27–52.

BAGNOLD, R. A. 1954. *The physics of blown sand and desert dunes.* 2nd edn, Methuen, London.

BALL, M. M., SHINN, E. A., and STOCKMAN, K. W. 1967. The geologic effects of hurricane Donna in South Florida. *J. Geol*, **75**, 583–97.

BARBER, N. F., and URSELL, F. 1948. The generation and propagation of ocean waves and swell. *Phil. Trans. Roy. Soc. London, Series A*, **240**, 527–60.

BARTRUM, J. A. 1926. 'Abnormal' shore platforms. *J. Geology*, **34**, 793–806.

BASCOM, W. N. 1951. The relationship between sand size and beach face slope. *Trans. Am. geophys. Un.*, **32**, 866–74.

BASCOM, W. N. 1954. The control of stream outlets by wave refraction. *J. Geol.*, **62**, 600–5.

BASCOM, W. N. 1964. *Waves and beaches.* New York.

BATES, C. C. 1953. Rational theory of delta formation. *Bull. Am. Ass. petrol. Geol.*, **37**, 2119–62.

BECKER, R. 1936. Dünung und Wind des Atlantischen Ozeans im Bereich des meteorologischen Äquators. *Ann. d. Hydrographie u. mar. Meteorologie*, Zweites Köppen-Heft, 1–4.

BELLKNAP, R. L. 1928. Some Greenland sand dunes. *Pap. Mich. Acad. Sci. Arts and Letters*, **10**, 198.

BELLY, P. 1964. Sand movement by wind. *Tech. Memo. Coastal Eng. Res. Center U.S.*, No. 1.

BIRD, E. C. F. 1963. The physiography of the Gippsland Lakes, Australia. *Zeit. f. Geomorph.*, **7**, 232–45.

BIRD, E. C. F. 1965. The formation of coastal dunes in the humid tropics: some evidence from North Queensland. *Austr. J. Sci.*, **27**, 258–9.

BIRD, E. C. F. 1967. Depositional features in estuaries and lagoons on the south coast of New South Wales. *Austr. Geogr. Studies*, **5**, 113–24.

BIRD, E. C. F. 1968 (2nd edn 1976). *Coasts.* Australian Nat. Univ. Press, Canberra.

BIRD, E. C. F. 1976. *Shoreline changes during the past century* I.G.U. Working Group on the dynamics of shoreline erosion, Melbourne (mimeo).

BIRD, E. C. F. 1978. The nature and source of beach materials on the Australian coast: *in* Davies, J. L. and Williams, M. A. J. (eds) *Landform evolution in Australasia*, 144–57.

BIRD, E. C. F., and HOPLEY, D. 1969. Geomorphological features on a humid tropical sector of the Australian coast. *Austr. Geogr. Studies*, **7**, 89–108.

BLOOM, A. L. 1967. Pleistocene shorelines: a new test of isostasy. *Bull. geol. Soc. Am.*, **78**, 1477–94.

BLOOM, A. L. 1974. Geomorphology of reef complexes: *in* Laporte, L. F. (ed.) *Reefs in time and space*, Soc. Econ. Pal. Min., Spec. Pub. 18, 1–8.

BLOOM, A. L., BROECKER, W. S. CHAPPELL, J. M. A., MATTHEWS, R. K. and MESOLELLA, K. J. 1974. Quaternary sea level fluctuations on a tectonic coast: new ^{230}Th/^{234}U dates from the Huon Peninsula, New Guinea. *Quaternary Res.*, **4**, 185–205.

BOUGHEY, A. S. 1957. Ecological studies of tropical coast-lines, 1. The Gold Coast, West Africa. *J. Ecology*, **45**, 665–87.

BOURCART, J. 1958. Les calcaires éocènes de la Manche et leur contribution aux sables des plages. *Eclogae Geologicae Helvetiae*, **51**, 505–8.

BOURGOIN, J., DEYRE, D., MAGLOIRE, P., and

KRICHEWSKY, M. 1963. Les canyons sous-marins du Cap Lopez (Gabon). *Cah. oceanogr.*, **15**, 372–97.

BOWEN, A. J. 1969. Rip currents, 1: theoretical investigations. *J. Geophys. Res.*, **74**, 5467–78.

BOWEN, A. J., and INMAN, D. L. 1966. Budget of littoral sands in the vicinity of Point Arguello, California. *Tech. Memo. Coastal Eng. Res. Center, U.S.*, No. 19.

BOWEN, A. J. and INMAN, D. L. 1969. Rip currents, 2: Laboratory and field observations. *J. Geophys. Res.*, **74**, 5479–90.

BRANNER, J. C. 1904. The stone reefs of Brazil: their geological and geographical relations. *Bull. Mus. Compar. Zool. Harv.*, **44**, 1–285.

BRETSCHNEIDER, C. L. 1952. The generation and decay of wind waves in deep water. *Trans. Am. geophys. Un.*, **33**, 381–9.

BRETSCHNEIDER, C. L. 1956. Wave forecasting relationships for the Gulf of Mexico. *Tech. Memo. Beach Eros. Bd., U.S.*, No. 84.

BRETZ, J. H. 1960. Bermuda, a partially drowned, late mature, Pleistocene karst. *Bull. geol. Soc. Am.*, **71**, 1729–54.

BROCHU, M. 1954. Un problème des rives du Saint-Laurent. Blocaux erratiques observés a la surface de terrasses marines. *Rev. Géom. dynamique*, **5**, 76–82.

BROUWER, A. 1953 Rhythmic depositional features of the East-Surinam coastal plain. *Geol. en Mijnbouw*, NS, **15**, 226–36.

BROWN, E. H. 1970. Man shapes the earth. *Geogr. J.*, **136**, 74–85.

BROWN, P. R. 1953. Wave data for the eastern North Atlantic. *Marine Observer*, **23**, 94.

BRUNS, E. 1953. *Handbuch der Wellen der Meere und Ozeane*. Berlin.

BRUUN, P. 1962. Sea level rise as a cause of shore erosion. *J. Waterways and Harbors Div., Proc. Am. soc. Civ. Eng.*, **88**, 117–30.

BURBRIDGE, N. 1944. Ecological notes on the vegetation of 80-mile beach. *Proc. Roy. Soc. W. Austr.*, **28**, 157–64.

BURKHART, M. D., and CLINE, C. W. 1961. The quality of tabulated deck-log swell observations. *Proc. 7th Conf. Coastal Eng.*, **1**, 41–52.

BURLING, R. W. 1955. Surface waves on enclosed bodies of water. *Proc. 5th Conf. Coastal Eng.*, 1–11.

CHAPMAN, V. J. 1960 (2nd edn 1974). *Salt marshes and salt deserts of the world*. London.

CHAPMAN, V. J. 1964 (2nd edn 1977). *Coastal vegetation*. Pergamon Press, Oxford.

CHAPMAN, V. J. 1966. Some factors involved in mangrove establishment. *Proc. Dacca Symp. Scientific problems of the humid tropical zone deltas and their implications*, 219–25.

CHERRY, J. A. 1966. Sand movement along equilibrium beaches north of San Francisco. *J. Sedim. Petrol.*, **36**, 341–57.

CLARKE, E. DE C., and PHILLIPS, H. T. 1953. Physiographic and other notes on a part of the south coast of Western Australia. *J. Roy. Soc. West. Austr.*, **37**, 59–90.

CLOUD, P. E. 1958. Nature and origin of atolls. *Proc. 8th Pac. Sci. Congr.*, **3A**, 1009–24.

CLOUD, P. E. 1965. Carbonate precipitation and dissolution in the marine environment: *in* Riley, J. P., and Skirrow, G. (eds) *Chemical oceanography*, 127–58. Academic Press, London.

COALDRAKE, J. E. 1962. The coastal sand dunes of southern Queensland. *Proc. Roy. Soc. Queensland*, **72**, 101–16.

COLBY, B. R. 1964. Discharge of sands and mean-velocity relationships in sand-bed streams. *Prof. Pap. U.S. Geol, Surv.*, **462-A**, 1–47.

COOPER, W. S. 1958. Coastal sand dunes of Oregon and Washington. *Mem. geol. Soc. Am.*, No. 72.

COOPER, W. S. 1967. Coastal dunes of California. *Mem. geol. Soc. Am.*, No. 104.

COTTON, C. A. 1955. *New Zealand geomorphology: reprints of collected papers of 1912–1925*. Wellington.

COTTON, C. A. 1967. Plunging cliffs and Pleistocene cliffing in the southern hemisphere: in *Mélanges de géographie physique, humaine, economique, appliquée offerts à M. Omer Tulippe*, **1**, 37–59.

COTTON, C. A. 1969. Marine cliffing according to Darwin's theory. *Trans. Roy. Soc. N.Z., Geology*, **6**, 187–208.

COX, D. C. 1963. Status of tsunami knowledge. *Proc. Tsunami meetings, 10th Pac. Sci. Congr. 1961*, 1–6.

CRONIN, L. E. (ed.) 1975. *Estuarine Research* 2 vols. Academic Press, New York.

CROSSLAND, C. 1965. The oecology and deposits of the Cape Verde marine fauna. *Proc. zool. Soc. Lond.*, 1905, 170–86.

CROWE, P. R. 1949. The tradewind circulation of the world. *Trans. Pap. Inst. Brit. Geogr.*, 1949, 37–56.

CROWE, P. R. 1950. The seasonal variation in the strength of the trades. *Trans. Pap. Inst. Brit. Geogr.*, 1950, 23–47.

CROWE, P. R. 1951. Wind and weather in the equatorial zone. *Trans. Pap. Inst. Brit. Geogr.*, 1951, 21–76.

DARBYSHIRE, J. 1957a. A note on the comparison of proposed wave spectrum formulae. *Deutsche hydrogr. Zeit.*, **10**, 184–90.

DARBYSHIRE, J. 1957b. Sea conditions at Tema Harbour. *Dock. Harb. Author.*, **38**, 277–8.

DAVIES, J. L. 1958. Wave refraction and the evolution of shoreline curves. *Geogr. Stud.*, **5**, No. 2, 1–14.

DAVIES, J. L. 1960. Beach alignment in southern Australia. *Austr. Geogr.*, **8**, 42–44.

DAVIES, J. L. 1964. A morphogenic approach to world shorelines. *Zeit. f. Geomorph.*, **8**, Mortensen Sonderheft, 127–42.

DAVIES, J. L. 1977. The coast: *in* Jeans, D. N. (ed.) *Australia: a geography*, 134–51.

DAVIS, J. H. 1940. The ecology and geologic role of mangroves in Florida. *Pap. Tortugas Lab.*, **32**, 303-412.

DAVIS, W. M. 1898. *Physical geography*. Boston.

DE GROOT, A. J. 1966. Mud transport studies using manganese as an accompanying element under temperate and tropical conditions. *Proc. Dacca Symp. Scientific problems of the humid tropical zone deltas and their implications*, 65–71.

DIETRICH, G. 1963. *General oceanography*. Wiley Interscience, New York.

DIETZ, R. S. 1963. Wave base, marine profile of equilibrium, and wave-built terraces: a critical appraisal. *Bull. geol. Soc. Am.*, **74**, 971–90.

DIONNE, J-C. 1968. Schorre morphology of the south shore of the St Lawrence estuary. *Am. J. Sci.*, **266**, 380–8.

DIONNE, J-C. 1969. Tidal flat erosion by ice at La Pocatière, St Lawrence estuary. *J. sedim. Petrol.*, **39**, 1174–81.

DOLAN, R. 1971. Coastal landforms: crescentic and rhythmic. *Bull. geol. Soc. Am.*, **82**, 177–80.

DONN, W. L. 1949. Studies of waves and swell in the western North Atlantic. *Trans. Amer. geophys. Un.*, **30**, 507–16.

DONN, W. L., and McGUINESS, W. T. 1959. Barbados storm swell. *J. Geophys. Res.*, **64**, 2341–9.

DOTY, M. S. 1953. Functions of the algae in the Central Pacific. *Proc. Ninth Pacif. Sci. Congr.* **4**, 148–155.

DOUGLAS, I. 1969. The efficiency of humid tropical denudation systems. *Trans. Inst. Brit. Geogr.*, **46**, 1–16.

DRAPER, L. 1967. Wave activity at the sea bed around north-western Europe. *Marine Geol.*, **5**, 133–40.

DRESCH, J. 1961. Observations sur le désert cotier du Perou. *Annls. Géogr.*, **70**, 179–84.

EKMAN, S. 1967. *Zoogeography of the Sea*. Sidgwick and Jackson, London.

ELIE DE BEAUMONT, L. 1845. *Leçons de Géologie pratique*. Paris.

EMERY, K. O. 1960. *The sea off southern California*. New York.

EMERY, K. O. 1962. Marine geology of Guam. *Prof. Pap. U.S. Geol. Surv.*, **403-B**.

EMERY, K. O. 1963. Organic transportation of marine sediments: *in* Hill (ed.) *The Sea*, **3**, 776–93. New York.

EMERY, K. O. 1968. Relict sediments on continental shelves of the world. *Bull. Am. Ass. petrol. Geol.*, **52**, 445–64.

EMERY, K. O., and STEVENSON, R. E. 1957. Estuaries and lagoons. *Mem. geol. Soc. Am.*, **67**, 673–750.

ESCOFFIER, F. F. 1954. Travelling forelands and the shoreline processes associated with them. *Bull. Beach Eros. Bd., U.S.*, **9**, 11–14.

EVANS, O. F. 1942. The origin of spits, bars and related structures. *J. Geol.*, **50**, 846–65.

FAIRBRIDGE, R. W. 1948. Notes on the geomorphology of the Pelsart Group of the Houtman's Abrolhos Islands. *J. Roy. Soc. West. Austr.*, **34**, 35–72.

FAIRBRIDGE, R. W. 1950. Recent and Pleistocene coral reefs of Australia. *J. Geol.*, **58**, 330–401.

FAIRBRIDGE, R. W. 1968. Coral reefs—morphology and theories: *in* Fairbridge (ed.) *Encyclopedia of Geomorphology*, 186–97. Reinhold, New York.

FAIRBRIDGE, R. W., and KREBS, O. A. 1962. Sea level and the southern oscillation. *Geophys. J.*, **6**, 532–45.

FAIRCHILD, J. C. 1959. Suspended sediment sampling in laboratory wave action. *Tech. Memo. Beach Eros. Bd., U.S.*, No. 115.

FISK, H. N. 1944. Geological investigation of the alluvial valley of the lower Mississippi River. *Miss. River Comm.*, Vicksburg, Miss.

FISK, H. N. 1959. Padre Island and the Laguna Madre flats, coastal south Texas. *Proc. 2nd. Coast. Geogr. Conf.*, 103–52.

FLEMING, C. A. 1965. Two-storied cliffs at the Auckland Islands. *Trans. Roy. Soc. N.Z., Geology*, **3**, 171–4.

FLEMING, W. L. S. 1940. Relic glacial forms on the west coast of Graham Land. *Geogr. J.*, **96**, 93–100.

FLORES SILVA, E. 1952. Observaciones de Costas en la Antàrtida chilena. *Informaciones geograficas*, **3**, 85–93.

FOLK, R. L., and WARD, W. C. 1957. Brazos River bar: a study in the significance of grain size parameters. *J. sedim. Petrol.*, **27**, 3–26.

FOSBERG, F. R. 1961. Vegetation free zones on dry mangrove coasts. *Prof. Pap. U.S. Geol. Surv.*, **424–D**, 216–18.

FOSBERG, F. R. 1966. Vegetation as a geological agent in tropical deltas. *Proc. Dacca Symp. Scientific problems of the humid tropical zone deltas and their implications*, 227–33.

FOURNIER, F. 1960. *Climat et erosion.* Paris.

GABIS, V. 1955. Les galets exotiques de la côtes Charentaise. *Bull. Soc. géol. France*, **5**, 71–88.

GADE, H. G. 1958. Effects of a nonrigid, impermeable bottom on plane surface waves in shallow water. *J. Marine Res.*, **16**, 61–82.

GALLOWAY, R. W. 1970. Coastal and shelf geomorphology and late Cenozoic sea levels. *J. Geol.*, **78**, 603–10.

GARDINER, J. S. 1931. *Coral reefs and atolls.* London.

GIERLOFF-EMDEN, H-G. 1959. *Die Küste von El Salvador.* Weisbaden.

GIERLOFF-EMDEN, H-G. 1961. Nehrungen und Lagunen. *Petermanns Geogr. Mitt.*, **105**, 81–92, 161–76.

GILBERT, G. K. 1885. Topographic features of lake shores. *Rep. U.S. geol. Surv.*, **5**.

GILBERT, G. K. 1890. Lake Bonneville. *U.S. geol. Surv., Monogr.*, **1**.

GILES, R. T., and PILKEY, O. H. 1965. Atlantic beach and dune sediments of the southern United States. *J. sedim. Petrol.*, **35**, 900–10.

GINSBURG, R. N. 1953. Intertidal erosion on the Florida Keys. *Bull. Mar. Sci. Gulf and Carib.*, **3**, 55–69.

GINSBURG, R. N. (ed.) 1975. *Tidal deposits.* Springer-Verlag, Berlin.

GINSBURG, R. N., LLOYD, R. M., STOCKMAN, K. W., and McCALLUM, J. S. 1963. Shallow-water carbonate sediments: *in* Hill (ed.) *The Sea*, **3**, 554–82. New York.

GINSBURG, R. N., and LOWENSTAM, H. A. 1958. The influence of marine bottom communities on the depositional environment of sediments. *J. Geol.*, **66**, 310–18.

GOODING, E. G. B. 1947. Observations on the sand dunes of Barbados, British West Indies. *J. Ecology*, **34**, 111–25.

GREIG-SMITH, P., GEMMELL, A. R., and GIMINGHAM, C. H. 1947. Tussock formation in *Ammophila arenaria* (L.) Link. *New Phyt.*, **46**, 262–8.

GROVE, A. T. 1968. The last 20,000 years in the tropics. *Geomorphology in a tropical environment, Brit. Geomorph. Res. Group, Occ. Pap.*, **5**, 51–60. (Mimeo.)

GUILCHER, A. 1953. Essai sur la zonation et la distribution des formes littorales de dissolution du calcaire. *Annls. Géogr.*, **62**, 161–79.

GUILCHER, A. 1954a. *Morphologie littorale et submarine.* Paris.

GUILCHER, A. 1954b. Presence de crêtes et sillons obliques sur la plage de la Langue de Barbarie. *C. r. Somm. Soc. Géol. Fr.*, 1954, 201–2.

GUILCHER, A. 1954c. Dynamique et morphologie des côtes sableuses de l'Afrique Atlantique. *Cah. Inform. Géogr.*, **1**, 57–68.

GUILCHER, A. 1958. *Coastal and submarine morphology.* London.

GUILCHER, A. 1959. Coastal sand ridges and marshes and their continental environment near Grand Popo and Ouidah, Dahomey. *Proc. 2nd Conf. Coast. Geogr., Baton Rouge*, 189–212.

GUILCHER, A. 1961. Le 'beachrock' ou grès de plage. *Annals. Géogr.*, **70**, 113–25.

GUILCHER, A. 1963. Estuaries, deltas, shelf, slope: *in* Hill (ed.) *The Sea* **3**, 620–54. New York.

GUILCHER, A., and KING, C. A. M. 1961. Spits, tombolos and tidal marshes in Connemara and West Kerry, Ireland. *Proc. Roy. Irish Acad., Sect. B*, **61**, 283–338.

GUILCHER, A., and PONT, P. 1957. Etude experimentale de la corrosion littorale des calcaires. *Bull. Ass. Geogr. Franc.*, No. 265–6, 48–62.

GULLIVER, F. P. 1899. Shoreline topography. *Proc. Am. Acad. Arts. Sci.*, **34**, 151–258.

GUPPY, H. B. 1906. *Observations of a naturalist in the Pacific between 1896 and 1899. II Plant dispersal.* London.

GURTNER, P. 1960. Development of a boat for India's surf coasts: in *Fishing boats of the world*. **2**, 585–96. Paris.

GUZA, R. T. and INMAN, D. L. 1975. Edge waves and beach cusps. *J. Geophys. Res.*, **80**, 2997–3012.

HALLIGAN, G. H. 1906. Sand movement on the New South Wales coast. *Proc. Linn. Soc. N.S.W.*, **31**, 619–40.

HANDIN, J. W. 1951. The source, transportation and deposition of beach sediments in southern California. *Tech. Memo. Beach Eros. Bd., U.S.*, No. 22.

HARDY, J. 1966. An ebb-flood channel system and coastal changes near Winterton, Norfolk. *East Midland Geogr.*, **4**, 24–30.

HARPER, J. R., OWENS, E. H. and WISEMAN, W. J. 1978. Arctic beach processes and the thaw of ice-bonded sediments in the littoral zone. *Proc. 3rd Int. Permafrost Conf.*, 195–9.

HARRISON, W. 1970. Prediction of beach changes. *Progress in geography*, **2**, 209–35.

HAYES, M. O. 1967a. Relationship between coastal climate and bottom sediment type on the inner continental shelf. *Marine Geol.*, **5**, 111–32.

HAYES, M. O. 1967b. Hurricanes as geological agents, south Texas coast. *Bull. Am. Soc. petrol. Geol.*, **51**, 937–42.

HAYES, M. O. 1975. Morphology of sand accumulation in estuaries: *in* Cronin, L. E. (ed.) *Estuarine Research*, **2**, 3–22.

HEDGPETH, J. L. 1967. Ecological aspects of the Laguna Madre, a hypersaline estuary: *in* Lauff (ed.) *Estuaries*, 408–19.

HELLE, J. R. 1958. Surf statistics for the coasts of the United States. *Tech. Memo. Beach Eros. Bd., U.S.*, No. 108.

HILL, R. D. 1966. Changes in beach form at Sri Pantai, north-east Johore, Malaysia. *J. Trop. Geogr.*, **23**, 19–27.

HILLS, E. S. 1949. Shore platforms. *Geol. Mag.*, **86**, 137–52.

HILLS, E. S. 1971. A study of cliffy coastal profiles based on examples in Victoria, Australia. *Zeit. f. Geomorph.*, **12**, 137–80.

HINES, A. C. 1975. Bedform distribution and migration patterns on tidal deltas in the Chatham Harbor estuary, Cape Cod, Massachusetts: *in* Cronin, L. E. (ed.) *Estuarine Research*, **2**, 235–52.

HODGKIN, E. P. 1964. Rate of erosion of inter-tidal limestone. *Zeit. f. Geomorph*, **8**, 385–92.

HODGKIN, E. P. 1970. Geomorphology and biological erosion of limestone coasts in Malaysia. *Bull. geol. Soc. Malaysia*, **3**, 27–51.

HOFFMEISTER, J. E., and WENTWORTH, C. K. 1942. Data for the recognition of changes of sea level. *Proc. 6th Pac. Sci. Congr.*, 839–48.

HOGBEN, N., and LUMB, F. E. 1967. *Ocean wave statistics*. London.

HOLCOMBE, R. M. 1958. Similarities and contrasts between the Arctic and Antarctic marine climates *in Polar Atmosphere Symposium, Part I, Meteorology*. London.

HOPLEY, D. 1968. Morphology of Curacoa Island spit, north Queensland. *Austr. J. Sci.*, **31**, 122–3.

HOPLEY, D. 1970. The geomorphology of the Burdekin delta, North Queensland. *Dept. Geogr., James Cook University, Monogr. Ser.*, No. 1.

HOYT, J. H. 1967. Barrier island formation. *Bull. geol. Soc. Am.*, **78**, 1125–36.

HUNKINS, K. 1962. Waves on the Arctic Ocean. *J. Geophys. Res.*, **67**, 2477–89.

HUNTLEY, D. A. 1976. Long period waves on a natural beach. *J. Geophys. Res.*, 81, 6441–49.

HUNTLEY, D. A. and BOWEN, A. J. 1975. Comparison of the hydrodynamics of steep and shallow beaches: *in* Hails, J. R. and Carr, A. P. (eds) *Nearshore sediment dynamics and sedimentation*, 69–109.

INMAN, D. L. 1960. Shore processes: *in McGraw-Hill Encyclopedia of Science and Technology*. New York.

INMAN, D. L., and BAGNOLD, R. A. 1963. Beach and nearshore processes. Part II Littoral processes: *in* Hill (ed.) *The Sea*, **3**, 529–53. New York.

INMAN, D. L., EWING, G. C., and CORLISS, J. B. 1966. Coastal sand dunes of Guerrero Negro, Baja California, Mexico. *Bull. geol. Soc. Am.*, **77**, 787–802.

INMAN, D. L., and FILLOUX, J. 1960. Beach cycles related to tide and local wind wave regime. *J. Geol.*, **68**, 225–31.

INMAN, D. L., GAYMAN, W. R., and COX, D. C. 1963. Littoral sedimentary processes on Kauai, a sub-tropical high island. *Pacific, Sci.*, **17**, 106–30.

INMAN, D. L., and NORDSTROM, C. E. 1971. On the tectonic and morphologic classification of coasts. *J. Geol.*, **79**, 1–21.

IPPEN, A. T. (ed.) 1966. *Estuary and coastline hydrodynamics*. McGraw-Hill, New York.

ISACKS, B., OLIVER, J., and SYKES, L. R. 1968. Seismology and the new global tectonics. *J. geophys. Res.*, **73**, 5855–99.

JAMES, P. E. 1961. *Latin America*. Cassell, London.

JENNINGS, J. N. 1955. The influence of wave action on coastal outline in plan. *Austr. Geogr.*, **6**, 36–44.

JENNINGS, J. N. 1957. On the orientation of parabolic or U-dunes. *Geogr. J.*, **123**, 474–80.

JENNINGS, J. N. 1964. The question of coastal dunes in humid tropical climates. *Zeit f. Geomorph.*, **8**, 150–4.

JENNINGS, J. N. 1965. Further discussion on factors affecting coastal dune formation in the tropics. *Austr. J. Sci.*, **28**, 166–7.

JESSEN, O. 1951. Dünung im Atlantik und an der Westküste Afrikas. *Petermanns Geogr. Mitt.*, **95**, 7–16.

JOGLEKAR, D. V., GOLE, C. V., and APTE, A. S. 1958. Some coastal engineering problems in India. *Proc. 6th Conf. Coastal Eng.*, 510–19.

JOHN, B. S. and SUGDEN, D. E. 1975. Coastal geomorphology of high latitudes. *Progress in Geography*, **7**, 53–132.

JOHNSON, D. W. 1919. *Shore processes and shoreline development*. New York. (Facsim. edn, Hafner, New York. 1965.)

JOHNSON, D. W. 1925. *New England—Acadian shoreline*. New York. (Facsim. edn, Hafner, New York. 1968.)

JOHNSON, J. H. 1961. *Limestone-building algae and algal limestones*. Boulder.

JOHNSON, J. W. 1956. Dynamics of nearshore sediment movement. *Bull. Am. Ass. petrol. Geol.*, **40**, 2211–32.

JOHNSON, J. W. 1959. The supply and loss of sand to the coast. *J. Am. Soc. Civ. Eng.*, **85**, 227–51.

JOHNSON, J. W., and EAGLESON, P. S. 1966. Coastal processes: *in* Ippen (ed.) 404–92.

JOYCE, J. R. F. 1950. Notes on ice-foot development, Neny Fjord, Graham Land, Antarctica. *J. Geol.*, **58**, 646–9.

JUDGE, C. W. 1971. Heavy minerals in beach and stream sediments as indicators of shore processes between Monterey and Los Angeles, California. *Tech. Memo. Coastal Eng. Res. Center*, No. 33.

KASSAS, M. 1957. On the ecology of the Red Sea coastal land. *J. Ecology*, **45**, 187–203.

KAYE, C. A. 1957. The effect of solvent motion on limestone solution. *J. Geol.*, **65**, 35–46.

KEARY, R. 1968. Biogenic carbonate in beach sediments of the west coast of Ireland. *Sci. Proc. Roy. Dublin Soc., Series A.*, **3**, 75–85.

KEARY, R. 1969. Variations in the biogenic carbonate content of sediments on the south coast of Ireland. *Sci. Proc. Roy. Dublin Soc., Series A*, **3**, 193–202.

KEMP, P. H. 1961. The relationship between wave action and beach profile characteristics. *Proc. 7th Conf. Coast. Eng.*, 262–77.

KEMP, P. H., and PLINSTON, D. T. 1968. Beaches produced by waves of low phase difference. *J. Hydraulics Div., Proc. Am. Soc. Civ. Eng.*, **94**, 1183–95.

KENDALL, C. G. STC., and SKIPWITH, P. A. D'E. 1968. Recent algal mats of a Persian Gulf lagoon. *J. sedim. Petrol.*, **38**, 1040–58.

KENYON, N. H. 1970. Sand ribbons of European tidal seas. *Marine Geol.*, **9**, 25–39.

KIDSON, C. 1960. The shingle complexes of Bridgewater Bay. *Trans. Pap. Inst. Brit. Geogr.*, 1960, 75–87.

KIDSON, C. 1963. The growth of sand and shingle spits across estuaries. *Zeit. f. Geomorph.*, **7**, 1–22.

KING, C. A. M. 1956. The coast of south-east Iceland near Ingolfhöfdi. *Geogr. J.*, **122**, 241–6.

KING, C. A. M. 1959 (2nd edn 1972). *Beaches and Coasts*. Arnold, London.

KING, C. A. M. 1963. Some problems concerning marine planation and the formation of erosion surfaces. *Trans. Pap. Inst. Brit. Geogr.*, 1963, 29–43.

KING, C. A. M. 1966. *Techniques in geomorphology*. Arnold, London.

KING, C. A. M. 1969. Some arctic coastal features around Foxe Basin and in Baffin Island, N.W.T., Canada. *Geografiska Annaler*, **51A**, 207–18.

KING, C. A. M. 1970. Changes in the spit at Gibraltar Point, Lincolnshire, 1951 to 1969. *Geographical essays in honour of K. C. Edwards*, 19–30

KINSMAN, B. 1965. *Wind waves—their generation and propagation on the ocean surface*. Prentice Hall, New York.

KOMAR, P. D. 1975. Nearshore currents: generation by obliquely incident waves and longshore variations in breaker heights: *in* Hails, J. R. and Carr, A. P. (eds) *Nearshore sediment dynamics and sedimentation*, 17–45.

KOMAR, P. D. 1976. *Beach processes and sedimentation*. Prentice-Hall, Englewood Cliffs.

KRAFT, J. C. 1971. Sedimentary facies pattern and geologic history of a Holocene marine transgression. *Bull. geol. Soc. Am.*, **82**, 2131–58.

KRUMBEIN, W. C. 1947. Shore processes and beach characteristics. *Tech. Memo. Beach Eros. Bd., U.S.*, No. 3.

KUENEN, P. H. 1950. *Marine geology*. New York.

LANGFORD-SMITH, T., and THOM, B. G. 1969.

New South Wales coastal morphology. *J. geol. Soc. Austr.*, **16**, 572–80.

LAUFF, G. H. (ed.) 1967. *Estuaries.* Pub. Am. Ass. Adv. Sci., 83.

LE BOURDIEC, P. 1958. Aspects de la morphogénése Plio-Quaternaire en Basse Côte d'Ivoire (A.O.F.) *Rev. Géomorph. dynamique*, **9**, 33–42.

LE PICHON, X. 1968. Sea-floor spreading and continental drift. *J. geophys. Res.*, **73**, 3661–97.

LEWIS, J. B. 1960. The fauna of the rocky shores of Barbados, West Indies. *Can. J. Zool.*, **38**, 391–435.

LEWIS, W. V. 1932. The formation of Dungeness foreland. *Geogr. J.*, **80**, 309–24.

LEWIS, W. V. 1938. The evolution of shoreline curves. *Proc. geol. Ass.*, **49**, 107–26.

LOGAN, B. W., DAVIES, G. R., READ, J. F., and CEBULSKI, D. E. 1970. Carbonate sedimentation and environments, Shark Bay, Western Australia. *Amer. Soc. Petrol. Geol., Mem.*, No. 13.

LOGAN, R. F. 1960. The central Namib desert, South West Africa. *Nat. Acad. Sci., Nat. Res. Council Washington, Pub.*, No. 758.

MABESOONE, J. M. 1966. Os 'recifes' do Brasil. *Bol. Soc. Bras. de Geologica*, **15**, 45–9.

McGILL, J. T. 1958. Map of coastal landforms of the world. *Geogr. Rev.*, **48**, 402–5.

McINTIRE, W. G., and WALKER, H. J. 1964. Tropical cyclones and coastal morphology in Mauritius. *Ann. Ass. Am. Geogr.*, **54**, 582–96.

MACKAY, J. R. 1963. The Mackenzie delta, N.W.T. *Geogr. Branch, Mines and Technical Surveys, Ottowa, Mem.*, No. 8.

McKENZIE, P. 1958. Rip-current systems. *J. Geol.*, **66**, 103–13.

McLEAN, R. F. 1967. Measurements of beach-rock erosion by some tropical marine gastropods. *Bull. Mar. Sci.*, **17**, 551–61.

McLEAN, R. F., and DAVIDSON, C. F. 1968. The role of mass movement in shore platform development along the Gisborne coastline, New Zealand. *Earth Sci. Jour.*, **2**, 15–25.

MACNAE, W. 1967. Zonation within mangroves associated with estuaries in North Queensland: *in* Lauff (ed.) *Estuaries*, 432–41.

MACNEIL, F. S. 1950. Planation of recent reef flats on Okinawa. *Bull. geol. Soc. Am.*, **61**, 1307–8.

MACNEIL, F. S. 1954. The shape of atolls: an inheritance from sub-aerial erosion forms. *Am. J. Sci.*, **252**, 402–27.

MANOHAR, M. 1958. Sediment movement at South Indian ports. *Proc. 6th Conf. Coastal Eng.*, 359–405.

MANOHAR, M. 1961. Sediment movement at Indian ports. *Proc. 7th Conf. Coastal Eng.*, 342–74.

MARMER, H. 1926. *The Tide.* New York.

MEADE, E. H. 1969. Landward transport of bottom sediments in estuaries of the Atlantic coastal plain. *J. sedim. Petrol.*, **39**, 222–34.

MEISBURGER, E. P. 1962. Frequency of occurrence of ocean surface waves in various height categories for coastal areas. *U.S. Army Engineer Research and Development Laboratories, Report* 1719–RR.

MELTON, F. A. 1940. A tentative classification of sand dunes. *J. Geol.*, **48**, 113–45.

MENARD, H. W. 1969. The deep-occan floor. *Sci. Am.*, **221**, 126–42.

MILLER, J. D. 1960. Giant waves in Lituya Bay, Alaska. *Prof. Pap. U.S. Geol. Surv.*, **354–C**, 51–86.

MILLIMAN, J. D. 1967. The geomorphology and history of Hogsty Reef, a Bahamian atoll. *Bull. Marine Sci.*, **17**, 519–43.

MITCHELL, A. H., and READING, H. G. 1969. Continental margins, geosynclines and ocean floor spreading. *J. Geol.*, **77**, 629–46

MOBERLY, R., BAVER, L. D., and MORRISON, A. 1965. Source and variation of Hawaiian littoral sand. *J. sedim. Petrol.*, **35**, 589–98.

MOIGU, A., and GUILCHER, A. 1967. Une flèche littorale en milieu périglaciaire arctique: la flèche de Sars (Spitsberg). *Norois*, **56**, 549–68.

MOORE, J. R. 1968. Recent sedimentation in northern Cardigan Bay, Wales. *Bull. Brit. Mus. nat. Hist. (Miner.)*, **2**, 21–131.

MORGAN, J. P., NICHOLS, L. G., and WRIGHT, M. 1958. Morphological effects of hurricane Audrey on the Louisiana coast. *Tech. Rep. Louisiana State Univ., Coastal Studies Inst.*, No. 10.

MORTON, J. K. 1957. Sand dune formation on a tropical shore. *J. Ecology*, **45**, 495–7.

MUIR, J. 1937. The seed-drift of South Africa and some influences of ocean currents on the strand vegetation. *Memo. S. African Bot. Surv.*, **16**, 1–108.

MUNK, W. H., and SARGENT, M. C. 1948. The adjustment of Bikini atoll to ocean waves. *Trans. Am. geophys. Un.*, **29**, 855–60.

MUNK, W. H., and SNODGRASS, F. E. 1957. Measurements of southern swell at Guadeloupe Island. *Deep Sea Res.*, **4**, 272–86.

MUNK, W. H., and TRAYLOR, M. A. 1947.

Refraction of ocean waves: a process linking underwater topography to beach erosion. *J. Geol.*, **55**, 1–26.

MURAOUR, P. 1953. Les phénomènes de sedimentation du cordon littoral situé à l'Ouest de Port-Gueydon (Algerie). *C. r. Acad. Sci.*, **236**, 2099–101.

NAGARAJA, V. N. 1966. Hydrometeorological and tidal problems of the deltaic areas in India. *Proc. Dacca Symp. Scientific problems of the humid tropical zone deltas and their implications*, 115–21.

NANSEN, F. 1922. The strandflat and isostasy. *Vidensk. Skrifter, I. Math-Naturw. Kl. 1921*, No. 11.

NEDECO. 1961. *The waters of the Niger delta.* The Hague.

NESTEROFF, W. 1956. Le substratum organique dans les depôts calcaires, sa signification. *Bull. Soc. géol. France*, **6**, 381–9.

NEWELL, N. D. 1956. Geological reconnaissance of Raroia (Kon Tiki) Atoll, Tuamotu archipelago. *Bull. Am. Mus. nat. Hist.*, **109**, 315–72.

NEWELL, N. D., and IMBRIE, J. 1955. Biogeological reconnaissance in the Bimini area, Great Bahama Bank. *Trans. N.Y. Acad. Sci.*, **18**, 3–14.

NEWELL, N. D., RIGBY, J. K., WHITEMAN, A. J., and BRADLEY, J. S. 1951. Shoal-water geology and environments, Eastern Andros Island, Bahamas. *Bull. Amer. Mus. Nat. Hist.*, 97, 1–29.

NICHOLS, R. L. 1961. Characteristics of beaches formed in polar climates. *Am. J. Sci.*, **259**, 694–708.

NICHOLS, R. L. 1968. Coastal geomorphology, McMurdo Sound Antarctica. *J. Glaciology*, **51**, 449–78.

NICOD, J. 1951. Le problème de la classification des 'calanques' parmi les formes de côtes de submersion. *Rev. Géomorph. dynamique*, **2**, 120–7.

NIELSEN, N. 1969. Morphological studies on the eastern coast of Disko, West Greenland. *Geogr. Tidsskr.*, **68**, 1–35.

NORRIS, R. M. 1964. Dams and beach-sand supply in southern California: *in* Miller (ed.) *Papers in marine geology*, 154–71. New York.

NOSSIN, J. J. 1961. Relief and coastal development in north-eastern Johore (Malaya). *J. trop. Geogr.*, **15**, 27–38.

NOSSIN, J. J. 1965. Analysis of younger beach ridge deposits in eastern Malaya. *Zeit. f. Geomorph.*, **9**, 186–208.

NOYE, J. 1967. Wave recording on the southern coast of Australia. *Horace Lamb. Centre for Oceanogr. Res., Survey Pap.* No. 3. (Mimeo.)

OFF, T. 1963. Rhythmic linear sand bodies caused by tidal currents. *Bull. Am. Ass. petrol. Geol.*, **47**, 324–41.

OTTER, G. W. 1937. Rock destroying organisms in relation to coral reefs. *Great Barrier Reef Exped. 1928–29, Sci. Rep.*, **1**, 323–52.

OTTMANN, F. 1965. *Introduction à la géologie marine et littorale.* Paris.

OTVOS, E. G. 1970. Development and migration of barrier islands, northern Gulf of Mexico. *Bull. geol. Soc. Am.*, **81**, 241–6.

OWENS, E. H., and MCCANN, S. B. 1970. The role of ice in the Arctic beach environment with special reference to Cape Ricketts, south-west Devon Island, north-west Territories, Canada. *Am. J. Sci*, **268**, 397–414.

PATERSON, D. E. 1956. Beach erosion at Durban, South Africa. *Bull. Beach Eros. Bd., U.S.*, **10**, 11–20.

PESTRONG, R. 1965. The development of drainage patterns on tidal marshes. *Stanford Univ. Publ. Geol. Sciences*, **10**, No. 2.

PHLEGER, F. B., and EWING, G. C. 1962. Sedimentology and oceanography of coastal lagoons in Baja California, Mexico. *Bull. Geol. Soc. Am.*, **73**, 145–82.

PIERCE, J. W. 1969. Sediment budget along a barrier island chain. *Sed. Geol.*, **3**, 5–16.

PIERSON, W. J., NEUMANN, G., and JAMES, R. W. 1960. *Practical methods for observing and forecasting ocean waves by means of wave spectra and statistics.* H.O. Pub. 603, Washington.

PIMIENTA, J. 1953. Sur les déplacements de l'embouchure de la Medjerda et les caractères de son delta. *C. r. Acad. Sci.*, **236**, 2326–8.

PRICE, W. A. 1954a. Correlation of shoreline type with offshore conditions in the Gulf of Mexico. *Proc. Coastal Geography Conf. 1954*, 11–30.

PRICE, W. A. 1954b. Shorelines and coasts of the Gulf of Mexico *in* Gulf of Mexico, its origin, waters and marine life. *U.S. Dept. Interior, Fish and Wildlife Serv., Fisheries Bull.*, No. 89, 39–65.

PRICE, W. A. 1955. Correlation of shoreline type with offshore bottom conditions. *A. and M. College of Texas, Dept. Oceanogr.*, Project 63.

PRIESTLY, R. E. 1922. The Antarctic ice-foot. *Brit. (Terra Nova) Antarctic Exped., Glaciology*, 295–324.

PRITCHARD, D. 1950. Notes on the dynamics of

estuarine waters. *Proc. Colloq. on the flushing of estuaries, U.S. Office of Naval Res.*, 49–60.

PURDY, E. G. 1974. Reef configurations: cause and effect: *in* Laporte, L. F. (ed.) *Reefs in time and space*, Soc. Econ. Pal. Min., Spec. Pub. 18, 9–76.

RANSON, G. 1959. Erosion biologique des calcaires côtiers et autres calcaires d'origine animale. *C. r. Acad. Sci.*, **249**, 438–40.

RATEEV, M. A., GOBBUNOVA, Z. N., LISITZYN, A. P., and NOSOV, G. L. 1969. The distribution of clay minerals in the oceans. *Sedimentology*, **13**, 21–43.

RAUNKIAER, C. 1934. *The life forms of plants and statistical plant geography*. Oxford.

REVELLE, R., and EMERY, K. O. 1957. Chemical erosion of beach rock and exposed reef rock. *Prof. Pap. U.S. Geol. Surv.*, **260–T**, 699–709.

REX, R. W. 1964. Arctic beaches, Barrow, Alaska: *in* Miller (ed.) *Papers in marine geology*, 384–400. New York.

ROBINSON, A. H. W. 1953. The storm surge of 31 Jan.—1 Feb. 1953. *Geography*, **38**, 134–41.

ROBINSON, A. H. W. 1955. The harbour entrances of Poole, Christchurch and Pagham. *Geogr. J.*, **121**, 33–50.

ROBINSON, A. H. W. 1960. Ebb-flood channel systems in sandy bays and estuaries. *Geography*, **45**, 183–99.

ROSSITER, J. R. 1954. The North Sea storm surge of 31 Jan. and 1 Feb. 1953. *Phil. Trans. Roy Soc. Lond. A.*, **246**, 371–99.

RUSSELL, R. J. 1963a. Beach rock. *J. trop. Louisiana salt marshes*. *Proc. Salt. Marsh Conf.*, *Sapelo Island*, 1958, 29–31.

RUSSELL, R. J. 1963a. Beach rock. *J. Trop. Geogr.*, **17**, 24–7.

RUSSELL, R. J. 1963b. Recent recession of tropical cliffy coasts. *Science*, **139**, 9–15.

RUSSELL, R. J. 1967. *River plains and sea coasts*. Berkeley and Los Angeles.

RUSSELL, R. J. 1969. South American marine energy. *Louisiana State Univ., Coastal Studies Inst., Tech. Rep.*, 73.

RUSSELL, R. J., and MCINTIRE, W. G. 1965. Southern hemisphere beach rock. *Geogr. Rev.*, **55**, 17–45.

RUSSELL, R. J., and MCINTIRE, W. G. 1966. Australian tidal flats. *Louisiana State Univ., Coastal Studies Series*, No. 13.

SAMOJLOV, I. 1956. *Die Flussmündungen*. Gotha (translated from Russian).

SANTEMA, P. 1966. The effect of tides, coastal currents, waves and storm surges on the natural conditions prevailing in deltas. *Proc. Dacca Symp., Scientific problems of the humid tropical zone deltas and their implications*, 109–13.

SAUER, J. D. 1961. Coastal plant geography of Mauritius. *Louisiana State Univ., Coastal Studies Series*, No. 5.

SAUER, J. D. 1962. Effects of recent tropical cyclones on the coastal vegetation of Mauritius. *J. Ecology*, **50**, 275–90.

SAUER, J. D. 1967. *Plants and man on the Seychelles coast*. Madison.

SAUVAGE DE SAINT MARC, M. G., and VINCENT, M. G. 1955. Transport littoral, formation de flèches et de tombolos. *Proc. 5th Conf. Coastal Eng.*, 296–328.

SAVILLE, T. 1950. Model study of sand transport along an infinitely long straight beach. *Trans. Am. geophys. Un.*, **31**, 555–65.

SAVILLE, T., and WATTS, G. M. 1969. Coastal regime recent U.S. experience. *22nd Internat. Navigation Congr., Paris* 1969.

SCHATTNER, I. 1967. Geomorphology of the northern coast of Israel. *Geografiska Annaler*, **49A**, 310–20.

SCHOU, A. 1945. *Det marine Forland*. Copenhagen.

SCHUBART, L., and MÖCKEL, W. 1949. Dünung im Atlantischen Ozean. *Deutsche Hydrographische Zeitschrift*, **2**, 280–5.

SCHUMM, S. A. 1963. The disparity between present rates of denudation and orogeny. *Prof. Pap. U.S. Geol. Surv.*, **454–H**, 1–13.

SCHWARTZ, M. L. 1971. The multiple causation of barrier islands. *J. Geol.*, **79**, 91–3.

SCHWEIGGER, E. 1959. *Die Westküste Sudamerikas im Bereich des Peru-Stroms*. Heidelberg.

SHEPARD, F. P. 1963 (3rd edn 1973). *Submarine geology*. 2nd ed. New York.

SHEPARD, F. P., and GRANT, U. S. 1947. Wave erosion along the Southern California coast. *Bull. geol. Soc. Am.*, **58**, 919–26.

SHORT, A. D. 1975. Multiple offshore bars and standing waves. *J. Geophys. Res.* **80**, 3838–40.

SHORT, A. D. 1979. Wave power and beach-stages: a global model. *Proc. 16th Conf. Coastal Eng.*, 1145–62.

SIDDIQUIE, H. N. 1966. Provenance of the dune sands of the Balasore coast, Orissa. *Rec. geol. Surv. India.*, **94**, 229–44.

SILVESTER, R. 1956. The use of cyclonicity charts in the study of littoral drift. *Trans. Am. geophys. Un.*, **37**, 694–6.

SILVESTER, R. 1960. Stabilization of sedimentary coastlines. *Nature*, **188**, 467–9.

SILVESTER, R. 1962. Sediment movement around the coastlines of the world. *Proc. Conf. on Civil Engineering Problems Overseas, London*, Paper No. 14.

SILVESTER, R. 1970. Growth of crenulate shaped bays to equilibrium. *J. Waterways and Harbors Div., Proc. Am. Soc. Civ. Eng.*, **96**, 275–87.

SILVESTER, R., and DE LA CRUZ, C. R. 1970. Pattern forming forces in deltas. *J. Waterways and Harbors Div.*, Proc. Am. Soc. Civ. Eng., **96**, 201–17.

SIMMONS, H. B. 1966. Field experience in estuaries: *in* Ippen, A. T., (ed.), *Estuary and coastline hydrodynamics*. New York.

SITARZ, J. 1960. Côtes Africaines—études des profiles d'equilibre de plages. *Trav. Centre d'Etudes Rech. océanogr.*, **3**, 43–62.

SMITH, H. T. U. 1954. Coastal dunes. *Proc. Coastal Geography Conf.*, 1954.

SNEAD, R. E. 1967. Recent morphological changes along the coast of West Pakistan. *Ann. Ass. Am. Geogr.*, **57**, 550–65.

SNODGRASS, F. E., GROVES, G. W., HASSELMANN, K. F., MILLER, G. R., MUNK, W. H., and POWERS, W. H. 1966. Propagation of ocean swell across the Pacific. *Phil. Trans. Roy. Soc. Lond., A*, **259**, 431–97.

SONU, C. J. 1972. Field observations of nearshore and meandering currents. *J. Geophys. Res.*, **77**, 3232–47.

STANLEY, K. W. 1968. Effects of the Alaska earthquake of March 27, 1964, on shore processes and beach morphology. *U.S. geol. Surv. Prof. Pap.*, **543-J**.

STAPOR, F. W. 1971. Sediment budgets on a compartmented low-to-moderate energy coast in north-west Florida. *Marine Geology*, **10**, M1–M7.

STEERS, J. A. 1946 (2nd edn 1964). *The coastline of England and Wales*. Cambridge Univ. Press, Cambridge.

STEERS, J. A. 1953. *The sea coast*. Collins, London.

STODDART, D. R. 1965. Re-survey of hurricane effects on the British Honduras reefs and cays. *Nature*, **207**, 589–92.

STODDART, D. R. 1968. Climatic geomorphology: review and reassessment. *Progress in geography*, **1**, 161–222.

STODDART, D. R. 1969a. World erosion and sedimentation: *in* Chorley (ed.) *Water, earth and man*. London.

STODDART, D. R. 1969b. Climatic geomorphology: *in* Chorley (ed.) *Water, earth and man*. London.

STODDART, D. R. 1969c. Ecology and morphology of Recent coral reefs. *Biol. Rev.*, **44**, 433–98.

STODDART, D. R., and CANN, J. R. 1965. Nature and origin of beach rock. *J. sedim. Petrol.*, **35**, 243–7

STOMMEL, H. M. 1966. The large-scale oceanic circulation: *in* Hurley (ed.) *Advances in earth science*. M.I.T. Press, Cambridge, Mass. 175–84.

STRAKHOV, N. M. 1967. *Principles of lithogenesis*. **1**. Trans. J. P. Fitzsimmons. Oliver and Boyd, Edinburgh.

STRICKLAND, C. 1940. *Deltaic formation*. Calcutta.

SUESS, E. 1892. *Das Antlitz der Erde*. **1**. Vienna.

SWAN, S. B. StC. 1967. Characteristics of coastal sands and their depositional environments in south-west Ceylon. *J. trop. Geogr.*, **24**, 30–42.

SWIFT, D. J. P. 1970. Quaternary shelves and the return to grade. *Marine Geol.*, **8**, 5–30.

SWIFT, D. J. P. 1975. Barrier-island genesis: evidence from the central Atlantic shelf, eastern USA. *Sed. Geol.*, **14**, 1–43.

TANNER, W. F. 1958. The equilibrium beach. *Trans. Am. geophys. Un.*, **39**, 889–91.

TANNER, W. F. 1960. Florida coastal classification. *Trans. Gulf Coast Ass. Geol. Soc.*, **10**, 259–66.

TANNER, W. F. 1961. Offshore shoals in area of energy deficit. *J. sedim. Petrol.*, **31**, 87–95.

TAYLOR, J. D. 1968. Coral reef and associated invertebrate communities (mainly molluscan) around Mahe, Seychelles. *Phil. Trans. R. Soc. London, B*, **254**, 129–206.

TERMIER, H., and TERMIER, G. 1963. *Erosion and sedimentation*. Van Nostrand, New York.

THOM, B. G. 1965. Late Quaternary coastal morphology of the Part Stephens—Myall Lakes area, New South Wales. *J. Proc. Roy. Soc. N.S.W.*, **98**, 23–36.

THOM, B. G. 1967. Mangrove ecology and deltaic geomorphology: Tabasco, Mexico. *J. Ecology*, **55**, 301–43.

THOM, B. G. 1968. Coastal erosion in eastern Australia. *Austr. geogr. studies*, **6**, 171–3.

THOM, B. G. 1974. Coastal erosion in eastern Australia. *Search*, **5**, 198–209.

THOM, B. G. 1978. Coastal sand deposition in

southeast Australia during the Holocene: *in* Davies, J. L. and Williams, M. A. J. (eds) *Landform evolution in Australia*, 197–214.

THOM, B. G., WRIGHT, L. D. and COLEMAN, J. M. 1975. Mangrove ecology and deltaic-estuarine geomorphology: Cambridge-Ord River region, Western Australia. *J. Ecology*, **63**, 203–32.

THOMPSON, R. W. 1968. Tidal flat sedimentation on the Colorado River delta, north-western Gulf of California. *Mem. geol. Soc. Am.*, **107**.

TIETZE, W. 1962. A contribution to the geomorphological problem of strandflats. *Petermanns geogr. Mitt.*, **106**, 1–20.

TODD, D. K., and WIEGEL, R. L. 1952. Near-coastal storms and associated waves. *Trans. Am. geophys. Un.*, **33**, 217–25.

TRASK, P. D. 1952. Source of beach sand at Santa Barbara, California as indicated by mineral grain studies. *Tech. Memo. Beach Eros. Bd., U.S.*, No. 28.

TRENHAILE, A. S. 1978. The shore platforms of Gaspé, Quebec. *Ann. Assoc. Amer. Geogr.*, **68**, 95–114.

TRICART, J. 1956. Aspects morphologiques du delta du Sénégal. *Rev. Géomorph. dynamique*, **7**, 65–85.

TRICART, J. 1957. Aspects et problèmes géomorphologiques du littoral occidental de la Côte d'Ivoire. *Bull. Inst. Franc. Afrique Noire*, Series A, **19**, 1–20.

TRICART, J. 1959. Problèmes géomorphologiques du littoral oriental du Brésil. *Cah. océanogr.*, **11**, 276–308.

TRICART, J. 1960. Experiences de desegregation de roches granitiques par la cristallisation du sel marin. *Zeit. f. Geomorph.*, Supp., **1**, 239–40.

TRICART, J. 1962. Observations de géomorphologie littorale à Mamba Point (Monrovia, Liberia). *Erdkunde*, **16**, 49–57.

TRICART, J. 1967. *Le modèle des régions periglaciaires*. Paris.

TRICART, J., and CAILLEUX, A. 1965. *Le modèle des régions chaudes forêts et Savanes*. Paris.

TWENHOFEL, W. H. 1946. Beach and river sands of the coastal region of south-west Oregon with particular reference to black sands. *Am. J. Sci.*, **244**, 114–39, 200–14.

UMBGROVE, J. H.F. 1947a. Origin of the Dutch coast. *Proc. Kon. Ned. Akad. Wet.*, **50**, 227–36.

UMBGROVE, J. H. F. 1947b. Coral reefs of the East Indies. *Bull. geol. Soc. A.*, **58**, 729–78.

VALENTIN, H. 1952. *Die Küsten der Erde*. Supplement to *Petermanns Geogr. Mitt.*, No. 246.

VALENTIN, H. 1954. Der Landverlust in Holderness, Ostengland von 1852 bis 1952. *Die Erde*, **3**, 296–315.

VALLIANOS, F. 1970. Recent history of erosion at Carolina Beach, N.C. *Proc. 12th Conf. Coastal Eng.*, **2**, 1223–42.

VANN, J. H. 1959. The geomorphology of the Guiana coast. *Proc. 2nd Coast. Geogr. Conf.*, 153–87.

VAN DIEREN, J. W. 1934. *Organogene Dunenbildung*. The Hague.

VAN STEENIS, C. G. G. J. 1941. Kustaanwas en Mangrove. *Nat. Wehensch. Tydschr. Ned. Indië*, **101**, 82–5.

VAN STRAATEN, L. M. J. U. 1954. Composition and structure of Recent marine sediments in the Netherlands. *Leid. geol. Meded.*, **19**, 1–110.

VAN STRAATEN, L. M. J. U. 1965. Coastal barrier deposits in south and north Holland. *Meded. Geol. Sticht.* NS 17, 41–75.

VAN VEEN, J. 1950. Eb- en vloedschaar systemen in de Nederlandse Getijwateren. *Tijd. Kon. Ned. Aard. Gen.*, **67**, 303–25.

VAUGHAN, T. W. 1909. The geologic work of mangroves in southern Florida. *Smithson, misc. Collns*, **52**, 461–4.

VERSTAPPEN, H. T. 1968. On the origin of longitudinal (seif) dunes. *Zeit. f. Geomorph.*, **12**, 200–20.

VESEY-FITZGERALD, D. F. 1955. Vegetation of the Red Sea coast south of Jedda, Saudi Arabia. *J. Ecology*, **43**, 477–89.

VESEY-FITZGERALD, D. F. 1957. The vegetation of the Red Sea coast north of Jedda, Saudi Arabia. *J. Ecology.*, **45**, 547–62.

VOLKER, A. 1966. Tentative classification and comparison with deltas of other climatic regions. *Proc. Dacca Symp. Scientific problems of the humid tropical zone deltas and their implications*, 399–408.

WALTER, H., and STEINER, M. 1936. Die Oekologie der ost-afrikanischen Mangroven. *Zeit. f. Bot.*, **30**, 65–193.

WATSON, J. D. 1928. Mangrove forests of the Malay Peninsula. *Malay. Forest Rec.*, **6**, 1–275.

WELLS, J. W. 1957. Coral reefs. *Mem. geol. Soc. Am.*, **67**, 609–31.

WENTWORTH, C. K. 1938. Marine bench forming processes; Part 1, Water-level weathering. *J. Geomorph.*, **1**, 6–32.

WEST, R. C. 1956. Mangrove swamps of the Pacific coast of Colombia. *Ann. Ass. Am. Geogr.*, **46**, 98–121.

WIEGEL, R. L. 1964. *Oceanographical engineering.* Prentice Hall, New York.

WIEHE, P. O. 1935. A quantitative study of the influence of the tide upon populations of *Salicornia europaea.* *J. Ecology*, **23**, 323–33.

WIENS, H. 1959. Atoll development and morphology. *Ann. Ass. Am. Geogr.*, **49**, 31–54.

WILLIAMS, W. W. 1956. An east coast survey: some recent changes in the coast of East Anglia. *Geogr. J.*, **122**, 317–34.

WILLIAMS, W. W. 1960. *Coastal changes.* Routledge and Kegan Paul, London.

WILSON, B. M. 1957. Hurricane and wave statistics for the Gulf of Mexico. *Tech. Memo. Beach. Eros. Bd., U.S.*, No. 98.

WILSON, J. T. 1965. A new class of faults and their bearing on continental drifts. *Nature*, **207**, 343–7.

WRIGHT, L. D., CHAPPELL, J., THOM, B. G., BRADSHAW, M. P. and COWELL, P. 1979. Morphodynamics of reflective and dissipative beach and inshore systems: south eastern Australia. *Marine Geology*, **31**, *in press.*

WRIGHT, L. D. and COLEMAN, J. M. 1973. Variations in morphology of major river deltas as functions of ocean wave and river discharge regimes. *Bull. Am. Ass. petrol. Geol.*, **57**, 370–98.

WRIGHT, L. D., THOM, B. G., COWELL, P., BRADSHAW, M. and CHAPPELL, J. 1977. Field observations of resonant surf and current spectra on a reflective beach and relationships to cusps. *Search*, **8**, 321–2.

WRIGHT, L. W. 1970. Variation in the level of the cliff/shore platform junction along the south coast of Great Britain. *Marine Geology*, **9**, 347–53.

YAALON, D. H. 1967. Factors affecting the lithification of eolianite and interpretation of its environmental significance in the coastal plain of Israel. *J. sedim. Petrol.*, **37**, 1189–99.

YASSO, W. E. 1965. Plan geometry of headland-bay beaches. *J. Geol.*, **73**, 702–14.

YONGE, C. M. 1951. Marine boring organisms. *Research*, **4**, 162–7.

YOSHIKAWA, T., KAIZUKA, S., and OTA, Y. 1968. Coastal development of the Japanese islands. *Means of correlation of Quaternary successions. Proc. Seventh Congr. Intern. Ass. Quat. Res.*, **8**, 457–65.

ZENKOVICHI, V. P. 1967. *Processes of coastal development.* Oliver and Boyd, Edinburgh.

INDEX